Blind People

SUNY Series, The Body in Culture,
History, and Religion
Howard Eilberg-Schwartz, Editor

and

SUNY Series in Anthropology and Judaic Studies
Walter P. Zenner, Editor

Blind People

The Private and Public Life of Sightless Israelis

Shlomo Deshen

STATE UNIVERSITY OF NEW YORK PRESS

Published by
State University of New York Press, Albany

Printed in the United States of America

For information, address State University of New York
Press, State University Plaza, Albany, N.Y. 12246

Production by Diane Ganeles
Marketing by Theresa A. Swierzowski

Library of Congress Cataloging-in-Publication Data

Deshen, Shlomo A.
    Blind people: the private and public life of sightless Israelis/
Shlomo Deshen.
        p.   cm.— (SUNY series, the body in culture, history,
and religion)
    Includes bibliographical references (p.   ) and index.
    ISBN 0-7914-1035-8 (CH: acid free).—ISBN 0-7914-1036-6 (PB:
acid-free)
    1. Blind—Israel—Social conditions. 2. Blind—Israel—Economic
conditions. 3. Blind—Israel—Family relationships. I. Title.
II. Series.
HV2078.5.D47   1992
362.4'1'095694—dc20   91-20397
                                                                CIP

10 9 8 7 6 5 4 3 2 1

In honor of
Suliman Hirbawy

Contents

Acknowledgments

I have invested in this monograph the major part of my research efforts in recent years. During 1983–84 I spent a sabbatical year in fieldwork, and thereafter until the summer of 1990, I read and wrote. During these years the project meandered with me to the several departments of sociology and anthropology with which I have been affiliated, first at Bar-Ilan University and later at Tel-Aviv University, my permanent bases, and to New York University, the University of Michigan, and the University of Florida, where I held visiting positions.

The fieldwork was supported by grants from the Tel-Aviv University Sapir Center for Development, and from the Jerusalem Center for Anthropological Research, directed by Dr. Edgar Siskin. I am very grateful for the confidence that the officers of these foundations gave me, in supporting a project that was far removed from the proposals that usually come before them. Even more than most ethnographic projects, this has been a solitary and often lonely one. I therefore deeply appreciate the pains that colleagues and friends in Israel and the United States have taken over the years, faithfully reading and commenting on drafts of papers that I inflicted upon them. I would like to single out the late Robert F. Murphy, the doyen of disability studies in anthropology, whose encouragement of the project has been of particular importance to me.

I am also thankful to numerous secretaries at four universities, who tolerated the idiosyncrasy of a writer, who still uses a ballpoint pen to produce longhand manuscripts. I name some of the long-suffering ones: Hadassah Raab, Roslyn Langbart, Pamela Yacobi, and Sylvia Weinberg.

Much of this study, particularly the fieldwork and some of the editing, was done jointly with my wife, Hilda Deshen, and four of the preliminary papers were actually authored jointly. Hilda is a biochemist who moved into anthropology in the course of family life with an anthropologist, such as Edith Turner, the late Mary Gluckman, and many others.

Like all anthropologists, I am profoundly indebted to the people whom I studied. Some of those who assisted me most, whom I came to like and respect deeply, figure prominently in the descriptions that follow. But I am reluctant to reveal the identity of any of them, and I must remain satisfied with this bald statement of acknowledgment. Suliman Hirbawy, who does not figure in the book, is a blinded veteran of the Israel Police Force. He was grievously injured under circumstances of tragic, mind boggling, convolution. The incident is described in his autobiography (Hirbawy 1987). Mr. Hirbawy encapsulates poignantly some of the complexities of Israeli society, which envelop the lives of the people described in this book. In dedicating it to him I seek to give due honor and to salute an individual blind Israeli.

The book is based partly on preliminary papers published in journals: "The Cultural Use of the Senses: The Case of Blind People", *Megamot* 32 (1990): 510–521 (Hebrew), partly incorporated in revised form in chapter 2; "On Social Aspects of the Usage of Guide-Dogs and Long-Canes", *Sociological Review* 37 (1989): 89–103, in chapter 3; "Coming of Age Among Blind People in Israel", *Disability, Handicap and Society* 2 (1987): 137–149, in chapter 4; "Managing at Home: Relationships between Blind Parents and Sighted Children", *Human Organization* 48 (1989): 262–267, in chapter 5; "Employment and Disability: The Quest for Work among Blind Israelis", *Journal of Visual Impairment and Blindness* 84 (1990): 80–84 , in chapter 6; "The Performance of Blind Israelis at Work", *Disability, Handicap and Society* 5 (1990): 269–280, in chapter 7; "Mutual Rejection and Association Among the Discredited: The Case of Blind People in Israel", *Human Organization* 50 (1991): 89–96, in chapter 10; "Ethnicity Among Blind People in Israel", *Ethnic Groups* 8 (1990): 235–247, in chapter 11; "Seeking Dignity and Independence: Toward an Ethnography of Blindness in Israel", *Journal of Visual Impairment and Blindness* 81 (1987): 209–212, in chapter 13.

Chapter One

Introduction:
The Field, the Questions,
and the Researcher

Throughout much of the world in our times there has been a dramatically heightened awareness of the existence, and the due rights, of people who have been traditionally repressed. These include people of ethnic minority status, people of various sex and age categories, people of unusual physiology, and others. Anthropological and sociological research has attempted to keep abreast of this tide, and considerable effort has been directed to pertinent areas of specialization, such as ethnicity and gender. The present work seeks to contribute to one of these emergent fields of inquiry—the anthropological study of disabled people.

Disability studies are one of the more recent of the new socio-anthropological specializations. The basic premise of disability studies is that physical conditions do not, by themselves, determine the roles and positions that disabled people fill in society. Rather, it is the culture of both able-bodied and disabled people in any given society that conceptualizes and moulds conditions of disability. According to this view, disabled people fill roles in society that are an outcome of cultural mediation. This theoretical anti-positivistic stance is not unique to disability studies. It pervades current studies of gender, ethnicity, and much of the range of contemporary social science. In the present work I extend that perspective, to explore in detail the social construction of one particular disabling condition, that of blindness.

The juxtaposition of apparently synonymous terms, "sightless" and "blind", that figure in the title of this work encapsulates the contemporary theme of disability studies, in the context of blindness. In both popular parlance and in that of professionals specializing in sightless people, the terms "blind" and "blindness" are much more common than the terms "sightless" and "sightlessness". This usage

1

reflects a particular facet of Western culture: people who lack sight are not viewed by the able-bodied as merely people who have a condition of limited physical disability. Rather, they tend to be viewed as people in whose existence sightlessness is all encompassing, overarching, total. The condition of sightlessness is symbolically enriched and magnified, sometimes mystified and even demonized.

Thus, in popular culture, delimited sightlessness becomes "blindness". That familiar term conveys much more than a particular condition of physical disability. It carries, in addition, a rich content of attributes—beliefs, prejudices, fears—that culture has associated with sightlessness in many (perhaps most) times and places. The peculiarity of the symbolic elaboration of sightlessness is not unique to that condition. Such conceptual elaboration of the environment in which humans live is a fundamental element of the cultural process, and lies at the root of belief and social order. Some of the finest achievements of cultural and social anthropology entail uncovering this process. In the context of the present study, it is notable that conceptual elaboration is common to many disabling conditions. The hearing impaired are considered "deaf" in popular parlance, sufferers of Hansen's disease are "lepers," and a great variety of muscular and orthopedic disorders lead people to become "cripples" in the general cultural understanding.

In a different but not unrelated way, some of the major diseases of our times, such as tuberculosis, cancer and AIDS, have become richly symbolized. These diseases have become metaphors for attributes that popular imagination attaches to patients, as has been eloquently described by Susan Sontag and others. Why some physical conditions capture the imagination in this way and others not, why some to a greater and others to a lesser extent, is imperfectly understood at this time and remain major open questions. There are great differences between various societies in these matters. Thus, deaf people were not considered at all remarkable in a nineteenth century New England locality described by Nora Groce (1985). Impairment of hearing was not much elaborated by culture and symbolized in that society.

Sometimes dramatic changes within the same society occur over time, as Zachary Gussow (1989) has demonstrated in connection with Hansen's disease in the United States, which became increasingly enriched in terms of symbolism in the nineteenth century. John Gwaltney (1970, 1980) who studied in the 1960s and 1970s a Mexican village afflicted with a high incidence of infectious blindness, has depicted the original remarkable social integration and acceptance of blind people among the sighted. However, as a result of certain socioeconomic developments in that village, the niche that blind people filled disappeared and their position in society changed markedly.

The upshot of this is that in real life one rarely encounters "sightlessness". The latter is primarily a heuristic term that can serve the description of human physiology. But it is not an apt term for medical discourse since that is infused with cultural and social considerations, as medical-anthropological research in general has demonstrated. In real life one usually encounters people whose sightlessness has been conceptualized and symbolized in various ways, in short—blind people. The term "sightless" is of even less use in a discourse, as the present study is, focused on socio-cultural matters, than it is in medical discourse. In fieldwork I did not encounter sightless humans, but blind people (more particularly, blind Israelis). Hence it is the latter term that figures in the main title of the study and that recurs throughout the discussions that follow. My purpose in retaining the bland physiological term in the subtitle is to highlight the analytical thrust of the study, the socio-cultural construction of a physical condition.

Blind people occupy a particularly salient position in the Western popular imagination. Of all people afflicted with disabilities and diseases, the blind probably attract the most attention from the able-bodied. The contents of a recent review of disability drama in television and film (Klobas 1988) illustrate this well. Of 435 pages of reviews, material featuring blindness fills 113 pages and constitutes the prime quantitative category of all disabilities. Blindness also constitutes, for those who are so inclined, a convenient avenue for the expression of altruism. Considerable resources often revolve around blind people, mediated by voluntary benevolent associations. Such associations are often well endowed, both in finances and in manpower of eager volunteers. This lies, I suggest, in the fact that blindness can be readily conceived as unambiguous, more so than other, far more common physically disabling conditions.

Many afflictions, such as muscular degeneration, brain damage, hearing impairment, not to mention debilitating internal conditions, are not readily visible. Often they are highly variable and undefined. To the extent that those conditions are visible, they manifest themselves through a broad range of symptoms that differ from person to person. In the Western popular imagination the overt behavioral manifestations of those conditions are not always readily linked to the conditions. Sometimes popular imagination links the manifestations to irrelevant moral attributes. Thus, the behavior of people with spastic disorders is prone to be popularly interpreted as clownish, that of brain-damaged people as immoral, that of deaf people as feebleminded. (In Jewish rabbinical law this is expressed formally: In many contexts the deaf are categorized together with the feebleminded and with minors.) The outcome of this is that there is a tendency in many times and places in Western society to arbitrarily impute various negative moral attributes to certain categories of disabled people (as demonstrated in the Klobas review; for two erudite reviews of the Jewish rabbinical material concerning blindness, see Cohen 1982 and Steinberg 1983).

Blindness is more varied than is popularly realized, and comprises a spectrum of visual impairments which includes many kinds and degrees of residual sight. Moreover, the sensation of the eyes as physical organs, even when sight is totally absent, is variegated, and people often suffer from pain in the organ. However, blindness has an essential distinctiveness and lack of ambiguity relative to other conditions. There is an immediate visible link between the condition and its behavioral manifestations, such as impaired mobility and lack of ability to read print. These clear-cut manifestations lead sighted people to overlook the forementioned details, within the condition of sightlessness, that blur the clear-cut image. The result is a stereotyped image of the condition which includes incorrect notions, such as most blind people being blind congenitally, and that they "live in darkness." This popular clear-cut image of blindness leads that disability to be an attractive object of philanthropic attention on the part of the able-bodied.

More precise elucidation of the problem of why and how various disabilities are conceptualized in society in different ways is a desideratum. Beyond its importance in the study of disability this problem leads on to some of the most profound issues of culture and society: the nature of symbolization, of fear and of belief, and the social sources of discrimination and disempowerment. But before significant advance can be made at the general level, we require limited and detailed accounts of symbolization of particular conditions, located in time and place. In the present work, my aim is to uncover how the social status of sightless people figures in social interactions; how sightlessness influences the exercise of tactile and other senses and at what social cost people engage in them; what stimulates sightless people to experience degradation and respect; what is the range of permissiveness that the sighted permit the sightless and what is permitted among the sightless themselves. In all these questions, the concern is to shed light on the symbolization process that occurs in interactions between able-bodied and disabled human beings who are situated in an environment that is governed by the former. In short, I seek to illuminate how sightless people act in a realistic context as blind people.

Such questions, varying in formulation along with different contexts and cultures, are the staples of the socio-anthropological endeavor. They are fundamental for understanding a vast array of human experience, irrespective of particular culture or specific physical condition. The focus in this study is on people, Israelis, who happen to be sightless. The disability is a very important element in their existential experience, but it is not the sole element. The aim is to convey the variety of humanity of these people, in a way similar to that in which anthropologists have described many other people, uncovering the commonality with other humans together with the uniqueness. This study aims to strike a balance between two extreme positions on blindness, both of which I consider misguided. One is the position of uninformed sighted people, who view the sightless in stigmatizing terms, mystifying the disability, and transforming specific sightlessness into diffuse blindness. The other position is that of some disability-rights activists who minimize disability, trivializing sightlessness by slogans such as, "Blind people are like everybody else; they just don't see," or "Blindness is an inconvenience, not a handicap."

The purpose of this monograph is to fill a lacuna in ethnographic coverage, the study of people who differ from most humans by having exceptional bodies, and whose culture usually disempowers them. The approach contrasts with that of remedial practices, such as rehabilitation and social work, not only because of the absence of a spotlight focus on disability, but also because in my role as anthropologist, I do not view blindness as "a problem" that requires eradication, so that people "cope" and "adapt successfully." In this study I adopt an intellectual stance that requires some courage: blindness is viewed dispassionately, as an interesting fact of life.

Despite the fact that socio-anthropological interest in disability is recent, there does exist a steadily growing body of literature. Several of the major disabling conditions have now been described by pioneering students who opened the field. On dwarfism there are two monographs by Joan Ablon (1984, 1988), on deafness the works of Gaylene Becker (1980), Paul Higgins (1980) and Nora Groce (1985), on epilepsy there is the work of Peter Conrad and Joseph Schneider (1983)[1], on mental illness Sue Estroff (1981), and on mental retardation Robert Edgerton (1967). These are just some of the monographs; there are also illuminating shorter accounts of other conditions. There are, for instance, notable papers on management strategies of stutterers among fluent speakers (Petrunik 1974), and of obese people among normal sized (Himelfarb and Evans 1974). In a more recent collection there are fine papers on identity management of people suffering from end-stage renal disease (Kutner 1987) and urinary incontinence (Mitteness 1987).

Also the socio-anthropological study of blindness has attracted some attention. The major study of the United States scene remains

Robert Scott's *The Making of Blind Men,* and there is the forementioned ethnography of blindness in a Mexican setting by John Gwaltney, *The Thrice-Shy,* both works of the late 1960s. In the past thirty years at least forty social science oriented doctoral dissertations on blindness have been approved in the U.S. Perhaps the most insightful are those of phenomenologically-oriented sociologists and social anthropologists, such as Stephen Ainley (1981) and Carol Goldin (1980). Most of the dissertations are frustrating, however. Their perspective is mostly that of individual psychology, which implies the examination of limited issues as dictated by the concerns of psychological theory. The other main line of research in the dissertations is that of social work, which is geared primarily to interventive practice, and only secondarily to an elucidation of social fields as such. A third line is that of demographically-oriented sociologists, who have gathered potentially valuable data, but due to their limited theoretical concern, the data do not bring much insight to the field.

The method of this study is that of informal ethnographic observation. One must address therefore the question as to whether Israeli blind people form social groups that are amenable to such observation. In general, although they are far from fully integrated into many of the relationships that engage sighted people, blind people do not usually congregate in secluded groups of their own. However, powerful impulses that emanate from the able-bodied aim to segregate blind people and to thrust them into particular social niches. The issue of grouping among blind people is therefore an important one, even in settings where no such grouping is overt, and it will be discussed later (chapter 10). At present it suffices to note that the conditions of the field lead me to engage in extensive individual visiting, and also to observe and often participate in organized public and semi-public settings in which blind people participated.

The study is based on fieldwork of about fifteen months' duration, from July 1983 to October 1983, and from January 1984 to January 1985, among a population of blind people in the Tel-Aviv area. The data and analyses that follow reflect the conditions of that period, but it is my general impression that changes since then have not been remarkable. All the people of the study were adults, the youngest being in their twenties and the oldest in their early sixties. I endeavored to uncover the nature of adult blindness: the population includes only people who lost their sight during their teens at the latest, before completing socialization to adulthood. These people had to grapple with concerns of adult life as blind people, including such crucial matters as the quest for work and spouses. The delimitation of the field thus excluded army veterans, among others, since they lost their sight as adults. Definition of blindness in terms of ophthalmology is complex, and actual conditions of so-called blindness are variegated. The working definition that determined my own selection of people in the field was a functional one: people who required one of the standard mobility aids when travelling.

The people whom I selected to visit and befriend, and sometimes just to interview, were not statistically random. My initial entries into the field were through initiating contacts, separately, with the sighted manager of a sheltered workshop, and with a blind activist who headed an advocacy group. Eventually, people befriended me and led me from one acquaintance to the next. My universe of blind people came to number fifty-seven individuals, spread over numerous socio-occupational niches, of varying family status, and differing ethnic background. These people are fairly representative of blind Israelis with the exception of two minority categories, people living in outlying areas in the north and south, far from the metropolitan areas, and Israeli Arabs.

With eight of the people of the study I maintained, together with my wife, a mutual family-based relationship and exchanged visits and many telephone conversations. In research practice I was as unobtrusive as possible. I tried to avoid posing direct questions and preferred eliciting information by leading conversation indirectly onto topics that intrigued me. In particular, I sought information that stemmed from behavioral and verbal interactions in which both my wife and I were relatively passive. Twenty individuals we came to know well, but less than those in the first category. We visited them a few times at home and/or observed and interacted with them frequently in other settings. Twenty-five of the remaining people I knew only superficially from single or small numbers of visits or observations in various settings. Information about four individuals whom I never visited is also occasionally introduced into the study. Most of these fifty-seven persons were between thirty-five and fifty years old, about equally divided by sex.

I participated in several locales of blind people. One was the sheltered-workshop in which I worked on the shop floor virtually daily, threading steel nails into plastic rings, for the duration of three months. Another such setting was a social club that operated thrice weekly, a third one was that of the national association of blind people. There was also a circle of people who met as a kind of encounter group (they called themselves "the psychology circle"), and in which I participated for over a year as the single sighted member. Several other groups that I visited only irregularly will be mentioned later in the accounts. In all I interacted with, and came to be known to, well over a hundred blind people.

In the course of this fieldwork I encountered reservations from my professional and social ambience, such as I had never faced before in the course of a professional career that has spanned three decades.

Virtually all my colleagues queried as to what could have brought me to study the blind of all people. In the past, when engaged in mainline Middle-Eastern anthropology, studying immigrants, I was rarely asked such a question. Some of my colleagues were skeptical of a sighted researcher being able to study blind people, and one distinguished colleague strongly advised that I ought to experience living with a blindfold. I continued to encounter reservations to the study at later stages when I submitted papers that emerged, for publication in general anthropological journals. Quite a few of the negative comments I received struck me as deficient in serious academic engagement. Amazingly, the editor of one mainline journal concluded her letter of rejection by commenting, that my work did not raise important anthropological questions. Although journals in applied anthropology and disability studies did eventually accept the early versions of the study, the experience was sobering for me. It reflected, in my understanding, the present state of the discipline.

This brings me to outline my personal motivations and positions in this field of research. I came to anthropology in the early 1960s after a childhood in European Holocaust conditions and a tumultuous adolescence. Since then I have invested many years of effort in the area of Middle-Eastern Jewish studies, focusing on the ethnography of North African Jews in Israel and on their historical background. My motivation was heavily romantic, entailing a personal search for roots. Also, I was moved by a feeling of profound affinity for people who were considered inferior by those of the dominant strata. With time, I have lost much of my attraction for this ethnographic field, but some of the old motivations have remained with me, and that has made me aware of the illuminating potential that lay in a study of the physically disabled. Prior to this project I had no particular interest in, or personal involvement with blind people. But by the early 1980s blind people struck me, for the popular reasons I outlined earlier, as saliently exotic.

Further, I brought to the field an attachment to traditional Judaism which entails commitment to charitable activities. However, my initially weak support of the disability rights movement has increased over the years of my involvement in this study. I am aware that some of the questions I consider may be objectionable from some perspectives of the movement (for instance where I discuss the question of the aversion of blind people to each other's company, or the occupation of blind beggars and low-status generally). My comments do, however, reflect realistic situations with which I am familiar, which disability-rights activists sometimes seem to ignore. It is possible that in Western countries such as the United States, the high visibility profile of the disability-rights movement and its achievements, result in obviating attention from morally reprehensible conditions under which many disabled people still live. Those conditions are ideologically unpalatable to the movement, and they clash with the public image that the movement seeks to project. Personally, I support the rights movement, but that ideological position does not preclude me from developing an analytical sociological perspective, in precisely the same way that religious commitment need not inhibit the development of an analytical perspective on religious phenomena.

Despite my attraction to the disability rights movement I have little patience for some of the infighting and quibbling within the movement over what I feel are trivialities, such as problems of terminology (e.g., the usage of the term "disability" in preference to "handicap"). I follow usages that are currently fashionable mainly out of respect for the people concerned, not out of personal conviction. Finally, I brought to the field a fear of blindness, and never ventured to experiment with the advice to play blind man's bluff. Such an exercise would, in my opinion, be futile in any event because, as I elaborate in this study, blindness is much more encompassing as an existential situation than sightlessness—and all the more so when simulated and the sightlessness is temporary.

Once anthropologists acknowledge such personal idiosyncrasies and prejudices, they may venture, I feel, onto whoever will tolerate their presence. The ensuing accounts should then be evaluated critically in the context of that personal background. There is no reason why a sighted researcher could not penetrate into the lives of blind people, just as a New York anthropologist can penetrate and uncover the nature of life in a Berber village, or of Harvard Business School alumni for that matter. Similar to conventional practice in traditional fields of study, the anthropologist of blind people will be expected to exhibit a measure of empathy—more than the superficiality that satisfies many sociologists, but less than might lead to full submergence and to "go native" in the culture that is being studied.

The latter point requires emphasis at this time. Much of contemporary socio-cultural anthropological writing is geared to a sensitive literary genre, that aims to evoke nuances of the atmosphere and of the drama of individual lives. In support of what Paul Stoller (1989) has termed "radical empiricism in ethnographic writing," the claim is currently being made, that optimally an ethnographic field project should extend over decades, virtually the lifetime of a researcher. Such immersion encourages vivid description and deep characterization, standards that anthropologists have frequently, if not always aimed for, and have attained with varying measures of success. I maintain however, that these emphases on empathy and literary quality, when linked to a second prevailing trend, that of reflexivity and

introspection, lead to a loss of vigor in the attainment of one of the
major traditional goals of anthropologists: the raising of general theoretical problems and the attempt to resolve them. The increasing lack
of coherence in the discipline ever since the early 1970s is, I suggest,
linked with a loss of balance between problem-oriented writing and
the striving for the production of descriptions that are of literary and
humanistic quality. The imbalance causes many anthropologists to
measure their achievements and those of their colleagues by the standards of others, namely of creative writers. Beyond doing themselves
ill-service by this evaluation, it leads anthropologists to sterility in
their own craft.

The present study is, in contrast, an apology for traditional social
anthropology, in the sense that it is concerned with analytical descriptions of major issues in the lives of people. Therefore, contrary to
the practice of many ethnographers of contemporary life, I deliberately refrain from presenting any detailed profiles of individuals. I
feel that no analytic purpose would be served thereby. Also the craft
of anthropology is not that of literary art, and anthropologists need
not try to practice it. I could not rival a writer such as Ved Mehta, to
offer the kind of profound insight into the lives of individual blind
people that he does. The anthropologist is however, able to provide a
picture that incorporates systematic linkages with facets of wider
culture and society, and that is usually beyond the depth of other
social commentators, including great literary artists. Though their
doings are fractured according to the various subtopics I explore,
individual people do nevertheless figure in this work. Anyone interested in them will be able to follow their traces by the help of the
index—and produce indifferent literary profiles.

I am anxious to protect not only the privacy of these people, but
also their sense of self-respect. Virtually any socio-anthropological
study that is not founded on the assumption of total immersion has
elements of debunking. The student's vision of people is bound to be
different from that which they have of themselves. The latter vision
is a result of laborious self-sustaining image-making, and chances are
that the student's image of a person may be painful. It is the
researcher's responsibility to avoid actually inflicting pain. Conven-
tionally, I have therefore disguised the names of most persons and
places. In some cases I have gone further, and also changed occupations, ages, ethnic identities, even gender—whenever these data were
not pertinent to analyses in which the individuals figured.

The order of the topics of this study aims to present an unfolding
of the life experience of blind people, starting from the most personal
and private, and leading onto broad public concerns. The book is
composed of four parts in which the lives of sightless people are

studied, beginning in part one with the immediate and intimate domain of the body. In part two the focus moves beyond the body, to the circle that is closest to the individual, that of the home and the family. In part three we follow people beyond the domestic setting, as they reach out to fill their material requirements. Part four focuses on the doings of people as they reach out for fulfillment, dignity, and integration, in circles beyond those of the home and work place; namely, activities and concerns in the areas of leisure, society and politics.

Part one is composed of two chapters. The first discusses problems inherent in the essential nature of the sightless body—how blind people manage it in a world that is governed by the sighted, specifically, the usage that blind people make of their unimpaired senses. The second chapter focuses on social problems that inhere in the usage of the main aids of blind people to compensate for their physical disability. Part two is composed of two chapters on relationships between parents and children. The first of these is devoted to the experience of growing up as a blind adolescent in a home governed by sighted parents, and the second deals with the problem of mature blind people who have come to raise their own sighted children.

The chapters that compose part three focus on the work situation and on the welfare system as it operates in the area of material needs. Chapter 6, the first of these chapters, describes the travails of obtaining employment, and in chapter 7 we enter the work place to describe the nature of that employment and the way employees experience it. Chapter 8 describes the nature of the social support system that sighted people, both public agents and private volunteers, provide. The impact of this system upon the blind clients and the way they experience it is described in chapter 9.

The four chapters that compose part four deal with public life. Chapter 10 focuses on the issue of socializing and reaching out for friendship, that is, the dilemma of disabled people associating with, or dissociating themselves from, people of similar condition. Chapter 11 focuses on a possibility of association that is common in Israel as an immigrant society, that of ethnic bonding, and discusses to what extent blind people are interested in such identities and divisions. In chapter 12, discussion shifts to what is in many ways the obverse of ethnic bonding; namely, nationalism and patriotism, and describes the views and doings of people concerning the latter. Finally, chapter 13 concludes with an examination of positions that lead to political activism, debates about the major public issue that blind people face, that of empowerment as against quiescence.

Part 1

The Body

Chapter Two

The Use of the Senses

Anthropologists agree that culture has a profound impact on the ways in which people govern their bodies. This thesis has been established in many studies hailing back to the school of Mauss and Hertz and particularly Hall (1966) and Montagu (1971). The pertinent literature is concerned mostly with culture referring to particular clusters of symbols held by ethnically discrete populations. But what of people who belong to a society that has an ethnic culture which is internally diversified, due to the radically different physiques and states of health of its members and to the cultural meaning attributed to these physical differences? Though not much discussed in the literature, this social situation is quite universal, since virtually all societies are heterogeneous in terms of human physique and health. Following the prevailing theory, as to the impact of culture on body management, may we assume that in a situation of physical heterogeneity the dominant able-bodied people will constrain the physically disabled to govern their bodies in particular ways?

In raising this question we take into account a variable that anthropologists have not commonly considered in the study of the impact of culture upon the management of the body. The impaired body is managed by disabled people under cultural conditions that include both the variable of ethnic culture common to all members of a given society, and the variable peculiar to the disabled, that of living in a situation dominated by the able-bodied. This chapter uncovers how the impaired body is managed in a realistic social context that encompasses both these major variables. It extends an anthropological perspective into the particular condition of blindness and sheds light on a problem that crosscuts disabling conditions in general: how one manages the impaired body under conditions where people are presumed to be normal, able-bodied.

The focus is upon the uses that blind, but otherwise able-bodied people, make of the unimpaired senses—audition, olfaction and tac-

15

tility. Blind people exercise these senses, some more and some less. The ways in which people manage their bodies appear on the surface to be rooted in primarily personal, idiosyncratic factors, and it is at this point that a socio-anthropological perspective is illuminating. While granting the salience of individual factors such as personality, innate ability and intelligence, I contend that the practices of blind people are not determined solely by them. The hand of culture weighs heavily upon all human action, that of blind people included. Hence this chapter argues, socio-cultural constraints common to blind and sighted mould the way blind people exercise their bodies.

Starting from observations on tactility and going on to olfaction and audition, I demonstrate the impingement of culture upon the exercise of the unimpaired senses of blind people and conclude by offering indications as to the parameters of this impingement.

I. Tactility

In Western European and North American societies people tend to avoid tactile contact and body odors to a greater extent than do people in Mediterranean and Middle Eastern societies (see Polhemus 1978 and citations there, and Watson 1970). Israelis in general are much exposed to Western mores and fashions, and people deliberately align their activities accordingly.[1] Therefore I apply to the field of the present study the basic datum of Western culture as being relatively averse to physical closeness.[2] In the interactions of blind people I observed, both among themselves and with sighted people, tactility was not common. The only times that blind people demonstrated such a practice regularly was when a number of people negotiated public thoroughfares together. On such occasions they linked arms so as not to lose one another. But that, importantly, does not constitute touching as an exploratory action to overcome sightlessness. Blind people have by-and-large adopted the common aversion to tactility.

There are, however, indications that the repression of tactility constitutes a problem. Rivqa Cohen, a sheltered workshop employee, when asked whether she did not sometimes feel the urge to touch people, so as to better apprehend them, reacted vehemently: "No! Never! Only primitive people do that! One does not go around touching people!" Another blind woman once confessed that she had an urge to touch the faces of people, but refrained from doing so for fear of offending. The fear of imposing unwanted tactility is well-founded. Many people experienced physical rejection when they needed to hold the hand of a sighted person. I received several accounts of incidents where, instead of the sighted guide holding the hand of the blind person, the former would hold only the blind person's sleeve, minimizing physical contact.[3]

One evening, Danny and Pirhiya Akram were regaling me with stories of such incidents. A couple with children, they managed their affairs competently. He held a job in a factory among sighted workers, and the couple moved in a higher social stratum than did the forementioned women.[4] Pirhiya remarked that she had no problem with regard to physical contact with guides on the street. Whenever she had to solicit help from a stranger, she said happily, she just locked arms with him. "Yes", remarked her husband ruefully, "but that doesn't work with me." He went on to recount an incident, in which a woman whom he had asked for guidance on the street, reacted by gingerly touching his sleeve with the tips of her fingers. Thereupon he had slipped his arm onto hers, but the woman reacted indignantly. She turned startled, and exclaimed, "How dare you?! Aren't you ashamed?!" Apparently she had interpreted Danny's gesture as a sexual advance.[5]

Repeatedly people reported having experienced sighted passengers recoiling from them as they took seats next to them on crowded buses. Sometimes, they reported, passengers vacated their seats, so as not to share a bench with the blind passenger. The extent to which these accounts are true is secondary to the fact, that in recounting them people express their feeling that the sighted wish to avoid physical contact. Sometimes this feeling is expressed in sarcasm, "The sighted think that my blindness is contagious!" The apprehension of imposing tactility thus runs deeper than expressed earlier by Rivqa. Not only do people not permit themselves any touching that is exploratory and diffuse, but they are sometimes ambivalent even about delimited physical contact which may be required for mobility needs. In talking about relationships with the sighted, some blind people said that one of the things that impaired mutual ties was the fact that in going out, the sighted had to hold hands with them, and they felt this was repugnant to the sighted. This phenomenon once arose with reference to me. Penina Danieli, a professional social welfare worker used to maintain a physical activities regime and participated in a group of sighted people who went on brisk weekly walks in parks. One person would walk hand-in-hand with Penina in order to guide her. She had difficulties retaining partners and was on the verge of dropping out. Upon suggesting vaguely that I might want to join the group Penina's retort was apologetic. She said that I ought to consider that joining her in these walks would entail holding hands and that "some people find this objectionable".

The foregoing are guarded, restrained, and apologetic expressions concerning the use of tactility. On extraordinary occasions only did I encounter expressions denoting a positive desire for tactility.

These incidents are important as deviant cases; they shed light on the particular circumstances that accompany the expression or repression of tactility, and afford us insight into the pertinent boundaries. One such incident involved Aharon Ben-Arsi, a switchboard operator in his forties whose standing among his peers, blind switchboard operators and blind acquaintances from his school years, was unusual. They considered Aharon to be both mentally disturbed and immoral, and held him in contempt. The reason for this was that Aharon was aggressive in pressing requests upon the welfare authorities. Several times he made a spectacle of himself and caused the media to publicize his grievances. The precise nature of these grievances need not concern us; the salient point is that Aharon had earned a bad reputation among many other blind people for what they considered unbecoming behavior.[6] Many blind people, while willing to take a stand concerning what they consider their lawful rights, are extremely apprehensive of behavior that might be linked by the sighted with mendicancy. The image of "the blind beggar" is appalling to them. Aharon Ben-Arsi had no such compunction. His behavior therefore raised a profoundly disturbing association.

It is striking that precisely this marginal person vehemently expressed the effectiveness of tactility, and the right of blind people to make use of it. Reminiscing about the time that he had spent in the Vocational Training Center for the Blind, Aharon recalled various people he had encountered there. Suddenly he exploded,

> There was one blind instructor there who pawed (*misheish*) every girl-trainee to see if she was pretty. But that very same fellow wanted to expel a student for doing precisely the same thing! I swore at him! I threatened to make public everything I knew about him! That got him off me!

More than Aharon's indignation at the perceived inequity, the frank recognition of the importance of tactility is remarkable.

Another expression of tactility emerged again in an extraordinary context: an experimental film, made by a sighted university student majoring in cinema, whose subject was a young blind student. The subject was shown in a variety of situations, mainly blindness-linked, such as visiting a haptically-designed botanic garden, dancing and socializing and, relevantly, recognizing people by tactile exploration of their faces. The heroine commented matter-of-factly that she had to touch people's faces in order to appreciate their features. The painstaking manner in which she did so accentuated her feeling. Here again, tactility was clearly bracketed off from ordinary day-to-day activities; this time by the artistic context.

Another occasion on which I observed confrontation of tactility was at a noisy Purim party,[7] given for the blind people of one locality by a local benevolent association, jointly with the local blind activists.[8] The party was attended by approximately two hundred people, a third of whom were blind, the others being sighted relatives, companions, and activists of benevolent associations. The program featured a succession of entertainers who broadcast their performances through a set of powerful loudspeakers. The evening also featured the sale of raffle tickets. The atmosphere became increasingly rowdy and excited, particularly towards the end when the time for announcing the results of the raffle drew near. This part of the program was being managed by Mazal Eini, a blind activist. Some twenty or thirty ticketholders, mostly blind, were noisily crowding around her, and Mazal tried, not very successfully, to maintain a semblance of order. Suddenly she raised her voice yet louder and called out jokingly, "If you don't go back to your seats right now, I'll paw everyone of you from top to bottom!" (*amasheish kol ehad mikem milema'ala 'ad lemata!*) Here again a direct reference to the use of tactility was elicited in an extraordinary context, a Purim party with its marked joking and carnival association.

While the exercise of tactility enhances the performance of blind people in society, it is notable that sensitivity to tactile experience can also be a cause of distress. The comments of Penina Danieli on homemaking were illuminating on this point. She remarked that stains of food and dirt, that might disturb a sighted person, did not bother her. She said that she took care to remove stains, when these were pointed out to her, but only for the sake of her sighted environment and to maintain respect. Dusty surfaces on the other hand, disturbed her personally because they were unpleasant to the touch.

II. Olfaction

In contrast to the tactile sense which is naturally exercised visibly, use of the olfactory sense among humans is usually not visibly evident. The use of the sense of smell therefore readily escapes the opprobrium imposed by the Western aversion for bodily expression. Consequently, blind people are able to enhance their capabilities by having recourse to smell to a much greater extent than they are by touching. The blind have been reported to orient themselves through odors that mark various points along routes they take (Steiner et al. 1988).

In a social group discussing the weight of visual attractiveness in heterosexual ties among the blind, most of the participants were young, single and sexually not very experienced. They minimized the importance of tactility and olfaction. They claimed that, with the assistance of sighted companions, they could use visual criteria and thus not differ from the sighted. The forementioned Rivqa Cohen was articulate in attributing weight to the unimpaired senses in heterosexual ties. She did not care about a man's appearance, she stated, but was concerned that he be clean and have a pleasant odor. Rivqa, a disillusioned mature woman in her forties, with a history of a long, unhappy marriage, stood in bold contrast to the other discussants. It is remarkable that Rivqa held a socially marginal position among the participants in the discussion. As with the sense of tactility, I note that where the values of the blind person are less subjugated to those of the sighted, the sense of olfaction is expressed more fully.

Of all the blind people I came to know Rivqa talked most freely about her use of the olfactory sense. She recalled how once on a visit to the Western Wall in Jerusalem where people come on pilgrimage, she chanced to be near a group who had come from a farming village. From the accent of their speech, Rivqa said, she identified the villagers as kinsmen; "they spoke just like we did at home". The pilgrims turned out to be the children of the sister of Rivqa's grandmother, and they took to her lovingly. Rivqa closed her account of the moving experience in terms of olfaction, "They had the odor of a farm!" (*reyah mesheq*).

The sighted are usually not aware of the extent to which the blind cultivate the sense of olfaction. This difference can be a source of pain as revealed by Sevia Aslan. A lonely single woman, the boundaries of her life were her parental home and the office where she worked as a switchboard operator. Sevia was sensitive to the failings of courtesy of people about her. She was pleased that some of her colleagues greeted her but was hurt by others who ignored her, and who, she imagined, believed that she did not notice their impoliteness. Sevia told me that in fact she was so sensitive to the odors of individuals and the sounds of their footsteps, that she easily recognized people passing her, even if they did not utter a word. Sevia claimed, that from the scent of the particular perfume that lingered there, she knew which of her female colleagues frequented the washroom before her.

III. Audition

In the popular imagination the use of the sense of audition is that most directly associated with blind people. In the categorization of infirmities the blind and the deaf are frequently linked, sometimes being conceived as similar, sometimes as contrasting.[9] There is no positive reason for this; in reality the conditions of blindness and deafness and their ramifications, are very different.[10] Blindness can be appositioned to any other disability such as epilepsy, Down's syndrome or poliomyelitis, with as much a logic as it can be appositioned to deafness. The nature of the cultural categorization of disabilities remains to be studied. Suffice it to note the relevance of disability categories to the question of the use of the senses. Namely, Western middle-class sensitivities accept wider exercise of sight and hearing than of the tactile and olfactory senses.

One need not be as guarded when seeing and hearing, and talking about this, as one has to be when touching and smelling. There are many more contexts in Western culture where glancing and looking, if not actually staring, are perfectly acceptable, than there are contexts that permit even subtle tactility. The same applies to listening, even though "eaves-dropping" is considered improper in certain contexts. Bluntly, the blind are therefore permitted to hear (and the deaf to see). Popular imagination actually exaggerates and glorifies the natural hearing ability of blind people.[11] The attitude of the sighted thus encourages the blind to develop the ability to listen to its fullest.[12] Some blind people are more sensitive than others to the range of experience that audition opens to them, and listen more carefully. There are also individual differences in the application of training and discipline to innate physiological capacities. But beyond limitations of that kind, Western culture imposes fewer limitations on hearing than it does on touching and smelling.

The superior hearing-performance of the blind can lead to dramatic leaps in social acceptance, as in an incident in which Yafa Makhluf was involved. A single woman in her forties, of Baghdadi background, whose friends and family lived mostly in an outlying city suburb, Yafa had moved to an upper middle-class city neighborhood in order to be closer to her work. She was fortunate to have found a small, inexpensive apartment, but she was exceptional among her neighbors. The other residents of the apartment building were older, well-to-do professionals of Central-European background. Thus there were contrasts of age, class, ethnicity, family status and physical condition. Yafa recalled that when she first moved into her home she had the feeling that her neighbors shunned her. This all changed when, one day, Yafa saved one of her neighbors from a burglary attempt. She heard the lock of the apartment door below her being forced, and suspecting a burglary, swiftly called the police. The neighbors appreciated their blind neighbor, "And after that", Yafa said, "I was a queen to them!" Since then, she said, she feels accepted by her neighbors.

In contrast to tactility and olfaction blind people overtly and directly express the exercise of their hearing sense, as did Ze'ev Gutman, saying "When it is noisy, I do not see you speaking to me."

Nuances of mood are conveyed to this sensitive person by mutations of tone exclusively, which the sighted notice primarily by changes in the facial expression of the speaker. Avraham San'ani is another such person. One evening when I was sitting in his apartment he remarked,

> Just now my neighbor is taking his waste bin downstairs to pour [its contents] into the refuse container. You didn't hear or see him. But I did! For me the closed door is no obstacle for seeing beyond it!

Avraham recognized his neighbor and his activities from having carefully listened to the latter's habits, the sound of footsteps and other noises he made when carrying down the garbage. Just as the sighted do not cultivate the olfactory sense as much as the blind, so also do they not sharpen their audition to the same extent. This may give rise to ill-feeling and misunderstandings between the sighted and the blind. Aharon Ben-Arsi was involved in quarrels at his place of employment with people whom he served as switchboard operator. On one occasion, Aharon's superior contacted him by phone to reprimand him about a complaint from one of the secretaries who had come to his office. Aharon asked that before he presented his side of the story, the secretary leave the manager's office, so that their conversation be private. The manager agreed to the request and told Aharon that the woman had left his room. Aharon then retorted that this was untrue because, if the secretary had walked out, he would have recognized her steps over the telephone. Thereupon the conversation degenerated into angry exchanges.

The salient point lies not in the actual ability of people such as Aharon, Avraham and Sevia to achieve remarkable feats of discernment. They may have been mistaken in their claims (I did not check whether indeed the neighbor was taking down his garbage, nor whether Aharon's suspicion was justified). The importance of the incidents lies in their conveying the image that these people have of themselves, of being endowed with superior sensitivity. This image gives Aharon the self-confidence to assume a position in a situation that his sighted interaction partner, the manager, did not anticipate. The latter did not attribute to Aharon extraordinary hearing ability. Consequently the manager dealt with the situation as he did: either he lied, concealing the fact that the secretary had not left the room, or if the woman had left the room unnoticed by Aharon, the superior reviled the latter for his extraordinary suspiciousness. Aharon's purported enhanced hearing ability, which was not shared by his superior, was a source of friction, and obviated smooth communication with his sighted partner.

The importance of audition leads many blind people to avoid doing violence to their hearing sense, such as by exposure to the high-volume music that is commonly blared from amplifiers at weddings and parties. Some sophisticated individuals are articulate in expressing their fear of damaging their hearing in such situations. Beyond that, people suffered directly from noise because it impaired their orientation and overall abilities. Very ordinary sources of noise also distress blind people. Frequently they complained about the loud radios in public buses which numbed their ability to orient themselves. Many stated that they preferred not to attend weddings and similar celebrations. However, since these affairs are usually organized by sighted hosts, absenting oneself from them implied self-imposed isolation for the blind. At noisy parties I encountered blind participants attempting to escape the din. This was particularly evident, ironically, at some of the large annual Purim and Hannuka[13] parties arranged by the benevolent associations for the blind. Some blind people stood forlornly in relatively quiet passageways. Once I noticed a woman who had turned her chair around to evade the direct blast of the amplifiers and sat facing a blank wall.

Conclusion

As with all human sensitivity, the cultivation and exercise of the unimpaired senses increase awareness. This also leads to apprehension of pain, as we saw in the case of Sevia Aslan on audition, and Penina Danieli on tactility. Of all the unimpaired senses, the blind are permitted, even encouraged, to use the audition widely. This difference we suggest, is rooted in Western culture that has principled objections to the exercise of audition in only few situations, while it discourages the exercise of tactility and olfaction in many more contexts. One important source for the limitation of the exercise of the sense of hearing lies in the contextual practice of hearing of the able-bodied. The latter conceive hearing within an overall context of senses that includes unimpaired vision. Hearing is relatively less important to the sighted than it is to the sightless. The former do not derive the maximum from their sense of hearing: they frequently even engage in practices that disturb their own hearing ability. The dominant culture imposes these practices upon blind people, thereby interfering with their ability to function effectively among the sighted. Relative to the exercise of audition, Western culture imposes itself even more heavily on tactility and olfaction. In the context of Western middle-class culture which restricts tactility, blind people are virtually prohibited from freely exercising that sense.[14]

These observations extend the perspective of labelling theory with respect to blindness. Robert Scott (1969) has cogently argued that the roles of blind men in society are anything but naturally given. They are socio-culturally constructed, more, imposed. It is now evident that the cultural construction of blindness runs deeper. Culture impinges not merely on occupational and other social roles of blind people, but also on what one might take as their human essence, the way they manage their bodies. This study demonstrates that elemental activities of blind people are by and large constructed by the general environmental culture, and only secondarily by the natural fact of sightlessness.[15]

Finally, some of the parameters that figure in this social construction have been uncovered. Wherever I observed relatively free exercise of the senses, this was linked to peripheral people or to conditions of peripherality, in relation to the dominant culture. Thus Aharon did not adhere to the public presentation of the blind self of his peers; Rivqa was a mature and experienced widowed woman in a group of immature young people; and the film and Purim incidents occurred in extraordinary settings. On the other hand, I encountered no incidents of unrepressed expressions of the unimpaired senses in ordinary situations and among people who conformed to their social setting. Such incidents might have occurred, but my field notes are eloquently silent on this point. This leads to the conclusion that restraints on the exercise of unimpaired senses are greater on people and in situations that are close to the institutionalized center of society. Restraints are weaker as people are removed from that center.

Having uncovered some of the social forces that impinge upon blind people's management of their bodies, we proceed in the next chapter to study how the usage of technical aids, to facilitate mobility, is also moulded by social constraints that emanate from the sighted environment.

Chapter Three

The Use of Guide Dogs and Long Canes

When physical disability is culturally constructed through concepts of stigma the physically impaired individual is prone to various forms of discredit. The elucidation of these social consequences constitutes a major trend in the literature on discredited people ever since Goffman.[1] In addition to the consequences of stigmatization of disabled individuals the literature also highlights the effect of stigma for individuals who are part of the ambience of the discredited person. Such individuals, although themselves able-bodied, are prone to be subjected to "courtesy stigma" (Jones et al. 1984: 71–76, and citations). Another major focus of the literature on discredited people is on the reaction to, or management of stigma, by individuals. Some of the ethnographies of physically disabling conditions mentioned in the introduction, provide vivid insight into various strategies that individuals employ.

The aim of this chapter is to draw attention to the fact that discredit does not pertain only to individuals, but also to material objects and, paradoxically, even to the implements of aid that disabled people use to assist themselves. This perspective on the study of physical disability is also pertinent to the more general socio-anthropological study of material culture. One approach to that area has been that of the classical Chicago school of urban sociology as exemplified by Ogburn 1933, and many associates, and now interestingly resuscitated by Claude Fischer 1985, 1988, and others.[2] These scholars seek to demonstrate the social effects of technologies. But whereas the older work was framed in generalities, the new work is relatively much more specific, both in terms of the problems formulated and of the empirical fields subjected to research. Material culture has also been approached from the anthropological angle. Scholars such as Douglas and Isherwood 1978, Csikszentmihaly and Rochberg-Halton 1981, and the contributors to the Appadurai 1986 collection have demonstrated that mundane household artifacts which

Blind People

people bring into their homes are pregnant with cultural meaning, often attributed idiosyncratically by their owners. According to this view a major, though certainly not the sole function of the acquisition and consumption of goods, is to make order and to discriminate. The sociological and anthropological approaches are thus complementary: the latter illuminates subtle, cultural and personal existential factors that operate beside the more overt social, organizational and material forces. The present study, dwelling upon a unique category of material objects, mobility aids for blind people, is part of the current wave of interest in material culture. In particular, it draws together the strands of disparate approaches, seeking thereby to underpin the theoretical significance of the various approaches.

Following upon the forementioned insights into material culture, one may concede to the general statement, that "medical technology is moulded in no straightforward sense by a simple goal of efficacious healing" (MacKenzie and Wajcman 1985:306). However, while socio-anthropological perspectives have enlightened our understanding of medical knowledge, they have on the whole not been brought to bear upon the study of the social shaping of the material artifacts and technology of medicine. MacKenzie and Wajcman go on to suggest plausibly:

> Prevailing medical theory, the social nature of the doctor-patient relation, institutional frameworks such as hospitals ... divides of gender, class and race, the role of the state—all these appear to have a place in shaping medical technology (op. cit.).

Focusing now upon the mobility aids of blind people, as part of the broad complex of technology designed to assist people with physical disorders, will contribute to fill this lacuna in our understanding of the dynamics of material culture.

I. Long Canes

Impaired mobility, caused by blindness, is a major component of the stigmatizing image that the sighted have of blind people and is a matter of crucial concern to blind people themselves. The writer, Ved Mehta, recalls in his memoirs an incident that highlights this. Mehta was a seventeen year-old graduate of a school for the blind, taking leave of a sighted teacher who had trained him many years:

> "Son, what's the most precious thing you're taking from us?" Mr. Wooly asked, breaking the little silence in the car—it seemed that none of us knew what to say. "Mobil-

ity," I said unhesitatingly. I was surprised at the baldness of my reply" (*New Yorker*, November 25, 1985, p. 129).

The era of electronics has brought with it promises that electronic pathfinders would revolutionize blindness-linked mobility. But certainly in Israel, and probably elsewhere too, this has not yet been realized. At present there are only half a dozen electronic canes in the country, and even these are not in constant operation because their fragility leads to breakdowns which necessitate servicing overseas.

The predominant mobility aids are of two types: long canes and guide dogs. Failing those, the blind person is destined either to depend on sighted guides or to immobility. For all its deceptive simplicity, the long cane is the single most important achievement of technology for the blind. Essentially it is an extended limb that enables blind pedestrians to ascertain the nature of the immediate space facing them. Being virtual extensions of limbs, collapsible long canes are very personal objects. The people whom we studied exhibited a possessive attitude toward them, rather similar to ladies' handbags. Usually they were careful to have them within reach, either in personal cases or handbags, or they actually clutched them for long stretches of time. Prior to the perfection of long cane mobility technique, blind people used ordinary canes. For guidance the value of such canes is very limited. They are helpful for orthopedic purposes but healthy blind people do not require this type of assistance.

For all its advantages long cane-aided mobility involves a number of tangible difficulties. It is stressful, demanding constant concentration in its implementation, and it is laboriously slow. Compared to other pedestrians, the cane-aided traveller requires inordinately large sidewalk territory. In heavy pedestrian traffic the blind person with a cane presents an obstruction to rushing sighted people who, in most instances, are unprepared for an encounter with this radically different type of pedestrian. Many blind people have had the traumatic experience of having their canes damaged by sighted pedestrians carelessly stepping on them; consequently some harbor a constant fear of such an occurrence. Not only impatient and uncouth pedestrians, but also patronizing and overly solicitous ones present hazards to the blind cane-user.

Such situations are exemplified by the following account by a computer operator:

> The routes that I travel regularly I can do very fast. I have my signs of street details, and I count my steps from one to the next. So my orientation is very good. The other day as I was rushing to get the bus to work, I hear a man shouting from a distance, '*Adoni! Adoni!* (Sir! Sir!)'. The man contin-

ued shouting while running towards me, so I stopped walking. When the man reached me panting, breathless, he just
asked, 'Sir! Sir! Where do you want to go?' That angers me!
That confuses me! I lose the signs I have of my route. If I
require assistance I ask for it!

Volunteered help on the street is thus a mixed blessing. The
unrequisited do-gooder assumes that a person, by the mere fact of
blindness, cannot manage without assistance. Such a volunteer, while
having good intentions, interferes and makes the adept cane-user's
task more difficult. On the other hand, for the inept cane-user, there
is frequently a paucity of volunteered help.

Cane-aided mobility has also created a highly visible marker of
the blind condition. In contrast to the short cane, the long cane is
unique to the blind. Since the former is also used by the aged and
halting, it is not so clearly a marker of the blind.[3] The new long cane
technique, while emancipating blind people from their previous association with other disabilities, has created a new clearly stigmatizing
marker, definitive for blind people. This is especially true when the
long cane is properly used in the fan motion, accompanied by characteristic tapping sounds. People using the improved mobility aid thus
pay a price, they are walking advertisements of their exception.

Blind people were often aware of this and expressed embarrassment, not only because of the visibility of the cane to the sighted but
also because of its audibility, the tapping sound. The latter property
was referred to in conversations on cane usage. The informants even
innovated linguistically to express this sound, by formulating the
natural sound as a Hebrew verb (*le'taqteiq*). People sometimes expressed a yearning to be able to escape using the cane. One woman,
Rivqa Cohen, persisted in her attempts to walk about in her neighborhood without mobility aids. She recounted that in doing so, she
repeatedly crashed into obstacles and that she had broken her dark
glasses four times. Thereafter she began to wear cheap plastic spec-
tacles. Rivqa explained her behavior by saying that her neighbors
used to encourage her to walk about unaided, "You walk so well.
What do you need a cane for?" Though Rivqa may or may not have
received such thoughtless encouragement, her behavior reflects how
much she yearned to escape usage of the cane.

Rivqa is a woman burdened with grave material and family problems who lives in a run-down neighborhood and works in a sheltered-
workshop. Another person, Yoram Peres, was a man whose situation
was very different from that of Rivqa, yet he behaved similarly. A
telephone switchboard operator who had contacts with middle-class
professionals, and lived in a comfortable supportive environment,

Yoram was free from overt burdens. He was an able person endowed with a superb memory and a good sense of direction who moved about efficiently with the aid of his cane. Yoram used to boast about his self-reliance and being superior in some ways to his sighted colleagues. Nevertheless, Yoram avoided using the cane whenever he could. Like Rivqa, he frequently negotiated routes familiar to him without a cane and, like her, he paid the price of suffering minor accidents (such as falls and a bruised nose).

The behavior of Yafa Makhluf, also a switchboard operator, while again illustrating attempts at evading cane usage, also demonstrates several modes of acceptance. For many years Yafa used to walk to work from her city apartment, a distance of a few blocks, without using a cane. The route did not entail any busy crossings and was not crowded with pedestrian traffic. At that time, collapsible long canes were not available in Israel, only cumbersome, one-piece canes. Two elements thus operated in Yafa's situation that encouraged her to move about unaided—the availability of only a particularly visible and, in her estimation, repulsive instrument, and the feasibility of an easy route. It is also possible that Yafa was endowed with a measure of "facial vision" which bolstered her confidence.[4] After some years Yafa changed her place of employment. Although this too was within walking distance of her home, it required negotiating major thoroughfares, crowded with children rushing to school and adults to work, and included several busy intersections. At that time collapsible canes had already become available in Israel, and Yafa resigned herself to cane usage.

However, Yafa's cane technique is not the standard fan spread. She explained that she only holds the cane in front of her in order to prevent hurrying people from bumping into her. Thus, she said, she spares herself the embarrassment of tapping her cane in public. But Yafa claims to forget her cane sometimes. Once, she recounted, she came home from a visit in an outlying distant suburb and noticed its absence only upon alighting from the bus, some blocks from her home. She walked home unaided. Yafa thus reports three modes of cane-usage for improved mobility: the standard fan technique, usage as a symbol only, and deliberate non-use. Her account reflects the ongoing struggle to attain independent mobility, while minimizing as much as possible usage of a stigmatizing aid.

II. Guide Dogs

The major alternative to cane-aided mobility are guide dogs. However, relatively few people in Israel avail themselves of this possibil-

ity. At the time of the study there were only about one hundred and
twenty guide dogs in the whole country, and of these about one-third
were owned by a particular category of blind people, veteran soldiers.
In fact, unless they suffer from additional disabilities such as impaired limbs which make the use of guide dogs impossible, most
blinded veterans employ this type of mobility aid. In this the veterans
are exceptional. Thousands of other blind Israelis do not employ guide
dogs. There are a number of reasons for this, one of them was the
difficulties involved in acquiring a guide dog. Dogs are obtained overseas and that is costly. This problem is usually solved by funds donated by public institutions and philanthropists. Applications for guide
dogs are screened by a committee of the Israel Guide Dog Association
which selects applicants who meet given prerequisites, such as physical fitness, understanding and ability for animal care, and ability to
bear the cost of maintenance of the dog. Successful candidates are
then assisted in acquiring a guide dog.

In view of this support system, the remarkably small number of
guide dog users in Israel does not seem to be rooted only in the
difficulties encountered in acquiring a dog. It probably also stems
from limited demand. In the course of fieldwork, I did not meet a
single cane-user, who earnestly sought to own a guide dog and had
failed to obtain one. On the other hand, there were a number of cane-
users who deliberately eschewed using guide dogs, and even one who
had had a guide dog and who had reverted to cane usage. On the
surface this is astonishing since it is generally accepted that usage of
guide dogs improves mobility performance.[5]

The clue lies in the different patterns of ownership of guide dogs
in Israel and the United States. This difference leads to an insight
into the socio-cultural moulding of mobility practices of the Israeli
blind. Israeli guide dog users are predominantly members of upper
strata (in terms of the stratification of blind people described later in
chapter 6). In the United States, however, guide dog users are to be
found not only in the upper strata: one commonly encounters guide
dogs on central city streets being used by blind persons who clearly
belong to low social strata, the poor and the racial minorities. Even
dog-guided beggars can be met on U.S. city streets. The social range
of Israeli guide dog users is comparatively small.

This limited spread of guide dog ownership is partly linked to the
particularly centralized Israeli system and its role in allocating support for acquiring guide dogs. But there is also an element rooted in
the culture and social life of Israelis. In Jewish culture there is a
repugnance of dogs as unclean beasts.[6] In Israel having dogs as domestic pets, while common now, still clashes with social impulses
rooted in tradition. This negative attitude towards dogs applies, by

and large, to guide dogs too. The feeling is particularly potent among people who are close to tradition, it declines as they distance themselves from tradition. The overall situation is very different from that of societies, such as those of Western countries, where the dog is romantically viewed as "man's best friend". Consequently, members of tradition-bound social strata in Israel, who for historical reasons (outlined in chapter 8), comprise most of the adult blind, have a sound cultural basis for refraining from having recourse to guide dogs as mobility aids.

In one of the social groups in which I participated, there was only one guide dog user, the rest were all cane-users. Some of the latter expressed repugnance at the presence of the dog in the room. Out of the dog owner's hearing, Rivqa Cohen repeatedly expressed her dislike of what she claimed was the dog's bad odor.[7] But dogs are problematic not only for people who have such strong aversions to them, but also for the owners themselves. Danny Akram exemplified this ambivalence. He was married to a woman who was blind since childhood, although he himself suffered from a condition that had permitted him a degree of unaided mobility until his early twenties. Thereafter, his eyesight deteriorated and he required an aid. He had not managed to become competent in the use of a long cane. When his little son grew up, Danny used him for street guidance, but that proved to be unsatisfactory. Danny felt that the child's service disrupted his other activities and perverted the overall relationship between father and child. Wisely, Danny was concerned that his family should not suffer from the development of what has come to be termed "a parental child". Therefore, although not being naturally predisposed to having a dog (he came from a traditional Middle-Eastern background), Danny resigned himself to acquiring a guide dog.

Danny was a satisfied guide dog user. But while waxing eloquent on the usefulness of the dog, he also elaborated on the difficulties he had reconciling family life with dog ownership. The presence of the large animal in his small apartment was disturbing. The children sometimes played with the dog as a pet, disrupting the animal's discipline and diminishing its usefulness. Danny believed that the dog was often unruly in the small apartment because of the children's doings. In the context of a tightly knit family, inexperienced with handling dogs, and particularly a meticulously trained guide dog, Danny's solution to his mobility problem is a mixed blessing which, in his case, clashed with harmonious family life.[7]

The experiences of other people parallel those of Danny. Yafa Makhluf, whom we met in the previous chapter, is a single woman living by herself far from her family and old friends. On the surface it would appear that Yafa has social characteristics, namely compounded isolation, that would lead to successful dog ownership. In fact, Yafa had reservations similar to those expressed by Danny. She said that basically she disliked dogs. She felt that were she to go visiting with a guide dog, she would harm relationships with her parents and married siblings, as they would not feel comfortable with a dog in their homes. Another woman, Yemima Kagan, used a guide dog because, like Danny, she felt inadequate at cane-aided mobility. Yemima was eloquent and reserved about dog-usage, in virtually the same breath. Using images drawn from Jewish mysticism, she waxed poetic about the faithfulness of her dog, "The soul of a very saintly person (*sadiq gadol*) has transmigrated into my dog!"[8] But immediately thereafter she would go on to talk about the inconvenience of dog guidance, elaborating on the many situations that did not permit the presence of a dog (such as formal visits on occasions of festivities and mourning, and at synagogue). The compound effect of a culture that has a negative attitude towards dogs, together with the kind of close social ties that blind people maintain with the sighted, is a major factor that inhibits the widespread usage of guide dogs.

Even when adopted, the efficient use of guide dogs is hampered by unfamiliarity with dogs in general, and guide dogs in particular. Owners of dogs must contend not only with the doings of family members, but also with those of their whole social ambience, people whose fundamentally negative attitude towards dogs is based on unfamiliarity with the animal. At the industrial plant where he was employed as an assembly worker, Danny Akram used his dog to move on the shop floor, threading his way between machines and irregularly placed equipment and materials. However, Danny complained, the behavior of his co-workers made using the dog difficult. Having shed their basic cultural disposition and lacking a tradition of maintaining and disciplining dogs, people such as Danny's co-workers are prone to indiscriminate petting. Both revulsion and improper handling are problems that inhibit the most effective usage.

III. Conclusion

The observations demonstrate that mobility aids are prone to symbolization like other artifacts in the domestic environment. This symbolization can lead people to stigmatize the artifacts and to shun them. That process, it needs hardly be said, is not universal; it is there potentially and only sometimes, in fact. Also in the ambience of the blind Israelis, mobility aids, particularly guide dogs, were often incorporated favorably, sometimes with love and warmth. The present discussion focuses upon only one form of incorporation of the material

aids of the handicapped in society, that of stigmatization. It is remarkable that the potential for this kind of symbolization can move
not only sighted, but also blind people. The existential situation of the
latter is radically different from that of the former, in reference to the
role of mobility aids in their lives. Nevertheless, the common culture
that both sighted and blind share in a given context can lead to
certain elements of symbolization being common to both kinds of
people.

At this point a comparative mention of the place of television in
the lives of blind people will be illuminating. In Israel people devote
relatively little time to television in comparison to that of many other
countries, Israelis are also highly-regimented viewers (about 80% of
television owners view a certain daily program, Kahanman 1986, p.
4). Among the blind people of this study however, I encountered many
negative expressions about televiewing. People said it caused them to
be superfluous among the sighted.[9] One man said,

> Abroad [in Baghdad] life was better for the blind. Sighted
> people used to accompany me. But now television intrudes
> (*mafria*); it separates (*marhiq*) the sighted from us. Tech-
> nology hurts us![10]

However in marked contrast to this and other such expressions, television sets were much in evidence in these same people's homes; even
in many households composed solely of blind couples or singles. One
rationale for this, offered by blind television set owners, was that the
sets served to entertain sighted guests who also provided running
commentaries for their blind hosts. Another rationale was that ownership of a television set permitted listening to the main evening
news broadcast on television. Both explanations are factually dubious. Many people own radios that have access to the television channel, making ownership of television sets superfluous. Secondly, many
sighted viewers are not sufficiently articulate to be able to give their
blind companions a running commentary. The purported explanations are actually part of a puzzling phenomenon, and themselves
require explaining. Gaining an insight into this is pertinent to our
understanding of the social construction of the usage of mobility aids
by blind people.

I was afforded such an insight while visiting a young man,
Shime'on Serussi, who lived in a distant part of the country, after a
mutual friend had made a telephone introduction. Shime'on had been
only vaguely informed of the purpose of the visit and was unsure
about how to host me. I was seated on a settee opposite the television
set and, after serving me a drink, Shime'on asked if I would like to
watch the evening news, which few people in Israel miss. But I was

not interested and onto my polite refusal I pegged an elaboration of the purpose of my visit. The man reacted with relief; he went on to say that he too was more interested in talking. He explained that he had thought I would not want to miss, what he surmised, was part of my daily routine. Shime'on went on to say that he kept the television set only for the needs of sighted visitors.

In being considerate of the putative wishes of his visitor, this man was thus willing to forego his personal convenience in his own home. The incident highlights the ambivalent, virtually dialectical effect of television in such situations. It both lessens and increases the gap between sighted and blind, depending upon the level and kind of interaction. It appears that there is a parallel in the roles that television and mobility aids play in the lives of blind people, even though the former is particular to the condition of the sighted and the latter to that of the blind. Blind people incorporate television into their lives to promote their integration, while in fact they bolster their marginality at one level of their interaction with the sighted. Similarly blind people sometimes reject mobility aids to enhance their integration among the sighted, while in fact they impair thereby their mobility.

The symbolization of material objects in society is linked to their being adopted and used in particular ways. One aspect of this is that when an object is widely adopted, even extraordinary individuals (in the present context—blind people), for whom it is unsuited, are driven to adopt it. On the other hand, objects that are designed for discredited people are prone to be symbolized accordingly, to be stigmatized. Mobility aids are incorporated into the symbolic system of the general culture, and are conceptualized similarly to the way that blind people are conceptualized. The implications of this conclusion range far beyond guide dogs and long canes. People in a great variety of physical conditions require technical aids, such as wheelchairs, hearing aids and respirators, and the social effects of these objects can be ambivalent. The elucidation of the effects of these developments of technology is a challenge for the socio-anthropological study of disability.

Having focused on the two major facets of body management by blind people, the exercise of the unimpaired senses and the use of aids to overcome the deficiency of the impaired sense, we move to Part Two, where we shall see blind people in action in the intimacy of the close family circle.

Part II

The Domestic Circle

Chapter Four

Coming of Age

The social study of disability in terms of labelling theory, and particularly in terms of the sociology of stigma as developed by Goffman (1963), remains to date the major viable approach to the field. According to this approach, disabled people are generally perceived by the able-bodied in terms of "a master status" of handicap, and not in terms of the other categorical attributes a person carries. An important ramification of this way of perceiving disabled people is that they are stereotyped in a condescending, often denigrating, manner. They are a priori considered to lack many of the skills, needs and desires of the able-bodied, in short, they are stigmatized.

The operation of the stigma of handicap has been studied primarily in public settings by Goffman himself and by scholars who followed him. Comparatively little effort has been expended on the study of stigma in the intimacy of domestic settings. On the one hand, one might presume that the parents of disabled children would relate to them differently from strangers, whose contacts with these children are incidental. On the part of parents whose relationships with their offspring are diffuse, not fragmented and specific, one might expect the attribution of a master status of handicap, and of stigmatizing, to be uncommon. On the other hand, there are indications that not only aliens, but also parents inculcate in their disabled children the feeling that their condition is stigmatized. Thus, in studies of epilepsy, parents are described as being "stigma coaches" (Schneider and Conrad 1980; Scambler and Hopkins 1986). Also an Israeli study of the parenting practices of parents of newborn malformed infants (Weiss 1986) supports this.

The objective of this chapter is to extend the study of stigma to the domestic setting, showing that among blind people parents play a role in inculcating stigma. Further, parental behavior has a dialectical effect on their blind children, particularly when the latter distance themselves from their parents. After describing some of the

37

patronizing practices of sighted parents, and some of the reactions
that young people develop, the chapter finally focuses on young people
as they move towards marriage, and demonstrate the effects of stigma
in marital choice.

I. Coping with Sighted Parents

    The people of the study were adults and they recounted their life
histories. A theme that recurred was their desire to escape anxious,
over-protective parents who restricted their activities. Many informants felt that their parents had had low aspirations for them. Both
in the areas of job-seeking and marriage-making, sighted parents
encouraged their blind offspring to reconcile themselves to undesirable alternatives—switchboard operating or sheltered workshop ca-
reers, and blind mates for marriage. As they grew to maturity, these
people made great efforts to leave the parental home and to attain
independence. The phenomenon is notable. Young Israelis of Middle
Eastern immigrant background, particularly those who are religiously
observant, are generally slow to move out of the parental home. Among
my blind informants, however, most reported striving with determination to be by themselves; many succeeded. Moreover, even people
lacking homemaking skills strove to have their own apartments. People
wanted to be independent, even though logistically this was sometimes very difficult for them. Therefore, they made compromises. A
case in point is that of Nehama Gadol. A woman in her early thirties,
she developed a *modus vivendi* wherein she formally had her own
home, but since she was apprehensive of being by herself at night,
she slept at her mother's. Since she could not cook, she ate dinner
there too. In fact, this person's apartment served her only during
those few hours, in the afternoon after work, when she happened not
to have any leisure activities away from home. Yet formally, she lived
independently.
    There were also many adult blind people who did not succeed in
severing their ties with the parental home. They remained single well
into middle age and continued to live with their aging parents. Some
of them were most deficient in domestic skills, mainly due to having
been deprived by their parents of opportunities to practice homemaking. Like Nehama, some were virtually incapable of preparing even
simple meals for themselves. A common refrain in the talk of sighted
parents, who had blind adult children living with them, concerned
the matter-of-course nurturing and caring. Esther Dadon, a vivacious
twenty-six year-old single woman, adept in mobility, lived at home.
Despite her considerable independence in mobility and her stable
employment in a sheltered workshop, Esther's mother used phrases

such as "I put her on the bus," "Her brother does . . . for her." Typically, Esther was inept in homemaking.

The patronage of blind children by their sighted parents was an important source of dependence among blind adults. At its extreme, it led to the pathetic phenomenon of doddering old parents extending personal services to their middle-aged children, preparing their food, and maintaining a home for them. One such parent died at the time of my research. Within a year of the woman's death, her blind daughter, who was rather helpless at home, suffered from undernourishment and a dramatic deterioration of health. The tendency of sighted parents to continue patronizing and thus to retain a measure of sovereignty over their children sometimes continued even after the latter married, moved into separate quarters and became parents themselves. One home included the blind husband's sighted mother, who monopolized much of the homemaking, although the blind daughter-in-law was quite capable (she did beautiful crocheting), and could probably have coped with more than she actually did.

However, there were also parents who encouraged their children by imparting skills and self-confidence. For such children, living at home did not constitute a threat to their independence. They did not assert themselves stressfully, and continued to live at home without overt conflict. Such were the cases of young blind people of particularly high aspirations (expressed for instance in ruling out blind marital candidates).

In the particular context of Israeli society, the repression of blind children is mitigated by the overall structure of education and society. Israeli society is primarily composed of a vast immigrant population that came to the country from Middle-Eastern and Eastern European countries over the past forty years. At the outset, the immigrants comprised the lower socio-economic strata of society, but over the years, most people have succeeded in ascending the socio-economic-ladder. The earlier phases of this process entailed shifts in occupations and living standards which were followed much later, and unevenly, by improved levels of education. The education of blind youngsters was different, however. It had the early advantage of an old, established and well-endowed facility, the Jerusalem School for the Blind. Blind youngsters from all parts of the country were encouraged to maximize benefits from this institution by using the School's dormitory. Thus, many of them lived for years in an institutional setting away from their homes. This, in turn, led to social mobility coupled with distancing from the family.

The sheer geographical distances and the logistic difficulties encountered when travelling by public transport tended to buttress the feeling of distance, social and physical, between family and hometown and the residential school. Sara Shmuel who, soon after finishing school in Jerusalem, married and moved to Haifa in the north of the country, expressed this well. She had been born in Beer-Sheba in the south, where her large family lived. In speaking of her home town she said, "I am not a Beer-Shebaite; I've been away so much from Beer-Sheba, that I don't know my way around there."

During the hectic early decades of statehood, the 1950s and 1960s, many of the siblings of blind youngsters were subjected to socialization in socio-economically deprived homes and in chaotic, mediocre schools, due to the conditions of mass immigration. The blind students however, enjoyed relatively superior education at that time. Many obtained a general humanistic education while their sighted siblings, at best, received schooling in crafts and often dropped out of school altogether. I met a number of blind college students and graduates from such families who were way ahead of their siblings and parents in terms of mental interests, though they lagged behind in terms of material achievements. These educated people were painfully aware of the gulf that had developed between them and their families. One such person, thirty-year-old Shlomo Deromi, single and with a Master's degree in philosophy, lacked a secure income. He claimed that he had no close rapport with anyone in his family and, when asked with whom he did have close contact, he replied, "My teachers at the university." That, in the Israeli context, where relationships between professors and students are usually aloof, is astonishing. Although Shlomo's experience may indeed have been exceptional, his comment might also reflect the wistfulness of an alienated person. Moshe Danino, who had majored in musicology, came from a traditional Moroccan family that lived in a faraway town populated mainly by North African immigrants of the 1950s and 1960s. Moshe felt that he had distanced himself from his family, because during the course of his life as a student, he had come to neglect religious practices.

Another student of similar background, Aliza Molkho, had many bitter things to say about the uncouthness of her parents and siblings. Coming from a large Moroccan family in a provincial town, she felt comfortable only with one brother; he too was a college student. Such people visited their families rarely, mainly during the major semi-annual festivals, and perforce, during university vacations. During term they lived on campus. Aliza complained that in her childhood she had never had any privacy, having had to share a bed with one of her sisters. Only recently had the home become less crowded and she had obtained a room for herself. However, Aliza still suffered from the fact that domestic arrangements at home were not considerate of her needs. Family members did not put things in their proper place, and the untidiness made it difficult for her to manage. She also said that at home she had to speak differently from the way she does elsewhere, otherwise people would not understand her. Aliza said that she deliberately shifted to a more colloquial language with her family. Such attenuation of kinship ties is linked to the overall mobility patterns of Israeli society. The material advancement of people such as Aliza's family is more marked than their educational advancement, while that of the blind family member typically lags behind her educational advancement.

The examples of family distancing described so far revolved mostly about the issue of youth developing middle-class traits against the background of a working-class home. Distancing rooted in youth shedding the middle-class practices of their parents is far less common. We proceed now to detail such a case. Binyamin Dayan was born in Morocco thirty-five years ago to a family of aristocratic rabbinical background. The family had adopted some traits of French colonial culture, in common with a stratum of such families that bridged upper-class traditional Jewish society and the colonial system.[1] As a young child Binyamin suffered from retinitis pigmentosa, but no suitable educational facility existed at the time in his Moroccan home town. The boy dropped out of school and spent his time roaming around the automobile workshops of the town. The parents did not comprehend the child's progressively deteriorating condition; they attempted to have him continue to attend a school which was unsuited to his requisites. But Binyamin, dressed in the neat, formal attire becoming a boy of his background, gave vent to his preference for things mechanical and not requiring acute eyesight. He regularly returned home with his fine clothing stained with grease.

Decades later, in his account to me, Binyamin recalled the daily punishments his parents used to mete out to him. Constructively nothing was done. Binyamin was not encouraged to carve a niche for himself in the manual labor that attracted him; nevertheless he slid out of the bourgeois groove that was naturally his. When I met Binyamin, he was a dependent person, deficient in skills. Although he worked in a sheltered workshop, all that had come of his old attraction for mechanical things was his habit of listening avidly to infrequent radio programs devoted to those subjects. Socially, Binyamin was isolated. His aged parents saw to his physical needs—food, clothing and shelter; beyond that he was often left to himself, largely immobile because of his deficiency in mobility, alone with his radio. Even at his age, Binyamin was permitted at home to listen to his favorite pop music only through earphones, and to smoke only in the yard. Relations between the bourgeois parents and the would-be work-

ing class son were such that I found him happiest only when alone—
the house filled with smoke, the stereo system blaring.

Another case of downward mobility evolved in a contrasting way.
Also about the same age as Binyamin, Re'uma Perah was the daughter of a successful businessman. The father, a cultured and well-
connected person, had invested much in his daughter and she developed wide ranging interests and good taste, expressed in the style of
her well furnished apartment and her fashionable dress. However,
whether due to lack of talent or insufficient application to studies,
Re'uma did not advance professionally beyond being a telephone
switchboard operator. She exemplifies descent from a decidedly upper
middle-class background to the low middle-class stratum occupied by
many blind people. But of all the blind switchboard operators I met,
she held the highest position. Not only was Re'uma employed in a
well-paying private firm, as compared to most of her peers who worked
in lower-salaried public institutions, but she was also the supervisor
of a number of other switchboard operators in her office. At one time
she was honored with a prize for excellence at work. The coincidence
is notable: of all the blind switchboard operators, the one with the
highest income and status at work came from an upper middle-class
family.[2] Her resourceful and sensible parents had directed their child's
natural abilities so as to obviate a status clash; Binyamin's parents,
also an upper middle-class family, did nothing to help their son find a
niche in a lower-class stratum. The results are reflected not only in
the type of employment the offspring attained, but also in the quality
of the respective family relationships: Binyamin's family relationships were deplorable, while Re'uma enjoyed the love of relatives and
friends.

The interrelationships between blind youths and their families
often lead to the emergence of powerful emotions towards parents,
emotions which ran the gamut from love to ambivalence to revulsion.[3]
A number of informants told me that they permitted themselves to
express anger only to their parents. One woman, Penina Danieli,
added that she never requested help from anyone for matters which
she could at all manage herself. She also permitted herself the luxury
of requesting assistance, that was not utterly essential, only from her
parents—and only towards them did she feel free to address words of
anger. As against this pattern of intergenerational relationships there
is also that of revulsion. One informant, Hava Dangur, expressed this
in a conversation about radio programs featuring Middle-Eastern music
and folklore. She and her husband were of Baghdadi background and
had come to Israel young and unmarried. Among many people of such
background these programs are very popular, but as I broached the
subject, Hava expressed disgust: No, they never tuned in to them

because they reminded her of her parental home! For reasons linked to these sentiments, the Dangurs also consciously broke with religious practices and considered themselves outrightly secular.

People as different as all these, who after having passed through the travails of adolescence, each in his or her individual way, all face the problem of adult intimacy. As they move towards the hurdle of finding a mate, they each have to contend again with the problem of their stigmatized condition.

II. Towards Marriage

As young blind people move towards establishing their own families, the initial aspiration is to find a sighted mate.[4] Usually they fail to realize this hope and eventually they resign themselves to marrying blind spouses or to remaining single. Among the latter there are individuals, mainly men, who deliberately rule out marriage with a blind partner. These individuals insist on attempting to deny their physical condition, oblivious to its socio-cultural facets—the inferior stereotyping. More commonly, blind people, particularly women, tend to compromise. They are willing to marry blind men, provided the candidate has other desirable features, i.e., good health, reasonable earning capacity, mobility, character, and integration into general society. Nevertheless, despite their readiness to compromise, many women have remained single, virtually having given up the search for a mate.

These disparate attitudes by blind men and women towards potential marital partners are rooted in the Israeli family system which has many traditional characteristics (Peres and Katz 1981). One is that women are required to bring greater resources to marriage than men, another is that women must be able and willing to perform servile domestic roles in marital life. However, the parallel requirement, that of men being successful breadwinners, is considered less essential in a situation where sexual inequality is widespread. Thus, a sighted woman is likely to accept a blind husband while the opposite is rare.[5] Stereotypically, the blind person is conceived as requiring domestic service and personal assistance. Where the wife is the blind partner, this compounds the reversal of the domestic roles, the husband having to assume the servile position vis-à-vis a mate who is inferior on two counts: being both blind and female. However, in couples where the wife is sighted and the husband blind, the traditional superior role of the male is somewhat compromised, but it places the wife in a position which, at least stereotypically, rivets her to a servile stance toward the husband.[6] That, in terms of the traditional family, is tolerable. The blind husband-sighted wife pattern of marriage is common and stable; I encountered only one divorce involving that kind of marriage. But the blind wife-sighted husband pattern is both rare and unstable. I encountered several marriages of this type that floundered and only of two that succeeded.

Marriages of the blind husband-sighted wife pattern prevail in two categories of people. The first is that of blind army veterans who number about one hundred men and, virtually none of whom married blind women.[7] This datum is significant and lends support to the contention that the marriage patterns of blind people follow the traditional attitudes prevailing in the Israeli family system. Blind veterans enjoy superior social and material status: their position in the marriage market (which altogether favors males) obviates the need for them to aspire to anything less than able-bodied women.

The second category of people in which blind husband-sighted wife marriages are common is that of elderly couples of Middle-Eastern background who married abroad or shortly after coming to Israel. This category requires a word of explanation. In the past, up to the 1950s, most Middle-Eastern Jewish marriages were arranged patrilocally by the parents. This pattern of matchmaking continued even when other facets of the traditional life had begun to disintegrate. The traditional marriage system entailed inferiority and relative passivity of youth in face of the old, and it is within this context that the father of a blind son sought to resolve the latter's marital needs. Also, the father of a sighted daughter, especially if he was penurious and the girl homely or sickly, might consider a match with a blind groom acceptable and thus a solution to his need to marry the daughter off. If, in addition, old ties of kinship existed between the two families or, if the father of the blind groom offered generous support for the young couple, and/or waived request for dowry, the pressure on the father of the sighted, prospective bride was great indeed. Such considerations would be bolstered by the inferiority of the young girl in relation to all the other people concerned. The readiness of parents to encourage such matches resulted in the integration of blind males into Middle-Eastern communities in traditional times. However, the corollary of this is that blind women in traditional Middle-Eastern communities did not have much access to blind men, not to mention the fact that their access to sighted mates was altogether blocked (for a pertinent description of the position of women in the traditional Middle-Eastern Jewish family, see Deshen 1989, ch. 7).

In present day Israel, many blind women and their kin realize early in life that their chances of finding a compatible mate, whether blind or sighted, are poor. This leads to social pressure to marry downwards, to compromise in terms of the physical and social attributes of the groom. This pressure is exercised by relatives of blind women who, engaging in matchmaking ventures, imbue stereotypic attitudes concerning blind inferiority.

Thus, an acquaintance of the parents of Penina Danieli, a vivacious and educated young woman, introduced her to a feebleminded sighted man, and tried to convince her of his compatibility as a husband. Penina's parents were exasperated by their daughter who repeatedly rejected such matches, and considered her to be unreasonably choosy. Nehama Gadol is a very different person, but her case is similar. A young woman, limited both physically and mentally, Nehama is quite resigned to marrying a blind man. However, she too has not yet found a suitable candidate since, for her, a desirable husband must work and lead an active life. Nehama has been repeatedly subjected to matchmaking propositions which were coupled with verbal pressure by relatives and friends. The propositions here also included blind men who had features that she considered objectionable—physical defects in addition to blindness, mental instability, and unemployment.

Parents differ in the extent to which they conformed to social conventions. The blind offspring interviewed, reported that some parents were less repressive than others. The mother of Devora Berkovitz, discussed below, reportedly advised against the disastrous marriage that her blind daughter eventually contracted. Some middle-aged women claimed that, in their youth, they had plunged into early marriages with blind husbands despite parental reservations as to the personal qualities of the spouses. Those cases, if factual, constitute parental direction towards personally desirable individuals within low-status categories of handicapped people. However, I never heard of parents who openly encouraged high marital aspirations in their blind offspring, in terms of socio-economic status.

In fact, blind women frequently marry downwards, whether to blind or occasionally, to sighted men. Such was the case of Devora Berkovitz, a fifty-five year-old woman who, judging from her present appearance, must have been a glamorous beauty in her youth. Devora stated that she used to work as a fashion model and, during that time, had attracted the attention of an unsavory, sighted character. Although she claimed that she was always aware of the man being degenerate, she nevertheless decided to marry him because she feared that otherwise she might never have another opportunity. She wanted to bear a child, and within wedlock. Devora said that, at the time, she realized that her marriage might break up, as in fact it soon did, but she had the satisfaction of raising a lovely daughter. The account illustrates the profound feeling of inequality of the blind in relation to the sighted in a marital context. The idea, accepted not only among the sighted, but also among many blind people, is that only a blemished sighted person would marry a blind spouse.

The feeling of inequality of blind people in heterogeneous, mixed sighted-blind marriages, is not reserved to women alone. It affects blind husbands too, as illustrated in an incident recalled by Asher Dalal, a sheltered workshop employee in his early fifties. Asher had met his sighted wife through relatives, a year or two after they both immigrated separately from Baghdad, early in the 1950s. He recalled how he had manipulated the welfare system at the time, drawing support both for himself and his wife by claiming that she was sickly. And when the officials expressed their doubts about the woman's purported poor health, Asher recalled that he heatedly argued: "If she is healthy why did she marry me, a blind man? Only a sickly woman would do that!"

The issue of the inferiority of being blind is expressed most markedly in matters concerning women in the marriage market. A case in point is that of Sara Shmuel, a young blind woman married to a man who was also blind. The notion that a blind woman can marry only a spouse who is less than she persisted even in that instance. Sara, who came from a traditional Syrian immigrant family, chose to marry a young man of Bulgarian Jewish background who was quite ignorant of orthodox practice. Sara told me that had any of her able-bodied siblings contracted such a match, her parents would have objected vehemently because of both the ethnic and the religious factors. However, in her case, they accepted the choice. Because of her condition they felt she could not aspire to contract a better marriage. Afterwards relations between many of the members of the two families, the couple and some of the in-laws, became tense, particularly on matters involving religious practice. Still, Sara reported, her parents remained resigned to the situation since they felt that her condition could only permit a less than optimal marriage.

III. Conclusion

The foregoing marital accounts should be considered within the overall context. In present day Israel, the traditional marriage patterns of Middle-Easterners are barely followed, mainly because parental control is much weaker. This trend is true also for blind people, and here it is enhanced by the Israeli educational system for blind youngsters which was discussed earlier. Today marriageable people, whether blind or sighted, are free of some of the pressures, but they are also denied some of the support that was part of the traditional situation. Numerous blind persons, including men of Middle-Eastern background, now either marry late or remain unmarried. But in the past, many of these men's fathers would have brought them sighted wives. This leads to an important conclusion: the current position of blind women of Middle-Eastern background, relative to that of their blind male peers, has improved. The latter do not now have such ready access to sighted women; consequently they are channelled more toward blind women than in the past. The marital prospects of blind women of Middle Eastern background have therefore improved.

On a more general level: in theory the permeability of the domestic setting to impulses of stigma toward the disabled member is an open question. On the one hand, it might be argued that the mutually diffuse roles of parents and children would obviate the parents stigmatizing their disabled kin. On the other hand, it might also be contended that since parents are part of the general society and therefore subject to its pervasive culture, their behavior vis-à-vis the disabled in their homes would follow the general, accepted pattern of society. The observations lend support to the second possibility. The role of parents thus emerges as being highly problematic, since it appears that qualitatively it is not very different from that of other able-bodied people in the social ambience of the disabled. Furthermore, the influence on their blind children continues into adulthood, notably into the sphere of matchmaking, where the attitudes of parents again dovetail with those prevailing among the able-bodied towards the disabled. However, the condescension of able-bodied parents is mitigated. In Israel young blind people are often able to obtain an education superior to that of their sighted kin and, as a result, they themselves develop feelings of alienation towards their families.

Is the impulse for distancing, of blind children from their sighted kin, inherent in the general situation of the disabled child among able-bodied kin? The foregoing observations do not lend themselves to an unqualified answer. The instances of distancing that we saw emerged in the specific Israeli immigration situation, which happened to offer young blind people better facilities and therefore swifter educational progress than their peers. Distancing from the family in the Israeli context may thus be due to the particular conditions extant here; they need not necessarily be inherent to blindness as such.

There are, however, indications in the literature that the phenomenon of distancing is a general one, extending beyond both the specifics of the Israeli situation, and possibly also beyond the particular condition of blindness. In an ethnography of U.S. blind people, Gaudreau (1963: 61 seq.) also reports that newly blinded people disengage themselves from their relatives. Hyman et al. (1973), in a survey study of the occupational aspirations of blind youngsters, found that class and racial background in their blind sample did not limit aspirations as much as in their sighted sample; the blind youngsters evinced more mobile characteristics. In terms of distancing, blind people are more detached from their surroundings than the sighted. The social ambience of blind people governs their social choices to a comparatively limited extent. Moving beyond blindness, Davis (1963), in a study of young polio patients after extended hospitalization, observed the phenomenon of distancing from families to the extent that the youngsters sometimes tried to delay their discharge home. Distancing would thus seem to be a property common to the situation of disability in the context of stigma and inequality.

One can only speculate as to the factors that underlie these expressions of social distancing. It is possible that we are viewing here the effects of institutionalized schooling and of hospitalization, effects that draw youth away from family and community. It is also possible that distancing is rooted in the leisure activities of the disabled. Traditionally, these included few physical activities, but centered more around white-collar, cultural and literary activities. Disabled people have been directed towards mental activities, more so than their able-bodied peers. Finally, I suggest that the coming of age of young disabled people may have a particular structure. Early in their lives, blind people are subjected to and shaped by the forces of stigmatization. As they grow to maturity and assert themselves, stigmatization reemerges, paradoxically, in the guise of the phenomenon of voluntary distancing from the family and community of origin.

Chapter Five

Raising Sighted Children

This chapter dwells on relationships between blind parents and their sighted children. These parents must contend with children who are exposed, like anyone else in society, to negative stereotyping of blind people. The latter (as disabled people generally) can, to a considerable extent, escape the tension of managing in a social environment dominated by the sighted by retreating into the privacy of their quarters. However, when the home is shared by blind and sighted kin, a point is reached that delimits escape. Blind parents, in facing their sighted children, must contend even at home with the problems of stigma. Moreover, in the area of blind parent-sighted children relationships, the disabled person is confronted by an able-bodied person who is clearly of subordinate status in the dimension of generation. In the literature on coping with stigma, there is ample documentation of the doings of the disabled in relation to able-bodied people of superior or equal status, but hardly any concerning disabled people vis-à-vis others who are structurally subordinate, but who are part of the overall socio-cultural ambience that stigmatizes. In this particular situation, disabled persons are in a position of command and relatively more powerful than they are in situations reported in the literature where they contend with peers or superiors.

The documentation of coping with stigma in the domestic situation leads us to a new frontier in the sociological study of stigma. In focusing on disabled parent/able-bodied child relationships, we encounter elements that conceivably might limit the power of stigma. This chapter addresses that possibility. The questions addressed are: How is stigma created in the family and how does it unfold? How do discredited parents react to stigma in their homes?

The population of the study are thirty-seven individuals who are or were married (mostly to blind spouses); most of them have children all of whom are, to my knowledge, visually healthy. The basic data of the chapter are accounts and analyses of interactions between sighted children or youths and their blind parents. These interactions are motivated by many forces. One, presumably, is the universal inter-generational clash discussed in psychoanalysis ever since Freud. Another is inter-generational confrontation at specific culture-associated levels, such as the discordance that is common in migration and culture-change situations. Blindness is one element among others that can lead to conflict between family members. This chapter will demonstrate the weight of the condition of blindness in the context of these additional more general factors. Following the premises of this research, the study of inter-generational actions involving blind people should not be reduced only to the factor of blindness, neither should it be reduced exclusively to factors other than blindness.

I. Blind Parent and Sighted Child

Two crucial processes mould the relationship between blind parent and sighted child: the child's comprehension of the nature of blindness and the parent's comprehension of the nature of sighted childhood. While the trauma of blind children who discover their condition has long been a concern of workers with the blind, the parallel experience—sighted children who become aware of their parent(s)' blindness—is virtually unknown.[1] The potential of this experience in moulding children's assessment of their parents, and of establishing relative status in the family, is weighty. The realization that one has sightless parents is difficult to contend with. In the early stages of this realization, the children view their parents as undifferentiated from other people, but they develop practices towards them that are unique to their condition.

The effect of blind parenthood upon sighted children is exemplified in an incident which took place late one evening when I was about to depart from a visit with the Eini family. Starting the farewell preliminaries I murmured to the hosts that I was going to pick up my coat. Suddenly seven year-old David Eini, who had been lounging in pajamas on the settee, half asleep, half listening to the adults, got up and wordlessly led me by the hand to where the coat was and placed my hand on it. Evidently, at that late hour, the sleepy child did not fully distinguish between the sighted visitor and his blind parents: he behaved to the former with the same anticipatory helpfulness with which he treated his parents. He knew, as his mother Mazal put it, that his parents "see with their hands."

These children, however, tend to become troubled as they gradually become fully cognizant of the distinctiveness of their parents. Following are a series of situations that document the unsettling quality of that discovery. A group of blind friends were entertaining each other, in the presence of their children, with stories of funny situations into which blind people blundered. One was about a blind man who had stepped onto merchandise that a streetwalk hawker had spread on the pavement. The merchandise consisted of plastic toys that squeaked and emitted a cacophony of odd noises on the pavement when the blind man trod on them. At that point, the informant said, one of the children in the room became frightened and upset at the outlandish doings of the adults and began to cry.

On another occasion, Rina Sadeh was talking about her mobility problems. Both she and her blind husband work in a busy downtown city street where pedestrian traffic on the narrow sidewalks is heavy. People are inconsiderate; they rush by, oblivious of her need to sweep an arc in front of her with her cane. One day a man accidentally stepped on Rina's cane and broke it. Thoughtlessly, he rushed on without bothering to help or apologize. The note in Rina's voice as she recounted this was one of seething anger that she had no way of expending. Her nine year-old son who was sitting with us reacted differently. He was concerned: "Ima, so how did you get home?" The child's reaction expressed anxiety at what might have been the loss of his mother. To an only child in a family of working parents, the absence of parents is a perennial source of worry. Blindness now intensified the problem.

The behavior of these children clearly attests to the turmoil they experience as they become fully aware of the difference between their parents and other people. On several occasions I observed that young children of blind parents, aged around seven to eleven, made sweeping motions with their hands in front of their parents' faces. Perhaps they may have been effecting primitive vision tests, as if they wished to verify that their parents did indeed not see anything. Sometimes there was an aggressive quality to the gesture. With a rapid movement the child would extend his or her arm to full length as if about to strike the parent. One might speculate that the distance between verifying whether one's parent is blind and pent-up anger and frustration at this condition, is not great. What is not in doubt is the blindness-linked ambiguity of relationships of the sighted child in face of the blind parent.

In the Sadeh family I saw the same child who, on another occasion, I had observed exhibiting anxiety and hostility, approach his father and attempt to show him a drawing he had made. The boy behaved just like a child with sighted parents. Perhaps he toyed with the idea that his parents had some vision, perhaps he wished to hide their blindness from the researcher by behaving as if they were sighted. Whatever the boy's reasons, the incident attests to the dilemmas such parents pose for their children. Hostile feelings of children towards their blind parents may be rooted in and exacerbated by a number of factors. Parents may use children at a tender age to serve them, particularly as guides. Even if they are not being directly exploited, sighted children are prone to developing ambiguous, if not outright negative feelings. A blind parent can be profoundly embarrassing to his or her children. They are viewed as unusual and odd by the children's peers whose parents are sighted. Some of the stigma that is the lot of the blind parents is also that of their sighted children.

Poverty is a phenomenon that frequently accompanies disability. Disabled parents are usually not in a position to give their children nearly as many material goods as their peers have. The children of blind people are usually unable to share with their schoolmates stories of joint physical activities with their parents, such as camping, outings, going for car rides. The latter deprivation is particularly visible and discomfitting: whereas the children of blind people walk on the street with their slow-moving parents, their schoolmates are picked up from school in the family car.[2] In short, theirs is Goffman's (1963) "courtesy stigma".

The basic condition of blindness is such that it may easily lead to danger, especially street accidents, and in fact, several such accidents occurred during fieldwork. One of the salient goals of mobility and orientation training of the blind is to enable them to operate efficiently under public thoroughfare conditions. Today, due to improved techniques and mobility aids, blind people evince remarkable mobility achievements. However, these are attained only after much effort and frustration. For the children of blind people, the mobility mishaps of their parents are worrying. This emerged from the account of a blind woman who was taking a three year-old child to nursery school. She held the child's hand, but he was not able to guide her efficiently. At the same time, his inept guidance disturbed her customary cane-mobility technique and she walked onto a pole hurting herself. The woman recalled that at that moment she felt the child's hand "freeze" in her grasp. "It became like a dead limb". Though I have only the adult's version of the event, the incident undoubtedly was frightening for the child. It is likely that such incidents will have a cumulative disruptive effect on the trust and security of the child in the blind parent.

As children grow and reach the stage of late childhood, their discernment increases and they are able to differentiate their blind parents from other people more clearly. They begin to introduce stigmatizing behavior into the relationship with their parents. Reuven Ovadia, sorely grieved by the fact that his eleven year-old daughter was ashamed of him, recalled how the problem began:

At first, as I walked with her in the street holding her hand, she would ask, 'Abba, why does everybody look at you?' Later, when she would see someone on the street whom she knew, she would withdraw her hand and stoop, saying that she had to tie a shoe lace.

In this account ambivalence is stark. The child is clearly ashamed of her father, yet she does not admit to him and perhaps also not to herself why she disengaged herself. She fabricates an excuse.

The pressure of society on these children is multifaceted. People in their ambience burden them with "courtesy stigma". But more than emitting a simple stigmatizing message which causes children to dissociate themselves from their parents, the sighted also convey a charitable patronizing message. Sighted people often erroneously assume the blind to be incapable of any achievement beyond a minimal level. This prompts them to urge self-righteously the sighted child of blind parents into giving unnecessary assistance. As a result, parent-child relationships can become painfully convoluted. This was the case in the family of Eliezer Ohayon, a piano tuner whose work required him to travel to his clients along familiar and often unfamiliar routes. Eliezer, who was self reliant and impressively mobile, felt that his children were embarrassed by their blind parents. He told me that his eleven year-old daughter was particularly troubled. People accosted her, telling her that she should be more helpful to her parents and that she should guide them to places. The blind father said that, in fact, he was perfectly able to accomplish his work and other errands unassisted. In this family, surrounded by an ambience of do-gooders, the children were reserved towards their parents. The oldest left home at the age of eleven, insisting on going to a boarding school. The next, though living at home, refused to have her parents visit her at school, saying that she resented having attention drawn to her.

The ability of parents to direct the attitude of their sighted children requires great parenting skills; in their absence blindness related problems can be compounded. Thus Sara Shmuel, the harrassed and sickly mother of three small children, interpreted the pranks of her seven year-old boy as follows: "Sometimes he plays tricks on us. He hides from us when we call him. He exploits our blindness *(menatzel et ha'ivaron shelanu)!*" Obviously, childish behavior at that age could also be interpreted differently. It is possible that the mother's harsh interpretation was not lost on the child and that his attitude could turn to hostility. Another instance of dubious parenting was voiced in a radio program featuring family problems. A blind nerve-wracked mother elaborated her problem: her blind husband was over-anxious that his children should not lack anything. He was apprehensive lest he be blamed that, due to his infirmity, he had not provided adequately for his family. He therefore spoiled the children by giving in to their every whim and wish. The oldest boy made it a practice to make a spectacle of himself in the supermarket and to scream whenever he was refused anything while shopping. In addition, when doing small errands for the family, the boy systematically demanded money to buy goodies for himself. All this resulted in public embarrassment and financial nuisance for the family.

The process of learning to live with blind parents and sighted children may be flawed in some families, but it is successful in others. People do sometimes manage to interact to their mutual satisfaction. Thus, Avraham San'ani's eight year-old daughter was proud of her father and told her friends about him. Avraham also was happy in his family life. Characteristically, upon elaborating, he specifically singled out the fact that his children had learned to be considerate of some of his particular requirements, namely to avoid keeping drawers and doors half-open, and playing TV or radio at high volume. Such habits hinder Avraham's mobility in the apartment and do not permit him to discern delicate sounds. I was witness to an incident in the Eini home that illustrates socialization to the needs of the blind. Mazal, who was seated with guests at the table, had momentarily risen from her seat to serve refreshments. In doing so she had moved her chair slightly. Her seven year-old child quietly came and replaced the chair so that his mother would not have a mishap when she sat down again.

Barring smooth relations between parent and child, the time of late childhood is one of transition from the complex of feelings that accompany the discovery of parental handicap to the onset of actual stigmatizing practices in adolescence.

II. Blind Parent and Sighted Adolescent

The results of different socialization processes and contrasting inter-personal relationships become evident as children reach adolescence. In some homes the stigmatization of the disabled parent developed clearly at this stage, with few or no allowances being made for the needs of the blind parent. I was frequently present in homes where families with teenagers sat around watching television, and the youngsters made no attempt to convey the visual content of programs to the blind person. The latter was relegated to the periphery.

The families that comprised the data base of this research are mainly of Middle-Eastern immigrant background. This implies that factors affecting the disparate cultural changes of young and old, and their relating to practices of the dominant culture (governed by people of Eastern European background) will be significant. Immigrant youth in that situation sometimes show disrespect for their elders, contending that they are out-of-touch and old-fashioned. The case of Rivqa Cohen's family affords insight into the contextual weight of blindness in intergenerational friction. The family, composed of three teenage children and their blind mother, was riddled with inter-generational conflict over life styles, work habits and consumer patterns. The children often had noisy jam sessions and parties at home, particularly in their mother's absence. This annoyed her. Therefore, whenever Rivqa visited her extended family, which was quite frequently, she did not inform her children in advance. She did this in order to try to prevent her children from planning social events in the home.

Rivqa was careful about her outward appearance: she dressed neatly and was careful to keep her hair well kempt. She participated in a physical fitness group for blind people which featured specially designed exercises. When she proudly demonstrated some of these exercises to her teenage children, they ridiculed her efforts and called them "exercises for idiots" (hit'amlut li'mefagrim). She mentioned that her children often vexed her by saying "You are primitive! You have no sense!" Rivqa told me that she had resigned herself to such behavior in the privacy of the home, but she insisted that the children behave properly in public so as not to cause her embarrassment.

These confrontations revolve around general inter-generational and migration type issues. Rivqa is concerned about the permissive behavior of her children; she would prefer them to conform to traditional mores. She would also like them to be industrious and save money. The children, on the other hand, tend to be light headed and pleasure seeking. The conflicts between the two Cohen generations cannot, however, be reduced to general issues only, unrelated to blindness. Clearly the youths are also expressing disdain at their mother's condition. They stigmatize actions that are specific to her as a blind woman. Thus, in addition to the general issues, blindness-related issues also fire the Cohen dissensions. The children's misconception of the nature of blindness dovetails with their mother's lack of empathy for the youth culture of her sighted offspring.

Another type of relationship between blind parent and sighted son is characterized by ambivalence rather than hostility. The Kagans' son had become an Air Force pilot, a signal achievement by Israeli standards. The mother said that at the time of the October 1973 war, when Israel suffered considerable losses in the air, the parents had gone beyond the call of duty in supporting their son's career. They could have requested that, in view of their condition, the son not be given particularly perilous assignments. The parents had refrained from doing so. The son, however, perceived the situation differently. He felt that he himself had hindered his promotion because of his consideration for his parents, that for their sake he had not accepted particularly dangerous missions.

Ambivalence is not restricted to the sighted youth. Blind parents also may entertain such feelings towards their offspring. This became salient in a discussion at a club meeting between Rivqa Cohen and Devora Berkovitz, a woman who lived with her daughter, a young woman in her early twenties. Rivqa told tales of woe about the unpleasantness of being guided by her teenage children. She complained that they were inconsiderate, would rush ahead without warning her of impending obstacles, such as steps or a curb. Devora countered by describing her own daughter. The girl respected her mother, behaved nicely to her, held a good job, and was liked by everyone. Devora was very proud of her. However, in the same breath, Devora continued to say that she felt uneasy when walking with her in the street: the daughter was always in command, directing her. Devora said she felt inhibited in expressing herself openly in her daughter's presence.

Strikingly, even within the same family, one encounters young people whose attitudes towards their parents differ dramatically. Of Miriam Aflalu's children, the eldest daughter who is in her early twenties, is attached to her parents. So little was she inhibited by her parents' condition that she brought her boyfriend home without warning him of her parents' blindness. Later, so Miriam claimed, the boy's parents made him break up with the girl because of their condition. The daughter did not appear to hold it against them. One afternoon I had occasion to observe the girl's behavior and indeed it was warm and engaging. She sailed into the house directly from the hairdresser. Delighted with her new hairdo, the girl came to her seated mother, and crouching, put her mother's hand on her head saying eagerly, "See! How do you like my new hairdo?" The girl's younger brother, on the other hand, evinces diametrically opposite behavior—he avoids being seen in public with his parents and never brings friends to his home.

As the sighted youngsters of blind parents grow into adolescence and maturity, the results of their parents' efforts are highly variegated. In evaluative terms they are as impressive or as dismal as those of sighted parents. At the time of research, one of the sighted sons was serving a jail sentence for rape, while another made headlines for courageously saving a drowning man. Some adolescents loafed around, out of school and work, and others were productively integrated into society.While the process of coming of age led many sighted youngsters to adopt the dominant social values with consequent active or implied stigmatization of blind parents, their behavior towards their parents was not uniform but varied significantly. This now brings us to consider the actions of parents.

III. Blind Parents and the Achievement of Status

Parents sometimes find ways to overcome their ambiguous position among the sighted in the family by contributing to the well-being of the latter. This entails actions which effectively make use of resources that blind parents have at their disposal. A number of cases will demonstrate this. Several blind adults, such as David Levi, told me that they were particularly active in helping their children and other young relatives with homework. The resources of blind people in the sphere of scholarship feature prominently in their families because, in Israel, the blind are frequently better educated than their sighted relatives (see chapter 4). Some people exploit this effectively and thus forge an important position for themselves in the family. Another activity which helps blind people attain status in their families was one in which Asher Dalal and his sighted wife engaged. Asher was careful to host his married children and grandchildren hospitably and with largesse when they visited him on Sabbaths. Asher happily noted that his home then "became a nursery school". He continued to say that he behaved in this manner so that in turn he would be treated respectfully by his children. Mordekhai Danino, an uneducated person employed in a sheltered workshop, contributed to his family's welfare in another manner. His married daughter, husband and three children lacked adequate housing. The family was entitled to some public assistance for housing, but the loan that was offered was insufficient for their needs. Mordekhai therefore staged a sit-down strike with his family at the pertinent government office. Mordekhai used his condition to try and elicit compassion from the officials. At the same time it showed the family that their father's blindness was not only a liability, but could also be an asset.

David Levi, Asher Dalal and Mordekhai Danino assumed disparate roles: scholar, dignified *pater familias,* and the afflicted man entitled to compassion. Despite the great differences between them, the common denominator of these roles was the traditional script they followed. Western culture generally offers these roles to the disabled and David, Asher and Mordekhai assumed them. A fourth way that some chose to contribute to the well-being of their sighted offspring, and this was not traditional, was to give public talks in the schools their children attended. In these talks parents would elaborate on the nature of blindness and demonstrate some of the accessories blind people use. Through these lectures the blind parents sought not only to counteract stigmatizing practices in general, but, more specifically, also to improve their status and that of their children among their peers. In summary, parents chose diverse means to assist their sighted children. These were deliberate attempts to break the ambiguity that surrounds blindness in the family.

Lastly, in many families there were overt indications that the blind parents commanded love and respect. Some of my most vivid impressions of family interactions are scenes in the Megidish family. There the six sighted children, aged ten to twenty-two, attended to their parents' needs, sat with them, respectfully listened. Another example is that of a mother of six children who was encouraged by her daughter to accept the position of chairperson of the workers' committee in her place of employment. The daughter was confident of her mother's ability to handle the position. Mazal Eini proudly told me that her children walked in the street hugging her. And a nursery school teacher once complained, that Avraham San'ani's little girl bragged too much about all the wonderful things her blind father could do.

IV. Conclusion

The ways of parenting sighted children by blind parents are, as we saw, highly variegated. The differences are rooted in disparate conditions of society and families, that are not related to blindness. But there are also contingencies, rooted in the peculiarity of the disability, which do affect the socialization process.

The relationship of the blind parent and sighted child is different from that of the parent-child relationship among the able-bodied, since the superiority of the parent relative to the subordination of the child is undermined by the physical disability of the parent. The confrontation of blind parent and sighted child often runs counter to ordinary domestic statuses because of the stigma that pervades relationships between the able-bodied and the disabled. Moreover, blind parents often make blindness linked requests of their children and that further emphasizes the contradiction. In their efforts to maintain the conventional status of generational superiority over their children, disabled parents face a problem that is particular to the experience of disability. We saw how blind parents coped with this problem in the foregoing accounts. They maximized blindness-linked elements in their situation in order to benefit their children.

The picture which emerges from this study differs from that reported in the American literature on the practices of disabled people. Following Goffman, writers such as Davis (1961) and Levitin (1975), on disability in general, Michalko (1982) on visual impairment in particular, and others on various disabilities, have dwelt on a general "disavowal of handicap" theme. They have documented disabled people insisting, in Levitin's words, that "others define them in preferred ways" and not in terms of their specific disabilities. According to the literature, "passing" as able-bodied is a major concern for many disabled people. In the privacy of their homes, however, the Israeli blind parents did not "disavow" their disability vis-à-vis their children. Rather they managed their disability in the terms of a world governed by the sighted, manipulating it as well as they could to their maximal benefit. Some parents succeeded in attaining status in their homes, others did not. Parenting under the conditions outlined requires great skill; it is also contingent on other, non-disability related variables. The variety of parental status that we observed in different families derives from that complex domain.

Much of the literature on the ethnography of disabilities is based on observations made in public settings in the United States. One may surmise that "passing" and "disavowing" would be more common in a public setting than in the intimacy of home. Also, in Israel, the disability rights movement is only weakly-developed, and the attendant lack of social awareness may account for salient behavioral differences.[3] In order to make cross-cultural comparisons, controls for situation specific elements must be introduced and only case material drawn from comparable settings should be compared. Possibly such cross-cultural research might reveal that the issue of generation superiority emphasized in the present chapter is culture bound and peculiar to the Israeli situation.

The value of Goffman's influence on the sociology of disability is undisputed, but his approach has lain too heavily on the field for many years. Thus, Gussow and Tracy (1968) described the practice of sufferers of Hansen's disease, similar to that of blind parents, lecturing in public about their condition. Gussow and Tracy however, discussed that in terms of coping with stigma in general. Already years ago Bynder and New (1976) argued that the Goffman paradigm may have exhausted itself, that the time was ripe to study disability in new ways, and this has been explicitly recognized in the special Journal of Social Issues (1988) volume entitled *After Goffman*. This chapter suggests that the actions of disabled people need not be viewed solely in the general terms of stigma. These actions are also linked to specific situational concerns, for example, the desire of parents to fill a superior role in relation to their children, and this particular desire is not one that is rooted in disability. The sociology and anthropology of disability now faces the issue of uncovering the ways that disabled people follow in coping with particular concerns.

Having discussed problems rooted in the intimacy of the domestic setting, the following section, part three of the study, examines the ways in which blind people attempt to meet their material needs.

Part III

Reaching for Material Needs

Chapter Six

Seeking Employment

The Israeli labor market is relatively small in terms of national economies and is characterized by heavy government regulation. This limits the scope of economic enterprise by non-government bodies. Competition between the relatively few private entrepreneurs is harsh and not many niches remain for competitors who are physically disabled. The latter are handicapped over and above their disability: Israeli welfare legislation does not extend deeply into the field of employment and employers are not obligated to reserve positions for disabled workers.[1] Welfare legislation in Israel differentiates between two categories of disabled people, veteran soldiers and others. Only veterans are accorded sweeping rights, similar to those in affluent Western countries, due to their unique position in the Israeli national ethos. For other disabled people, the blind included, the authorities have been less forthcoming.

These two elements of the economy, the weakness of private enterprise and the limited intervention of government on behalf of disabled people in general, cause blind people to engage in a limited number and range of occupations. The two main occupations are telephone switchboard operating and working in sheltered workshops. Each of these draws several hundred blind workers, the former about 500 and the latter, 300. The computer industry engages about 25 blind programmers,[2] and a few individuals are employed as assembly workers in regular industries. There are also individual professionals in social counselling, the arts and piano tuning, and a few self-employed businessmen. Near the bottom of the socio-professional scale, a few individuals make a living as public beggars. Married blind women are mostly homemakers. The figures ought to be seen in the context of general statistics of the blind population in the country, but reliable data are not available. According to a recent official estimate the population of blind people of working age reaches over 3,000 (State of Israel 1989).

The prominence of a particular occupation, switchboard operating, in Israel parallels the situation in some other societies; in France, for instance, blind people figure prominently as stenographers. The structure and hierarchy of office management and automation in France is such, that managers commonly relegate to their secretaries the finalizing of correspondence, which they dictate directly or via dictaphones. Many blind clerks have moved into this occupational niche, so that this is an important source of livelihood. In Israel, however, the development of an independent secretarial role has been lagging. Until quite recently managers wrote drafts of their correspondence in longhand which their secretaries copied; this did not constitute a convenient niche for a blind secretary. While a more modern secretarial role has been developing, the welfare authorities and blind people have not yet adapted themselves to the emerging possibilities. In the United States another occupation is common among blind people—the operating of vending stalls (for newspapers, cigarettes, sandwiches, etc.), on the premises of federal offices.

In some traditional societies, blind people were prominent in music-making, basketry, as well as professional begging. For many blind Israelis, a large proportion of whom were socialized in quasi-traditional Middle Eastern countries before emigrating to Israel, such niches are familiar. Blind players of the 'ud, the one-string Middle Eastern violin, were well known in Baghdad musical life, and frequently appeared in popular radio programs. Many of these artists were Jews, who came to Israel in 1950–51 with the mass migration. They tried to implement their craft in the new country, but their art was not appreciated and they seldom performed on radio programs.

Middle Eastern traditions were altogether not highly regarded at that time and the immigrant artists performed mainly at private celebrations, such as weddings. Even here it was difficult for blind immigrant musicians because they were scattered throughout the country, so that they usually performed one-man shows rather than in bands as in Baghdad. The eventual demise of traditional music-making by blind players in Israel was due to the increasing affluence and Westernization of the immigrants with time. They began to hold their celebrations in glittering wedding halls; the old-fashioned blind 'ud players could not withstand the competition of the modern bands using electronic equipment and their western pop and Greek-style melodies. The 'ud players neglected their art, and some of them can now be met assembling plastic parts in sheltered workshops.

Switchboard operating in Israel, as a niche for blind workers, is similarly rooted in given conditions. The standard of telephone equipment in the country lags behind that of more affluent countries; there has been relatively little automation and there is a chronic shortage of access lines. This has enabled blind people to work in the interstices of the system, in particular in operating the manual telephone switchboards of large offices. A hospital or factory often maintains a switchboard that operates twenty-four hours a day, and, if the equipment is adapted to the needs of the blind, it can provide employment for several workers.

The two specific occupations of blind people—assembly of parts in sheltered workshops and switchboard operating, are marked by grinding routine and sometimes by nerve-wracking pressure. Sometimes workers may have waited, unemployed, for years until obtaining work as switchboard operators, only to be frustrated after a while. They must then struggle to maintain their motivation and standard of work. But the aptitudes of blind employees are diverse and individual. Often there is a glaring contrast between a worker's mental quality and the routine of the job. The concentrated employment in basically unstimulating and undemanding occupations is therefore often a source of great frustration for blind workers.

The search for employment is essentially a process in which the blind person must adapt to existing job opportunities, that the public rehabilitation agencies offer. As blind workers seek to enter the labor market, they are screened for training in one of three tracks: switchboard operating, handicrafts, and academic studies. The first two entail training for about one year at a government vocational school for blind adults. Upon completion of the course the students are helped by the rehabilitation authorities to obtain work for which they have been trained. The third track is designed for a very small select number of young people, who are considered by the rehabilitation officers as suited for university studies, and who are granted funds for that purpose. Formally, nothing prevents ambitious people from trying to train for whatever career they choose, but in practice, they are inhibited from doing so because the alternative way of accepting the guidance of rehabilitation officers automatically entails material assistance.

After the completion of training, the rehabilitation officers act as placement officers. They first search for employers willing to take on blind switchboard operators; they then invest public funds to adapt the employer's equipment to the needs of a blind operator. Such aid is extended less rapidly to blind people who act independently of the rehabilitation officers, or worse, who run afoul of them. But the assistance is not withheld. In the case of blind trainees who trained for manual work in sheltered workshops or who studied at university, the role of rehabilitation workers is less crucial. In sheltered workshops, the salary is so poor that there is not much pressure for the jobs, and little assistance is required to acquire one. In fact, it is often the rehabilitation workers who try to encourage the blind person to accept a sheltered workshop position in the absence of a better offer. As to university graduates, the employment problems they face have often been so difficult that the rehabilitation authorities have usually not been able to assist. Altogether the number of university graduates does not exceed a few dozen; some have had to resign themselves to lesser work, even to operating telephone switchboards. But many of them have succeeded in entering the fields they have chosen, such as social and educational counselling.

A great deal of perseverance is required on the part of any blind person seeking work. One who aims for switchboard work might be relatively passive, but will still have to exhibit considerable persistence and resourcefulness in nudging the officials to exert themselves on his or her behalf. The university graduate will, in addition, have to be imaginative in initiating contacts with prospective employers, and to have sufficient resilience to bear slights and rebuffs. Avia Degani, a thirty year-old prospective history teacher, recounted such an experience. Answering an advertisement for a school position, she scheduled a meeting with the principal and presented herself to the secretary at the school. Upon asking to see the principal, the secretary told Avia that she would have to wait because the principal had scheduled a meeting at that time. When Avia explained that she was the person expected, the secretary called out loudly in the direction of her superior's room, "There's a blind woman here who says she's a candidate for teaching. Is that O.K.?"

Another prospective teacher, Elisheva Dann, a mathematician, had been a university teaching assistant and now sought a position teaching evening school. When Elisheva presented herself at the evening school without first announcing her blindness, the secretary was amazed and took her for an applicant to study rather than to teach. On another occasion, Elisheva tried her luck with a computer center linked to the defense establishment. There she was rebuffed by the argument that she was not long enough in the country to qualify for a sensitive installation. At the time she had been in Israel for ten years and immigrants of that duration fill many sensitive positions.

Similarly, Penina Danieli who had graduated in social work, failed for years to obtain employment. A prospective employer who had been informed that she was blind, called her for an interview, but thereafter turned her down because she did not own a vehicle—the latter was not a prerequisite for the job. Another prospective employer, whom Penina had informed of her blindness, turned her down at the interview, explaining that he was really seeking a male for the position—this despite the fact that Penina's name was clearly that of a woman. Such rejections incensed Penina because, she explained, these employers evaded confronting her as a person. Her blindness as a realistic condition was ignored. No pertinent question was raised as to her capabilities to perform her duties, such as coping with paper work or overcoming possible negative attitudes towards her by clients of the agency. The rejections struck Penina as being rationalized by frivolous arguments. Another kind of rejection that Penina reported was that of the director of an agency who explained that he could not hire her because, if occasion arose, he would not be able to bring himself to criticize her work and possibly even to dismiss her. Although Penina felt that this rejection too was outright discrimination, she considered it less demeaning than the previous ones because here at least the employer admitted the discrimination.

Experiences such as these were common to aspiring professionals who sought to enter occupations that were not the preserve of the blind. While people who were satisfied to work at telephone switchboards did not have to contend with such slights, they did have to suffer extended periods of inactivity, waiting for job openings. Such periods sometimes lasted for years. This was particularly true for married women, for whom the rehabilitation officials exerted themselves less than for married men or for single people. The officials maintained that if one person in a household was gainfully employed acute need was resolved.[3]

In many cases the rehabilitation officials succeeded in sustaining the motivation and patience of their job-seeking clients, and eventually in obtaining work for them. But sometimes people became discouraged. Thus Zekharia Dayan, a young man then in his twenties, trained for industrial assembly work for eight months in 1964 at a rehabilitation center. But thereafter he did not find work in a regular plant, and was reluctant to go to a sheltered workshop. In 1967 Zekharia was directed back to the center for retraining as a switchboard operator, but once again, upon completing the course, he found no work. In 1968 Zekharia accepted a position in a weaving plant; he worked there for nine years. During that period, National Insurance relief payments rose while salaries in the textile industry did not. The margin of income between gainfully employed people and those on relief became slim. Eventually Zekharia resigned his position and since then has lived, not unhappily, on his relief income only. This is how Zekharia described his last years as an employee:

> When I worked at the weaving plant the machines were operated by hand, not by electric power. I got sick from the hard labor; rheumatic fever and other conditions. That work was not even fit for convicted terrorists! Everybody fell sick there; some died! Only Satan can describe what

went on! People just worked because they got paid a bit more than they would have received from relief. But I couldn't take it anymore!

Obtaining work sometimes entails activation of social ties, popularly known as *proteksia*. In the case of professionals, ties are sought with persons who can influence an employer to take a blind person. Such string-pulling is not uncommon in Israel. In the early years of mass immigration, during the 1950s, the manipulation of personal ties to obtain work or housing was notoriously overt. Such nepotism was structured by the immigrant context, where one and all desperately scrambled seeking anchors of familiarity in a sea of strangers. During the 1960s and 70s proteksia became less overt and came to be considered increasingly askance, and the bureaucracy became more formalized and sophisticated (see Danet 1988, for a treatment of the phenomenon).

These generalizations, however, do not apply to those blind people who sought employment in the professions. They were often driven to try and resolve their problem by mobilizing whatever ties they had to activate old-time proteksia. Among them I never encountered any favorable evaluation of the efforts of rehabilitation officials on their behalf, in contrast to positive evaluations of the latter that I encountered among some switchboard operators. The experience of professionals in seeking work beyond the preserves of the blind altogether tended to be one of great frustration.

Thus Arye Greenberg, currently a computer operator in a local municipality office, did not succeed in finding work by applying directly to numerous employers, although the computer industry was booming at the time. Arye also failed to obtain a job through the mediation of welfare agencies. Eventually he obtained his present position by activating an uncle who had the ears of senior city officials, and the uncle persuaded the latter to hire Arye. But Arye felt that obtaining work in this way was degrading, and though years have since passed, he is still bitter about the incident. Similarly, Ze'ev Gutman, an educational counselor in his thirties, in describing his travails in finding work, recalled the time he was forced to have recourse to proteksia as one of emotional turmoil. The friend to whom Ze'ev had turned had a friend who was a senior in the education bureaucracy in a local municipality. That friend turned to a parallel official in another city and the latter prevailed on a school principal in his area, who had previously rebuffed Ze'ev, to now hire him.

The particular frustration inherent in such incidents is that people who failed to obtain work on their own merits, require the support of others who proffer arguments that are not related to the basic relationship of employer and employee, arguments which in the decades after the 1950s, had become overtly less acceptable. Blind professionals seeking work are particularly careful that feelings of patronizing pity for their disability should not govern their relationships with peers. When employment is obtained through activating non-professional ties and considerations, the professional's status at work, in his or her own eyes and that of others, may be dubious. In addition to that, blind proteksia seekers relegate themselves to act in a way that is overtly degrading, since it is associated with being a newcomer in the country. Nepotism of the proteksia type is far from unusual but for the blind work-seeker, having recourse to it, is linked with particular feelings of helplessness.

The situation of people who seek employment in one of the preserves of blind workers is very different. The employers of switchboard operators, if personally acquainted with blind operators, will have a notion as to how to handle such an employee. They will not be as shaken and astounded at the possibility, as was Avia's school secretary. Furthermore, such job-seekers have the advantage of scouting a field that is well known, since the rehabilitation officers exert themselves to discover openings for their clients. Precisely in this advantage, however, lies the problem with which these job-seekers have to contend—the indignity of dependence on officials. Job-seekers compete for a limited number of positions, and the officials decide to whom to allocate these.

The involvement of officials is less direct in cases of job-seekers who are already employed, but wish to change and improve their positions. In view of the nature of their job, switchboard operators maintain a wide network of contacts with their parallels in other places of employment. Frequently they are able to monitor information about job openings more quickly than the rehabilitation officials; agile operators can use this information to advantage. But job-seekers who are not part of the network of operators lack this advantage, and they are subordinate to the officials.

The involvement of the rehabilitation officers among different categories of job-seekers emerges in the case of the telephone exchange of the Manpower office in the Tel-Aviv suburb of Aliya. When a position became available there, the rehabilitation officers wished to offer it to Nissim Trabelsi, recently graduated from training, who was married to a visually impaired woman and the father of four children. However there was also Yoram Peres, who was single. While Nissim did not hold a position, Yoram had established himself elsewhere as a superb operator. He worked in a factory in the town of Yeruka, at some distance from his home in Aliya. This required

Yoram to make a complicated journey to work, involving several buses and crowded street negotiation. Wishing to work closer to home, Yoram contacted the management of the Manpower office with whom he had had indirect ties through his job at the factory. Circumventing the rehabilitation officials, Yoram secured the position for himself. The position at Yeruka was subsequently taken by a sighted operator. Eventually an insurance firm established offices in the same vicinity as Manpower and a new opening materialized. Nissim's competitor this time was Hava Dangur, a married childless woman who had the reputation of being irascible—and this time Nissim got the job. Meanwhile, Yoram was berated by the rehabilitation officers for having "burnt a position" *(saraf maqom)* in Yeruka. This, in the parlance of the blindness system means, that the Yeruka position was lost for blind people, since the changes were made without consideration of the needs of blind job-seekers. Yoram himself is extremely critical of the blindness system, but Nissim has remained appreciative of the efforts that the officials made on his behalf and speaks warmly of them.

A similar case is that of Reuven Ovadia and his wife Lea, an attractive blind couple, at the time in their early thirties with two small children. Reuven was a switchboard operator at a hospital near their home but Lea was out of work. They needed additional income and Lea also wished to get away from home. Reuven managed to obtain a better position elsewhere so that his job in the hospital became vacant. The rehabilitation officials wished to give Aharon Ben-Arsi the hospital position, since he had recently finished training and was about to get married. But Reuven and his wife thwarted the officials by arranging to have Reuven's former employer hire Lea.

Such behavior arouses recrimination among job-seekers and rehabilitation officers. The job-seeker is bitter at the officers' ineptitude and the latter accuse people such as Yoram, Reuven and Lea of wreaking havoc with their efforts to assist job-seekers. Also no love is lost between people such as Aharon and the Ovadias.

The dependence of some job-seekers on the officials, linked with the possibility of the official's judging a job-seeker in terms of past performance as a "position burner", can be ominous. The case of Yael Hadad reflects that situation. A single woman in her forties, Yael ran afoul of the rehabilitation officials and of employers: she was too familiar with her superiors, primarily male, and with people in general. During the years she was employed as a switchboard operator, Yael's behavior was unusual for a blind person and for a woman among colleagues who had conservative attitudes concerning proper feminine behavior. Yael's employers came to consider her an embarrassment and she lost jobs twice. The rehabilitation officers took a grim view of this as "position burning". Over time, relationships between the officers and Yael deteriorated reaching a point where she expressed her frustration by verbal abuse and a mild physical assault on one of them. The officials reacted by refraining from investing any more efforts on her behalf. This, in effect amounted to Yael having to resign herself to either working in a sheltered workshop or to remaining permanently unemployed. In bitterness, she chose the second alternative. For years Yael tried to appeal her case but this has not changed her situation. "Burning a position" in this case entails failure to comply with established norms considered proper for a blind female worker. Such failure can effectively paralyze the job-seeker's chances.

The discussion so far has focused on employed, salaried blind people. Altogether self-employed people are comparatively few in Israel and self-employed blind people are very rare. Successful private enterprise, in the comparatively repressive Israeli economy, requires great resourcefulness in manipulating financial assets and exceptional physical and mental prowess. Blind people have a command of these resources as infrequently as the sighted; the few self-employed blind people I encountered were people of superior abilities. One such person was Yehezqel Mazuz. He received his high school education in an ordinary school among sighted pupils where he coped with problems of acceptance among peers by lecturing on his blindness. While still a teenager at school, he made his first steps in the business world. Yehezqel prepared slides on activities of the blind and made money by showing these and lecturing to audiences. Later he promoted young singers who performed to the audiences with whom he had forged ties.

Upon finishing school, Yehezqel started to study for a psychology degree. The particular college department he chose had experience with blind students and that is what led Yehezqel to study there. But the field did not attract him, he later told me. Yehezqel dropped out of college and sought the help of the rehabilitation officers, who directed him to take a year long course in switchboard operating. Yehezqel did not wish to attend that course, and instead he found an opening for himself as a switchboard operator at a warehouse. There, he claimed, he was trained on the job by a friend in a mere two days. After Yehezqel had made independent arrangements for his employment, the rehabilitation officers, though annoyed at his having evaded the training course, invested the necessary funds to adapt the equipment of the warehouse's switchboard to the needs of a blind operator. Once on the job, however, Yehezqel suffered from the boredom of the work. As he recounted to me, "All day it went, 'Warehouse, shalom.

May I help you?' The day dragged on for an eternity". He used to call his girlfriend (later his wife) every so often, asking her for the time.

After a while Yehezqel prevailed on the manager of the nearby dispatching department of the warehouse to let him assist in wrapping goods for dispatch. At first the superiors were not happy with this, but eventually they acquiesced. At the same time Yehezqel learned the precise layout of the streets in the vicinity. He made the acquaintance of some gift shop owners and after hours, worked as an agent selling them cheap mass-produced pictures. Yehezqel recalled that in two or three hours he used to earn more than he earned all day at the warehouse. Eventually he resigned his salaried position, developed his agency, and opened a storeroom of his own. He later engaged sub-agents and drivers and operated throughout the country. Some years later Yehezqel shifted into the basic foods business. He purchased a large food store in a good residential area where he currently engages four employees. When I visited the store it was packed with customers, thriving and undercutting competitors. Yehezqel had also moved with his family to a new modern apartment.

While Yehezqel may have embellished and exaggerated the details of his history, the basic outline is supported by my observations and by independent accounts. This person began his course in life by using to advantage the natural resource that he had, his blindness. He offered lectures that commanded a fee, then continued by going to college through the blindness system. There again he trod an original path, moving away from studies that did not interest him. For a while he still had contacts with the blindness system through his work as a switchboard operator, but here again he evinced independence, and eventually struck out completely on his own. This history lacks accounts of frustration that commonly figure in the accounts of job-seekers.

The case of Yehezqel ought to be linked to the social situation of self-employment. That situation obviates the need to be indebted to employers and to be dependent on rehabilitation officials. But this road is open only to individuals who are endowed with extraordinary abilities and personality. The situation of self-employment has the potential for obviating the pain of the social ramifications of blindness. But the majority of blind people do not fall within this category. They are deeply embedded within the society of the sighted that on the whole views them patronizingly. They contend with the problem of seeking integration within a society that tends to segregate in delimited niches.

Chapter Seven

The Work Experience

The category "blind people" encompasses individuals of great diversity in terms of intelligence, ability, and preferences. Due both to the innate physical disability and to the socio-cultural structuring of that disability, blind people are channelled into a very limited range of occupations, primarily at the switchboards and in the sheltered-workshops. Sighted people who engage in these occupations are either individuals of limited abilities, or temporary employees, primarily women, for whom they are transient positions, awaiting more desirable permanent opportunities. Since telephone switchboards and sheltered-workshops are mainline opportunities for blind employees, the blind who engage in this work often have superior individual qualities relative to their sighted co-workers. Many are men, and for them, the position is their main and permanent source of income. The situation therefore creates a problem: many of the blind workers are imaginative and gifted, while the jobs are routine and undemanding. This often gives rise to frustration, alienating people from their work. But blind workers have hardly any realistic option to change jobs. How then do they maintain a reasonable degree of motivation for their work over many years?

In this chapter I document the frustration and alienation, and also the ways that people have developed for overcoming them. The topic is a classical one in the sociology of labor, but it has been explored mainly in the context of low-level manual laborers. One such instance is Roy's "banana time" study (1960, also Handelman 1975), where we see how unskilled workers punctuate meaningfully the time extent of a dreary job. But the present study entails a more complex scene. The workers are not unskilled or unlettered, on the contrary, in many ways they are superior. The frustrations are therefore severe, and the techniques the workers employ for coping with them are peculiar to the situation.

I. Sheltered-Workshop Employees

A major salient factor that eases the workers' resigning themselves to their occupation is the labor ethos that they hold. This ethos extols industriousness and shuns self-indulgence and laziness. There are indications that this ethos is expressed in the deep revulsion that blind Israelis have of the image of the blind beggar. This is a powerful image that was universally abhorent to the people of this study and moved them to act so as to avoid any association with it. But not only begging was repugnant: any kind of living off others evoked strong emotions (see the previous chapter, also chapter ten). In conversations about labor conditions, blind people who worked for their living would comment derogatively, that numerous others lived off society by drawing relief money. Subsequently, in the course of fieldwork, I searched to find such people, but encountered far less than my informants had led me to believe. The majority of blind Israelis of working age do in fact work, and of the others, many make efforts to do so; few are content to be idle.

The labor ethos, being a fundamental constituent of peoples' values, emerges and expresses itself particularly in situations of anger and emotion, when people drop their reserves. Thus, a conversation with a switchboard operator once turned to a blind person whom he did not like. As my informant referred to the man's shady doings, he exclaimed angrily, "That fellow?! a thief! an exploiter! *lo-oveid* (does not work)!!!" Not to work was for my companion equal to or worse than the other less than admirable characteristics that he attributed to the man. The mild words "does not work," in this parlance, attain symbolic weight and become a sharp epithet.

The labor ethos sometimes comes to positive expression, as when a couple were talking about the rights of the disabled and their problems in finding employment. The woman had come out with the slogan, "The sighted must realize that we are just like them, but we don't see." Upon this the husband exclaimed emotionally,

Yes, the blind person sinks his heart into his work! (*notein ha'lev shelo ba'avoda!*) He doesn't just want to take money!

The information that came to me highlighted the salience of the labor ethos, not only in verbiage but also in practice. Repeatedly I was struck by notable devotion of blind workers to their work. One of the switchboard operators, working in a large office employing hundreds of people, was selected by management as "outstanding worker" of the year. Another was selected by her co-workers to be chairperson of their workers' committee. Among workers in industry, the labor ethos was exemplified by one who, because of problems in the overall production system, was often left idle from his task of assembling plastic parts. At such times the shopfloor manager would ignore him, but the man's reaction was to scout through various departments of the plant, to find where he might make himself useful. Upon visiting this man on the shopfloor, I was struck by the quiet pride that marked his demonstration of his activities.

I was best positioned to observe the dedication of workers in sheltered-workshops, during the three months' period that I participated in workshop routine. There were two departments in the workshop. One was the assembly room in which plastic components were assembled. About ten men and women, mostly elderly or frail, worked there. In the second department, also employing about ten workers, there were heavy, noisy compressors and metal-cutting machines. Whereas in the first department workers sat around a long work table, in the machine room each person operated his own machine. Men only, most of them vigorous and healthy, were employed at the machines. The salary in both departments was by piecework, and was intended to slightly supplement the relief payments which were the mainstay of the workers' livelihood. However, in the machine room, due to the kind of product, the payment was slightly higher.

The differences between the two departments are sociologically significant, but for the present the notable point is that labor morale was equally impressive in both departments. The workers started at 7:30 A.M., took a half-hour recess at 9:30, and continued until 1 P.M. There was virtually no loafing around, little chatter, and workers were punctual about resuming work after the recess. For some individuals at the workshop the tempo slackened toward the end of the day when they began to relax, moved to straighten their backs, and smoked a cigarette. But others continued to work all day at the same pace. Many sheltered-workshop people underwent considerable inconvenience for the sake of their work: the profoundly boring job (the complaint is theirs) and the demanding trip. Though the workers were picked üp from their homes by a workshop bus, this entailed one hour trips each way. By Israeli standards those were long journeys. Although people did communicate at work, they did not usually permit conversation to dominate their activities. Some people set impressive quotas for themselves. Thus one man, Asher Dalal, packed forty boxes of a certain component daily. Two years later he had raised his productivity to sixty boxes daily. (When I worked there assembling parts I produced about half a dozen boxes of that component per day.)

The labor ethos expressed itself not only in the attitude towards work but, remarkably, also towards the remuneration. People in the workshop were aware that they were being paid poorly, but Asher

Dalal claimed that they did not work just for the money, rather they worked *lesheim shamayim*. The traditional phrase, literally meaning "for the sake of God," stems from the realm of piety. It is normally used in reference to a *mitzva,* a pious deed done for its own sake and not for an extrinsic aim such as gaining material reward. Transposing this idiom to the novel context of the labor situation, Asher innovated creatively, and expressed in a powerful way, the act of labor for its intrinsic sake.

The workers do also get extrinsic rewards. First there is the salary. However, the difference of income between people who do not work and subsist on relief only and those employed in sheltered-workshops, is not large enough to permit a significant increase in standard of living. Then there are the social ties established at work. But here again these are not very significant: hardly any close friendships flourished in the workshop, and none of the ties that existed there spilled over to leisure time. Some of the workers were actually explicit about their lack of interest in their co-workers. All this indicates that a major factor which weds people to their occupation is its intrinsic worth, the sense of dignity that it gives them. Work per se is valued. A man like Asher may lack ideological concepts to express the value he attributes to labor, but by using a religious idiom he articulated it well.

II. Telephone Switchboard Operators

Of the two main categories of blind employees, switchboard operators were most expressive of the frustrations inherent in their work. A fifty year-old switchboard operator, talking of the vicissitudes of his peer group who had gone through school together and later moved into similar occupations, expressed himself as follows,

> I was the first one of us to be rehabilitated, when the rehabilitation people *dafku* me here at this job.

The term used is a sharp colloquial expression approximating "did me in," and reflects a frustration of decades on the job.

There are differences between various kinds of switchboards, some of which are particularly annoying to operators. They dislike old inefficient equipment which has few access lines for callers. This gives rise to irascible tempers, and anger that is sometimes vented on the operator. The salary of operators is partially determined by the number of parties that their equipment serves: a more complex switchboard entails a higher salary. Further, such equipment will often also require a number of operators, working shifts around the clock, this, in turn, may be linked to shorter working hours. In contrast, a switchboard for which a single operator is sufficient is likely to cause more responsibility to be placed on the operator and to permit little flexibility, in terms of taking occasional hours or a day off.

The rehabilitation officials in charge of placing people at work do not judge all their clients equally capable of operating complex equipment. They were dubious about Nissim Trabelsi even though he insisted that he could cope with a large switchboard. Nissim threatened that if the rehabilitation officials did not acquiesce he would not accept any other position and go on relief. Eventually he persuaded the officials of his good memory and dexterity, and obtained the particular position he wanted. The regional rehabilitation official then came to observe and evaluate Nissim's performance. This is routine practice for newly employed operators whereby rehabilitation officials seek to obviate any misunderstanding with employers, that might arise from unsatisfactory performance at work. When the official came to see him, Nissim recalled with satisfaction, she was pleased with his performance.

> There I was placing calls. The switchboard was buzzing: Trakh! Trakh! Trakh! Trakh! That's how I hit the keys! There were no delays, and she had hardly anything to say![1]

One of the difficulties of switchboard operators is the need to be constantly ready to respond to calls, particularly when numerous parties require service simultaneously; this is exacerbated even more when lines are congested. Not all operators are equally efficient, some remember breaking down under the pressure. One operator, Efrat Ohayon, was confronted by her employer who complained of the quality of her service. Efrat retorted that she was "not an automat, but a human being," and could not cope faster with the load of requests. The employer however insisted, she claimed, that she must work "like a machine." Whereupon Efrat said, she broke down and wept. The effect of such an incident on the person involved is dehumanizing and alienating.

Another expression of the complaint of switchboard operators concerning dehumanization is that of Yael Hadad. This woman recalled that she constantly felt slighted at work, because officials used to leave their offices without notifying her. Yael felt that she should be informed of their departures in order to preclude forwarding calls to vacant offices. A frustration of this type, which actually led to violence, was recounted by a male operator who, in the course of service he was giving, was reprimanded by a female official. The case escalated to a confrontation in which the official hurled a biblical epithet at the operator, that he behaved like "a slave who came to rule" (*'eved ki yimlokh,* Prov. XXX:22), implying that he was just a blind person who happened to be in a position of providing an essential service. With smug satisfaction the man recounted, that he thereupon slapped the woman in the face.

Switchboard operators grapple in various ways with their frustrations. Some, like Efrat, fall into emotional crisis, but other exhibit resilience. Thus when an impatient caller complained to Yafa Makhluf, that judging from her tardy response she seemed to be hard of hearing, Yafa replied with irony, "Sure, blindness has affected my hearing too!" To me Yafa added, that she deliberately intended to shock the caller. She did so by volunteering personal information to the caller, thus blunting the edge of depersonalization and alienation. Another operator, Yoram Peres, does this even more overtly. He told me that he encourages friends to call him at his busy exchange. He maintains conversations with them, punctuated every few seconds by swift responses on the switchboard to the requests of parties. Yoram explained this candidly,

> When someone speaks to me personally, and a call comes—
> well, that call can just wait a moment!

Although the pressure of work severely limits the possibility of engaging in such private conversations, operators nevertheless strove to maintain communication among themselves. Many of the activists in the Associations of the Blind (AB) (discussed in later chapters) are employed as switchboard operators; they frequently engaged in public activities over the telephone during slack times at work. These activities were at times extensive, as in late spring when the welfare associations for the blind made plans for the annual summer vacations, in which hundreds of blind workers and their families participated. The registration and the arrangements for payment entailed a lot of administrative work which was effected mainly by these switchboard operators. The AB activists mastered much of this while simultaneously carrying out their regular jobs. But not everyone could cope well all the time: sometimes the pressure became too much. Thus a veteran activist once requested to be relieved of part of his administrative load because his equipment had just been changed; he had received "a stupid new semi-automatic switchboard," and it was giving him difficulties. Because of the delays in his responses at the switchboard the man reported that he suffered the indignity of having callers comment to him sarcastically, that he seemed to have fallen asleep at work.

The extent to which operators occupy themselves with public activities of the blind community while on the job, is influenced by idiosyncratic factors. One is the ability of a given operator to undertake and effect additional, and formally illicit, work. Another is the real and legitimate load of work at a given switchboard, and a third factor is the tolerance of the employer. Operators whose private calls exceed the boundaries that an employer deems tolerable may be reprimanded. Rumors circulated that some operators had lost their positions because of poor response to calls, due to exaggerated use of the switchboard for conversations unrelated to the job. Whatever the basis for those rumors, the issue of employers' reactions to the doings of their employees is pertinent to the sociology of the particular role of blind switchboard operators. Crucially, reprimands by employers may force operators out of the communication network of colleagues. Thus one man said that he did not attend an annual Purim party, attended by hundreds of blind people and their families. His colleagues had not informed him of the date and his employer had prohibited him both to make and to accept private calls. For blind employees, operating the switchboard thus involves more than the actual work situation. It tends to broaden the social, public and even political activities of the employees.

Another creative way whereby switchboard operators overcame alienation on the job was by carving out for themselves niches of greater importance than those of their formal position. Thus Yoram Peres worked in a plant that operated around the clock and employed people who needed sometimes to be consulted at home at odd hours. Yoram said that he memorized their telephone numbers and also those of many other people and institutions who were occasionally required. He proudly recounted that he was sometimes called after work hours for information to effect urgent connections. A deep devotion to his work led Yoram to have a positive attitude to such incidents which might otherwise be considered impositions. This relationship also lies behind a visit that Yoram paid to the plant while on his annual vacation. He explained that he "had wanted to see how they were managing." Essentially, Yoram's technique entails elaborating the role of switchboard operator beyond that of solely being an operator for calls.

There were also remarkable imaginative ways of elaborating the role of switchboard operator which entailed stepping beyond the boundary of the role as technically defined, and encroaching on the activities of a totally different, and more prestigious, work role. This was the case of Menahem Bergman, who worked as switchboard operator at a rehabilitation agency. Coming from a relatively well-to-do family and living in an affluent area, this man's situation was removed from both that of the clients of the agency and from that of many of the officials. In terms of social status Menahem was out of place. His way of trying to reconcile the dissonance was to develop a view of himself as a superior provider of social services, not merely a transmittor of depersonalized calls. In his words:

The officials depend on me. I inform them of addresses and phone numbers of the clients. I tell them in which area of the city the file of a particular client should be processed. I remember numerous details. Sometimes I exert myself for the client. I go after the officials trying to help. I behave nicely to clients because I am on their side of the barricade. But the officials are negligent. I get angry at them. I tell them, 'What kind of behavior is this?!' Once when I was walking on the main street a man came rushing, panting, up to me. It turned out that he was a client of the agency whom I had assisted, and he came to greet me. People of deprived classes know how to appreciate help. Whenever I do so they shower me with blessings. 'Menahem, you should be healthy! All the best to you! Your children should be well!' I am more veteran at my job than the officials. I show them that I am more than a messenger boy!

This account conveys the feelings of a man who finds his permanent job degrading and who considers his superiors inferior—a situation of multi-dimensional dissonance. Menahem structures his role, so as to overcome the contradictions. Thus his role of switchboard operator changes from being "a messenger boy," to an important one in terms of the services that the agency provides.

A radical instance of expansion and personalization of the work role was that of Miriam Aflalu, also a switchboard operator at a welfare agency. Like Menahem she was materially comfortable, due to the business activities of her partly-sighted husband, but in contrast to Menahem, Miriam lived in a low-income area and had personal contact with many clients. Miriam was much involved with blind people and their organizations, at both her local and the national levels. This, together with Miriam's work in the welfare agency, led her to promote herself as an advocate of the clients at the agency. She claimed to me that she had been instrumental in mediating material benefits for needy people, that she was able to help because of her personal knowledge of individual clients, and that people used to come to her home with their problems, so much that it interfered with her family life and she had to put an end to it. Miriam actually complained to me that she ought to have been given a position as a social worker, in view of all that she did. Whatever the realities behind this self-presentation, we have here a worker who views her occupation in terms of human pertinence, way beyond its essential barrenness.

The individuals who figure in these cases are articulate and successful; in terms of social practice they are "well adapted." This might lead one to view their doings as idiosyncratic, rooted in the vagaries of personality. My thesis, however, is that here we face a sociological dimension of the working-role of blind people which is not reducible to personal factors. This argument is underlined by two cases involving people who are very different from those we have seen. One is David Levy who works as switchboard operator in a bank. Despite his being close to fifty years-old, David still resides with his aged parents who care for his daily needs in a poor immigrant neighborhood. He takes medication, probably for emotional disturbances, and expresses his anguish in writing undistinguished verses. Though David would like to marry, his idiosyncrasies are such that even blind women, who themselves have few chances to marry, have rejected his advances (see chapter 4). But crucially in the context of the present argument, David, like the other workers, reported imaginative expansion of his role at work. He reported a situation in which a customer required urgent information but could not get through to the clerk who handled her account, and he, David, was able to assist. Having committed to memory the customer's account number and home phone number, he obtained the information and swiftly conveyed it to her. David claimed that his work gave him satisfaction whenever he was able to offer such service.

Similar personalization of the work role is evinced by Nehama Gadol, a person of even more extreme personal characteristics, who worked as operator of a small switchboard in a rehabilitation service. A thirty-five year-old single woman, Nehama is frail, sickly, of borderline intelligence, and insecure about herself. She barely coped with even her minimal mobility and personal needs. In a manner reminiscent of the forementioned very different people, Nehama used her position to try and promote the welfare of clients. An acquaintance of hers had arranged to obtain tickets to a swimming pool at discount prices for blind people: for this he required a list of the eligible local people. The officials were reluctant to release this information for reasons of professional ethics. Nehama acquiesced to her acquaintance's request and gave him the names that she remembered. Normally subdued and anxious vis-à-vis her superiors, Nehama seized the opportunity to make her work more meaningful, to be more than an impersonal switchboard operator.

III. The Ambiguity of the Labor Ethos

The thread that runs through the doings of numerous blind workers, very disparate in terms of occupation and other sociological categories, is the salience of the ethos of labor. It is apparent, however, that adherence to the labor ethos is ridden with ambiguity; there is an element of inhibition in the labor ethos of the workers. This is part of the social situation of blind workers, perhaps of disabled workers generally. Because the sighted are by and large unfamiliar with blind people, the latter realize that they are subject to the formation of stereotypes. Many blind workers therefore felt, that any one of them who makes an unfavorable impression on the sighted damages the image of blind people as a whole. Blind workers frequently told me that blind individuals must consider themselves as representatives of blind people in general. Some expressed this in a slogan, that individual blind people ought "to feel responsible for the community *(sibbur)* they represent."[2] They burdened themselves in a manner typical of a minority group. The devotion of blind workers to their jobs is thus linked with their conception of the way in which the sighted view them.

The paradoxical and frustrating effect that the ethos of labor can have under such conditions is demonstrated in the case of switchboard operator Shime'on Serussi. Shime'on was hired by a man for whom this was the first exposure to a blind employee, and he was efficient and well-liked. Subsequently, the employer expanded his office and hired another blind switchboard operator. However, the new worker was an elderly sickly person and did not cope well with the job. In addition, he was once caught coming to the office after his shift to make a private long-distance call. Thereupon the employer decided not to hire any more blind operators. Shime'on felt he was the cause of the employer's new prejudice because, he believed, that his own superior performance at work had led the employer to develop unrealistic stereotypical expectations of other blind operators. Shime'on felt that he had damaged the chances of blind people of average or mediocre performance from being able to make a living at his place of employment.

This kind of frustration is not the idiosyncrasy of an individual, but a recurring phenomenon. Successful blind people face a problem: to what extent should they seek success? For while success is desirable, it entails drawing attention to oneself, and one of the anguishes of blindness is asymmetric visibility: one is seen by others, but one cannot see them. Success highlights one of the fundamental existential features of blindness. It therefore entails a price for the successful blind person, namely, being singled out as "the blind genius." This anxiety is implicit in comments made to me by a successful self-employed businessman, Yehezqel Mazuz, whom we met in the previous chapter. In the course of many meetings, I had been trying to elicit from him accounts of incidents in which he had experienced frustration or failure. But Yehezqel was not very helpful. His was a story of constant good judgment, sparkling ability, and success. This was all corroborated by information from other people.

But Yehezqel did relate a series of frustrating incidents which were concerned with thefts, that he suffered occasionally at the hands of drivers whom he used to hire to deliver merchandise. Though Yehezqel was positive of the identity of the thieves, he was helpless to do anything. However, Yehezqel told me that, paradoxically, beside being frustrated, he was also pleased. The thefts, he explained, showed him that as far as the thieves were concerned, he had succeeded in making his mark as an ordinary person, and that they did not give him any consideration linked to his disability. Had "the shady characters" (so he called them) whom he employed not stolen from him, he would have suspected them of pitying him, and that he would have considered demeaning.[3]

The pattern of thought exhibited by Shime'on and Yehezqel gives an insight into the doings of blind workers who are less able and articulate. Like many able-bodied workers, some of the latter are presumably inept and negligent. However, it is possible that some of the inept doings of blind workers may be rooted in their specific condition as blind people. Blind people want to succeed just like everyone else, but they also reserve for themselves the right not to be asymmetrically exposed, the right not to be outstanding. This interpretation illuminates the extraordinary behavior of the ensuing case.

Nissim Trabelsi, the father of four children and husband of a visually-impaired wife, maintained his large family as a switchboard operator after having had considerable difficulty in finding a job. Nissim told me quite proudly that he had disciplinary problems at work, particularly because he sometimes failed to arrive on time. When his superior reprimanded him for this Nissim told me, he would retort sharply: "You don't do me a favor by keeping me on the job!" This kind of insolence is not unknown in the context of the Israeli labor relations system that strongly favors tenured employees (of which Nissim was one). But it is rather unexpected in a worker as weightily burdened as Nissim. However, in the light of the foregoing considerations, his behavior is understandable. Nissim courts failure, rather than modifying his behavior to one that might befit a person employed out of charity. He chooses to act like a person who has a choice. Nissim bolstered his self-respect by acts of brinksmanship on the job.

The three men whom we have been considering lead very different lives. In contrast to Nissim's straitened conditions, Yehezqel lives comfortably as a successful businessman, and Shime'on, though earning only a switchboard operator's salary, is single and supports only himself. These differences, and other personal ones in conjunction with the similar pattern of conceptualization that I have indicated, underscore the thesis that we are encountering an issue of sociological import and not mere individual idiosyncrasies.

IV. Conclusion

The two major occupations of blind Israelis, at the telephone switchboards and in sheltered-workshops, give rise to feelings of alienation and discredit, nevertheless both types of workers are dedicated to and involved with their work. Given these elements of commonality, there are differences between the two categories of blind employees. Whereas the work of sheltered-workshop employees is in many ways monotonous and unstimulating, we encountered there neither expressions of emotional crisis beyond verbal complaints, nor creative acts of symbolical transformation of the job. We did encounter such doings among switchboard operators. The difference between the two main categories of blind employees should not be dismissed in reductive terms, such as their being rooted in disparities of individual intelligence and culture. The works of Roy and Handelman clearly demonstrate the possibility of transformative activities even by people who are very low achievers. Rather we ought to search for a clue in organizational features of the two occupations that pertain to the existential situation of the people engaged in them.

Operating a telephone switchboard entails specific problems for blind employees, problems that are rooted in the particular institutional structure of this work role. Saliently prominent among these is the fact that for most sighted people switchboard work is a transitional, low-status, woman's job, whereas for blind people it is not. In addition, among blind people the importance of orality is disproportionately greater than it is in the lives of sighted people, as argued earlier in chapter two. Moreover, switchboard operating requires the use of the telephone, a boon of modern technology which enables blind people to overcome problems that stem from their disability. The telephone is important in the lives of blind people, it improves the quality of life, and telephone conversations figure prominently in daily routines. However, blind operators while working at the switchboard, are called upon to employ the instrument that otherwise, is existentially so enriching in a way that is impoverishing. I suggest that this complex of predicaments is a motivating force behind the actions of blind employees who enrich and extend their telephone-connected work. The workshop and switchboard employees of this study evince different work patterns, the origins of which can thus be traced to the overt social structures and to particular job roles.

Chapter Eight

The Experience of Support I:
The Blindness System

Philanthropy and work related to blind people in Israel is so institutionalized as to constitute what Robert Scott, who studied the American scene, has termed "a blindness system." In Israel the blindness system comprises two main branches. One is the public welfare system, such as the Ministry of Welfare, the National Insurance Institute, the educational network, and rehabilitation centers for the blind. The other branch is that of volunteers most of whom are organized in about twenty-five local benevolent associations for the blind, in each of the major cities and towns of the country. There are also several voluntary associations and institutions that aim for a nationwide clientele: the Netanya Library for the Blind, the National Guide-Dog Association, a group that maintains a nursery school for blind infants, and others. The number of Israeli organizations focused on blind people is thus at least thirty-five. Considering that the overall number of blind clients in the country is 8,000 at most, this means that on the average, there is approximately one organization for every 200 blind individuals.[1] Some of the activities of the voluntary associations, in particular those that are localized, are loosely coordinated by a central organ, the Center for the Blind (CB) which is located in Tel-Aviv. In this first of two chapters on the experience of support, I discuss the general organizational features of the blindness system, and dwell upon differences of detail between its two main branches.

Each local association terms itself "The Association for the Blind in Town X," and maintains clubrooms where blind people are encouraged to meet with other blind people. The associations also run sheltered-workshops in many localities. Occasionally they arrange large functions, such as Hannuka and Purim parties for their clients and day trips to resorts. The associations often provide miscellaneous minor material assistance, such as part of the expenses for summer vacation projects of groups of blind people, special expenditures for medication, schooling, housing, and extraordinary needs.[2] The volunteers are sometimes instrumental in mediating between their blind clients and various bureaucratic welfare agencies. Occasionally they provide basic human support to those in despair. The public welfare agencies also provide assistance in some of the aforementioned areas, but the major area in which the public agencies specialize is training blind people for employment and funding jobs for them. There is some overlap in the areas of activity of the two branches of the blindness system.

Over the years, some institutions founded by volunteers, such as the Netanya Library for the Blind and the Jerusalem School for the Jewish Blind, have adopted traits of public bureaucracies. The Jerusalem School, founded close to a century ago, has served the needs of generations of people who came from many parts of the Middle East, suffering from trachoma and other eye diseases. With time, the school established itself by endowments and, though remaining a private philanthropic foundation, became a large organization managed by an entrenched salaried staff. The latter successfully resisted the attempts of the welfare authorities to encroach upon the school's activities. This independence subsequently attracted the critical attention of the State Comptroller (State of Israel 1986: State Comptroller's Report, p. 720). The local benevolent associations, usually much smaller and more recently established, are mostly run by unpaid non-professional volunteers. But external bureaucracy sometimes succeeds in penetrating them. Thus the Ministry of Welfare prevailed upon the managers of local sheltered-workshops to accept some of their other clients, specifically people with minor brain damage and motor co-ordination problems. In exchange the Ministry extended material support to the facilities of the local associations. The needs of blind people fall within the provinces of numerous institutions and associations, officials, professionals and volunteers, that are not always clearly demarcated. However, the amount of centralization and co-ordination in Israel is greater than that reported of the American situation.[3]

Most of the organs of the Israeli blindness system are managed by sighted people, including those who deal with rehabilitation. Although there are some blind welfare professionals in Israel, they do not specialize in blind clients. Only the educational system employs a few blind professionals who specialize in work with blind clients. The local benevolent associations are also run by sighted workers, but there, one occasionally encounters influential blind people whom the sighted managers consult. Sometimes blind activists and sighted volunteers work together in local associations. Rapport between blind and sighted, based on personal ties, is altogether closer in this section of the blindness system than in that of the public authorities. At the national coordinating level of the local benevolent associations, the Center for the Blind (CB), one encounters prominent blind activists. The board of the CB is composed of an equal number of sighted representatives of the local associations and of blind activists of the Association of the Blind (AB), a countrywide advocacy association of blind people. Moreover, the CB is managed by a representative of the AB who is blind, and by a representative of the sighted volunteers. The blind activist is the one most involved in the daily affairs; altogether, the blind representatives of the AB tend to dominate the CB.

The Israeli blindness system is grounded in the age old conception that blind people constitute worthy objects of philanthropy. Hence, historically, welfare policies for the blind emphasized social activities and traditional charity; the former were geared to nurse people out of presumed despondent isolation, and the latter to assist them materially. Prior to the mid-1950s, welfare policy did encompass some rehabilitation activities, but the goals were limited. The main gainful occupation into which people were channelled at that time was the traditional one—basketry. Of the two branches of the Israeli blindness system, the public and the volunteer, the former was, until the mid-1950s, the less developed. The scope of public activities was limited mainly to providing small sums of money for relief to the needy. The volunteer associations on the other hand operated on bases that were established long before State independence and before bureaucracy mushroomed. There were a number of reasons for the rudimentary public services to the blind. The years following independence in 1948 saw chaotic mass immigration to the country. Thousands of people afflicted with eye disease came from Middle Eastern countries. In Baghdad trachoma was virtually endemic; the mass migration in 1950–1951 of the large Jewish community from that city substantially increased the number of blind people in Israel. During the years of mass migration, the number of blind in the country rose more than twelve-fold (from about 600 to about 8000), whereas the increase in the general population, although massive, was much less, six-fold (from 600,000 to 3.5 million). As a result public welfare services of all kinds, including those for the blind, were quite inadequate.

The early 1950s were years of imaginative improvisation in matters of social policy, some of this eventually proved to be successful and some, misguided. In the area of blindness the authorities experimented with an improvisation of the latter type. They attempted to segregate a large number of blind people and their dependents in one locality, in a place they actually named "Village of the Blind," *Kfar*

Ha'ivrim, and the residents were to be employed in basketry by state-promoted enterprises. The venture never succeeded. Lingering on for a decade, it represented an extreme case of segregative welfare policy. At the same time local associations and public officials founded many sheltered-workshops and expanded existing ones in order to cater to the many needs that had arisen. In particular, the local volunteers engaged in charitable activities, operating clubs, distributing second-hand clothing, providing monetary assistance. Often, the same premises served as workshop, clubroom, offices and store-rooms for charitable activities.

After the years of mass immigration the rate of expansion of the blind population declined. Since the 1960s, the epidemic sources of visual impairment have been under firm control, there are relatively few new blind people, and older ones have begun to leave the scene. Two developments at this time resulted in significant changes in the blindness system. One was the professionalization of welfare practice due to the establishment of professional schools for social work. The second was the decline of the traditional craft of basketry mainly because of the increasing availability of cheap plastic products. These developments caused blindness workers to seek new avenues of occupation for their clients: in the 1960s they attempted to integrate them into the textile industry. At the time of the study, the Orah weaving plant in Netanya still operated with a largely blind work force, about fifteen weavers, and was a financially sound enterprise. However, the textile industry in Israel, as a whole, has suffered from competition of Far East countries. Blind workers have been particularly vulnerable: their relatively recent entry into the industry and their special adaptive needs make their employment expensive. Consequently, most of the fledgling blind textile workers soon had to shift again to other occupations. Through the initiative of the public welfare authorities they established new niches for themselves, as telephone switchboard operators. The local sheltered-workshops also adapted to the new conditions: basketry was phased out and replaced by the assembly of components for the plastics industry.

Both the sheltered-workshops and the switchboard offices retain links with the traditional system of charity. In the switchboard offices this is demonstrated by the practice of placement officers visiting new employees on the job and scrutinizing their performance. By this action the officials make an emphatic statement concerning their domination of the switchboard job market. Also in the workshops the linkage with the old system is prominent. Although the workshops have the trappings of industrial formality, such as clocking devices to mark individual working time, and although high labor morale is notable, the workshops are still viewed as clubs of a kind. Character-istically, the term used for sheltered-workshop, in the parlance of both officials and workers, is "occupational club," *moadon ta'asuqa.* The term insinuates that the work being performed has social rather than economic connotations. In fact, the employees of the sheltered-workshops occupy the lowest rungs of the work of blind people, both in their own esteem and in that of others.

There are shades of difference between the situation of sheltered-workshop employees and that of telephone switchboard operators. The field of the latter, in the popular imagination, is not viewed as a segregated occupation. In fact there are probably more sighted than blind switchboard operators in Israel. Hence, moving into this occu-pation is a significant change, from a segregated into an integrated occupation. The blind switchboard operators themselves, while often unhappy with their work, are aware that it is located in an integrated niche of the economy, and that, in itself, is a source of deep satisfac-tion to them. Typically, switchboard operators whom I met for the first time, would introduce themselves in terms of their place of em-ployment and not of their occupation. Thus, "I work at bank X (or factory Y, or the municipality, or the hospital, or the university)"—all integrated places of work and some, prestigious. But people in shel-tered-workshops, working just as hard and sometimes even with heavy industrial equipment, would refer to themselves as working in "the club-house," *ha'moadon.*

The two occupations are embedded in the blindness system to a differing extent, and this is reflected in the way ancillary benefits come to the workers. Most workers at one time or another receive grants, loans, and particularly tax refunds mediated by the Center for the Blind. People who worked as switchboard operators usually received these payments impersonally through the mail, and not through local volunteers in person. People who worked in sheltered-workshops more frequently received such payments at work from the local volunteers who supervised and visited the workshops. Thus, in the case of switchboard operators, there was a clear separation be-tween their work roles and their roles as welfare clients, whereas in the case of the workshop employees these roles tended to merge. The fusion became compounded by the Israeli practice of giving workers gifts on the occasion of the two major annual holidays, New Year and Passover. For most salaried Israelis this is considered a regular fringe benefit. But it is also a venerable Jewish practice to make gifts to the poor on the eve of holidays. Therefore, in the case of welfare clients who are needy, holiday gift-giving is munificence to enable poor people to enjoy the holidays. Strikingly then, the identical practice of gift-giving in the two work situations has different attributes. While for the switchboard operators it is a regular fringe benefit that all workers enjoy, for the workshop employees it has the tinge of philanthropy.

The different nuances of practice of the two branches of the blindness system reflect a deeper issue which is debated among blind people and among blindness workers, namely that of the social role of disabled people. The traditional position has been to accept implicitly and categorically the inferiority of the blind in relation to the sighted. This has tended to lead toward segregation of blind people. This position has also given rise to charitable benevolence toward the inferior handicapped. The more progressive position entails an emphatic notion of human rights. It struggles to achieve integration and is impatient, often scornful, of traditional charity. According to these conflicting positions blind, and disabled people in general, are called upon to pay different prices to maintain themselves in society. The progressive position is expressed by the attempts of public welfare authorities to change the employment market, and to accommodate it to the special needs of the blind.

The authorities' major success to date has been to persuade numerous employers to adapt their telephone switchboards technically, so as to cater to the needs of blind operators, and to provide employers with monetary assistance for this expense. The authorities have also had some success of this kind in the field of computer operating. In other fields, the textile industry, x-ray photography developing, and physiotherapy, the authorities' efforts have met with indifferent results only. In contrast to the public welfare system, many of the activities of the volunteers take the socially inferior and materially depressed conditions of the clients as given facts. The volunteers do not seek to affect the general societal framework, but rather operate within its contours. They prefer to carve out niches for the blind that provide some measure of comfort and income, and these niches usually tend to be segregated.

A characteristic service which the local benevolent associations offer, is to help their clients to go on annual vacations to a popular resort. For most Israelis such a vacation is a fringe benefit paid mostly from a fund to which employees and employers contribute. However, the income of many blind workers, particularly those in sheltered workshops (not to mention the unemployed) is so low that they cannot benefit from this arrangement. The local associations therefore exert themselves to provide this benefit for many hundreds of blind people. What concerns us here are the venues for the vacations. Many hotels are reluctant to accept blind vacationers, and virtually none will accept such clients in large numbers. The hoteliers feel that a clientele of blind people will upset sighted patrons and this might affect business adversely. The local associations and their clients are resigned to this situation and do not make any significant efforts to alter it. Instead, the associations negotiate with vacation resorts that will cater exclusively to blind patrons during part of the season. Many practical problems are thus simultaneously resolved: the collective handling lowers costs impressively, special activities tailored for sightless people can be arranged more easily and group transportation can be provided conveniently.[4] Crucially however, the program is radically segregative.

The differences between the two branches of the blindness system are not absolute: the public authorities also support the vacation program, though indirectly, by providing funds. The difference between the branches is one of emphasis. This is particularly evident in activities related to direct material support for the needy. Here, the local associations are more than just active, they exhibit a particular kind of sensitivity. The case of Hava Dangur and her husband demonstrates this. About fifty years old, Iraqi-born and partly educated in Israel, the Dangurs were trained to be switchboard operators, but for many years have lived on relief. They are rather bitter, reclusive people and their social and familial ties are poor. In this context, the Dangurs' home is very important to them. Though the furnishings are worn and out of fashion, the Dangurs take great care of them; everything is spotlessly clean and tidy. At one point Hava Dangur sought to refurbish her apartment. However, the expense was well beyond her means and she turned to the CB for a grant.

Hava Dangur's application was processed by the blind activists of the CB who do not particularly care for the Dangurs. They are the antithesis of the CB activists who are vital, working people involved in public affairs. The activists view the Dangurs as people who could have found employment but make no effort to do so, preferring to live on relief. Moreover, the CB co-ordinates activities with government welfare officials who also look askance at people who do not work. The Dangur request involved a relatively large sum, intended for people whom they did not respect and for a need that the CB activists considered unessential. It was promptly rejected. However, and this is the salient point, when the Dangurs approached one of the local voluntary associations, not connected with the CB—the request was promptly granted.

The volunteers of the local association lacked the scope to evaluate the Dangurs' case in the context of numerous other requests. They also were not sensitive to issues of the overall situation of blind people, such as rehabilitation and disability rights. But the volunteers did have empathy for the need of the individual in the tradition of philanthropy, and in this case the particular tradition of Jewish charity. Disregarding considerations of blind people and their needs in general, the volunteers realized the importance of the Dangurs' home to them in their particular circumstances. And they allocated a substantial sum to enable the Dangurs to replace some of their old furniture. The consideration that governed this decision was far removed from both those of modern blind advocacy movements and of the public blindness system. Rather it followed Jewish tradition which, more than requiring to give handouts, specifies that gifts should be commensurate with the subjective requirements of the beneficent.[5]

The characteristic of local volunteers as purveyors of charity expressed itself well at deliberations of the CB, in preparation for the annual gala evening of the CB, which featured popular entertainers who donated their talents. One of the volunteers suggested that all income from the event be specifically earmarked for loans and gifts to the needy. But the blind activists of the AB who participated reacted vociferously, and rejected the idea outright. Income from the event, they exclaimed, should be used for routine expenses of the CB, which are all kinds of welfare for blind people, and not just for direct personal assistance. The volunteers acquiesced passively.

A similar incident occurred at a meeting of volunteers discussing general policy of the local associations. One of the volunteer women called on the meeting to adopt various resolutions aimed at improving the working conditions of blind people. One proposal was to act so as to impress on employers the fact that blind employees have mobility problems, and that these might cause them occasionally to come late to work. The volunteer proposed that employers be asked to show leniency and understanding for their blind workers in such circumstances. The proposal was so retrogressive in terms of rehabilitation and integration policy that it was promptly rejected, but the mere suggestion reflects the world of values, in relation to social policy, out of which many volunteers have come. In contrast to this, among public welfare officials there was keen awareness, that linking employment with a presentation of the client as anything less than fully capable of the job, was bound to lead to repression.

Having uncovered the differing conceptions of welfare that motivate the activities of the two branches of the blindness system, the volunteers and the public officials, we now turn to their actual procedures in pursuing their various policies. The officers of both branches of the system are inconsistent in the pursuit of their policies. The declared aim of the officials is "to rehabilitate" *(leshaqeim)* their clients, which they understand as providing them with gainful employment. In public discussions the senior officials claim being able to provide work for "all who seriously desire to rehabilitate themselves." To these claims both the blind clients and the volunteers express indignant dissent, as they name people who have not succeeded in obtaining work. The hard fact is, that despite the efforts of placements officers, the labor market is not geared to absorb each and every blind person. Similarly, local volunteers seeking to provide their clients with personal benefits often have cause to be embarrassed. Frequently the payments of the volunteers to their employees in local sheltered-workshops is beneath the legal minimum wage, agreed upon between the national trade unions and the employers. The reasons for that too are again beyond the control of the volunteers. The workshops that they manage are dependent upon other factories to supply them with materials to process. Frequently, the conditions of those suppliers are unfavorable to the sheltered-workshops, and the latter's managers are then driven to supplement workers' salaries from their charitable resources. Since those are commonly insufficient, the volunteers are reduced to underpay their employees.

The local volunteers often evince notable devotion to their clients, but this trait often makes them less than fully effective in the handling of affairs of blind people in general. On the personal level, I heard many accounts of blind people for whom sighted volunteers truly cared. Young blind mothers who were assisted by volunteers, and guided into unfamiliar tasks, people assisted through the Byzantine complications of bureaucracies, others who benefited by material aid. The personal care of local volunteers is extended to deliberations that take place at the CB. At these meetings, requests for loans and grants by individuals are periodically discussed. There might be requests for support to participate in the vacation program, to replace a washing machine that was breaking down, to pay for unusual medication or to assist in moving an apartment. When a local volunteer who was personally knowledgeable of the case was present, the petition had a better chance. The volunteer would then flesh out verbally the bare details stated on the official application form, and press for a decision favorable to the client. Yitzhaq Mizrahi, a blind activist experienced with such deliberations, once exploded at a meeting of the Association of the Blind:

> A strong person is needed at these discussions. Control is required! The ladies are all *yiddeshe mammes*. If there's an applicant from X, Mrs. X will press for him; if there's one from Y, Mrs. Y. will chime in, saying that he's such a poor guy. They just support the applicants of their own places! They don't check the applicants' declarations of income. They don't look at salary slips. But I know of applicants who earn twice as much as declared in the applications! They have nothing to contribute to the common concern!

Jointly with the representatives of the local volunteer associations, the CB was managed by representatives of the Association of the Blind (AB) who were themselves blind. These people were in a unique position. On the one hand they were part of an organ of the blindness system that governed the lives of disabled people, but on the other hand they were themselves part of the stratum of the disabled, thus objects of their organization's activities. The AB activists who were members of the CB board and participated regularly numbered about seven men and women. They were homogeneous from certain crucial aspects. In terms of age, they were mostly in their early and mid forties. In terms of occupation they were mostly telephone switchboard operators. In terms of ethnicity and family they were mostly of Middle Eastern background and heads of families. And crucially, they were mostly lifelong friends who had gone together through the Jerusalem School for the Blind, at a time when schooling was segregated and that institution served as the national boarding school. Such old-boy ties, in Israeli parlance being part of a circle of *hevre,* are saliently potent. The ties figure in many areas of life: backroom politics, employment, the structure of reserve Army units, and pervasively in friendship and leisure activities. In all these, Israelis have a tendency to select partners and invest in relationships, with people with whom they have an old comfortable tie, namely being part of a hevre network.[6]

Crucially, the AB activists also shared the institutional background with many other blind people of their generation who were the clients of the CB. Being one of the hevre of the blind entailed exposure to expectations on the part of one's fellows to show spontaneity and equality in relationships. Frequently, however, these expectations were frustrated. Blind people in positions of authority over their fellows, such as those on the CB board, were led by their social roles, as we have seen, to behavior that contradicted spontaneity and equality. They did not share the philanthropic and patronizing generosity of their sighted co-workers on the CB board, nor did they wish to give free reign to feelings of fellowship and warmth among the hevre who required CB services. The blind members of the blindness system tried to operate according to impersonal bureaucratic notions of equity. The clients, however, considered the activists as similar to themselves; expectations were thus frustrated and often gave rise to anger. Sometimes ordinary human failings, such as insensitivity and ineptness on the part of the activists, magnified problems. The activities of Reuven Ovadia and of Mazal Eini who attained prominence, one in a welfare office dealing with blind clients, and one in a local club for blind people, exemplify this. Reuven's position was salaried, and Mazal was an unpaid volunteer. Both Reuven and Mazal were devoted to their tasks, spending long hours at them, way beyond the call of duty. At the same time neither of these people was very efficient nor particularly tactful to their clients. People complained that upon coming to Reuven's office they were not always assisted, and sometimes just left standing helplessly.

Viewed by the often dubious standards of Israeli civil servants in general, of whom these people have much experience, the practices of Reuven and Mazal were unexceptional; still, people complained repeatedly. Even Pamela Samukha, a close friend of Mazal, grumbled that she was tired of hearing her friend declaring publicly at club meetings how much she did for people. Other people in the club intrigued against Mazal, both amongst local members and at the national AB, and eventually Mazal was driven to resign. Reuven, assisted by sighted office employees, supplied accessories for blind clients, such as canes and watches, and also mediated monetary support for needy individuals. But there were complaints about the operation of the office by clients who failed to obtain the item or the support that they sought. Sometimes there were confrontations with people who came at other than office hours, and who then received lesser treatment than they felt entitled to. Clients occasionally abused Reuven and the clerks, over the phone and in person, and in turn Reuven threatened to call the police. The recurring refrain in the clients' complaints was about impersonality and coldness. Remarkably, the clients never complained that the operations of the blind officials were worse than those of other bureaucracies. Rather, the bitterness was linked to the feeling that in an office dealing specifically with their needs, blind people were entitled to more considerate treatment.

There are indications that the grievances of the clients were fuelled by their frustration at the fact, that their credentials in terms of hevre-ties were ignored. In the case of Reuven verbal abuse did not primarily involve anonymous clients, for whom this was a first or rare contact with the official. On the contrary, these were old acquaintances, clients who had maintained regular contact with the office for years, and who had much in common with Reuven. One such person was a rival who, like Reuven, was involved in welfare activities for the blind. When the position of manager of the CB became vacant one of the blind candidates to whom it was offered rejected the position, arguing that he was too well-known among blind people. He had been educated at the Jerusalem School for the Blind, and he would find it difficult to resist the demands that his old friends might impose upon him. He was apprehensive that "first they would come back-slapping, and then they would leave in anger."

The phenomenon of Israelis being situated in old-boy type networks is not unique to those who are blind. Individuals who are so situated fill many managerial positions, operating either with total equity, or arriving at some kind of compromise between universalism and particularism. Blind activists appear to operate differently. They lean backwards, either avoiding managerial positions involving other blind people, or managing in a style of cold bureaucracy. Why are they so sensitive to insinuations of inequity? I suggest that the reason is rooted in the social isolation and depressed status of blind people, and perhaps of disabled people in general. Virtually none of the people of this study held any public position (the exception is one man who was active in his synagogue). Even the most successful, in terms of profession and income, did not move beyond activities that their family and professional doings imposed.

The reason for this isolation is dual. Sighted people are uncomfortable with blind people, prefer to segregate them, and are uneasy to have them as equals, not to mention superiors, wherever this is avoidable (such as in voluntary and political associations, as against employment situations that are considered an essential); in short— discrimination. The other source for the reticence of blind people in voluntary affairs is the condition of limited energy inherent in the situation of blindness. The achievements of blind people, in most of their endeavors, require much more time and energy than do similar achievements of able-bodied people. Therefore blind people expend relatively little energy in matters they consider inessential.

The result is that the scope of public activities of blind people is narrow. To the extent that they exert themselves in voluntary blindness work their doings attain an importance to them which comparable public activities do not have for able-bodied people. Moreover, the one arena where blind public activists operate, the blindness system, is that to which great numbers of blind people are drawn as clients. This contrasts the general situation of sighted public activists, who will operate in arenas that normally attract a variety of people, and not primarily members of their particular old-boy network. Thus blind activists in the blindness system are highly exposed to the pressures of their hevre, and their situation is relatively stressful.

The sighted volunteers who co-operate with blind activists on the CB board are not sensitive to the social constraints that hamper their colleagues. Therefore they evaluate doings of the latter that they deem objectionable in terms of prejudice and stereotype. Those emerged particularly over CB discussions where the position of the blind activists concerning allocations to applicants was more severe than that of the sighted volunteers. The latter, in private, would later comment to me that their colleagues, "the blind," were inordinately suspicious, jealous, and mean toward each other. Once a sighted volunteer actually insulted her blind colleagues at a discussion, saying that they were "merely switchboard operators."

The stereotypic conceptions that sighted volunteers have of their clients inhibits them from inviting the latter to participate in running the benevolent associations. The local volunteers generally seclude the clients and maintain a strict differentiation between themselves and the latter. One chairperson of a local association explained, "It might be desirable to have blind people in our administration, but in practice that is impossible. I know them too well." She went on to detail the reputed sexual initiatives of some of her clients. She had witnessed such doings, she recounted, while participating once in an overnight trip with her clients, and to her indignation, even women had behaved in inappropriate fashion. She regaled me with stories of particular individuals. One man was said to have maintained sexual liaisons with women at a time when his wife was sick. Another man had broken his engagement just a week before his scheduled marriage to a blind woman, in favor of another woman who was sighted. Although the first man did not actually abandon his sick wife, and the man who married a sighted instead of a blind woman greatly improved the quality of his life—both were judged severely. Yet many able-bodied people have acted in such all too human ways.

The local sighted volunteers thus combined contrasting attributes: warmth and compassion together with prejudice. Both sets of attributes are rooted in the traditional view, that dominant people have of what in social service parlance is often termed "the deserving poor." In the particular case of the local volunteers these attributes are compounded by the fact that they were also in positions of management of organizations, albeit small and struggling, but organizations nevertheless. Sometimes the volunteers evinced tendencies of organization managers, with vested interests and requirements of their own. An indication of this was an incident in which a volunteer considered that she required certain information about a client, which was recorded in the latter's file in the social welfare office. However, in the name of confidentiality and professional ethics, access to such files is restricted to all but professional staff, and the request was denied. According to the account given to me by a social worker,

> Mrs. Druyanov was furious! She clamored that she understood things better than the social workers, and that she was entitled to access. She boiled with anger!

The volunteer did not delimit her role. She ventured into territory that others had successfully staked out for themselves, and suffered rebuff. Issues of demarcation of territory sometimes arose among the volunteers themselves. In a particular case involving the allocation of certain urban sections there was one association that served a large, heavily populated area, and barely coped with its numerous clients. But when a new association established itself in the area, and sought to stake for itself a territory of activity, the effort was strenuously resisted by the veteran association.

For their part, the blind activists operate in a very different social field, that of carving out a role for themselves as assertive and dignified individuals. There is only very limited mutual understanding for the complexities of the disparate situations of the volunteers and of the activists. Consequently the blind activists and the sighted volunteers co-working in the CB constitute a partnership of strange bedfellows. Having described the general features of the blindness system and the different nuances of its branches and operators, the next chapter will describe how the system impinged upon the clients and how they experienced it.

Chapter Nine

The Experience of Support II:
Living with the Blindness System

Two important facets of the blindness system emerged in the previous chapter: one, the dynamics of organizations in general that moved managers of volunteer associations, and second, the persistence of stereotypes among operators of the system. This chapter will bring these facets to bear upon the question as to how the clients lived with and experienced the blindness system. Focussing upon these features of the blindness system that invite negative value judgement, it is salutary to recall the general context of the relationship between the blindness workers and their clients: this includes much dedication and devotion on the part of the former. Both the officials and the volunteers often invested tedious and altruistic work for their clients, as in the case of the sickly woman who required extended treatment at an inconvenient location, and who for many months was unfailingly driven there by a volunteer. The trip and waiting time constituted a chore of several hours per week, undertaken without any attendant publicity. Such assistance was appreciated by the clients; some of the moving moments in field work occurred when clients spoke warmly of volunteers among themselves and to me. Also at meetings of the AB blind activists spoke well of the volunteers in their various localities.

We proceed with the first facet of the blindness system, and consider the way clients experienced the tendency of local volunteers to ramify the activities of their associations. This is evident in a case that occurred in a physical activities group of blind people, which numbered about twelve members and met twice weekly. The group was composed of men and women aged 25 to 45, some of them married couples and some single. At the meetings, usually after engaging in light athletics, the group formed two competing teams of gateball players.[1] Each team was composed of three players, and in order to enable all members to participate, the instructor would periodically retire some of the players, and bring into the game others who were standing on the side. The instructor was careful that the teams should be matched more or less equally in terms of physique. Thus, women would usually not be made to face men, and vigorous young men would not usually be made to face older men. Participants enjoyed the sports group; banter and laughter was frequent despite the seriousness with which the players exerted themselves.

The instructor however, was a professional in physical training for the disabled, and for her the sports group was more than a mere recreational activity. She had set herself the task to promote, virtually create, a particular sub-field in sports activities that she had initiated in the country. At one point therefore, the instructor decided to train the sports group to play competitively against other teams. Thereupon she began to manage the gateball games more systematically and professionally, such as by timing performance with a precision timer. Eventually, she judged some of the players to be up to a standard that enabled them to play against a superior team of blind veterans, who were trained in their exclusive private club. The instructor explained that she had in mind the possibility that her team might excel, and eventually represent the disabled of Israel at international competitions.

Some members of the sports group were pleased to be upgraded and to play against a prestigious team, but others grumbled. The new policy entailed the eventual elimination of about half the regular gateball players, older men and the women who were not up to standard. The group now travelled regularly to train at the veterans' club, and there half of the members were relegated to be a passive audience. Even some of the superior players who were selected for the competing team were unhappy. One of them complained that he had no interest in competitive playing. He participated in the group not only for the physical activity, but because he had friends there, and he disliked the prospect of shattering the group. He also grumbled about time that now needed to be spent travelling to the veterans' club. Even those who were flattered at having access to the facilities of the veterans and rub shoulders with members of a high status category of blind people, were not enthusiastic. The sports instructor's extension of her work, from a mere health and leisure activity, to quasi-expert sport reflects an organizational force that is not rooted in the needs and desires of clients. Eventually the attempt failed. The sports group refrained from meeting the veterans' team, and the instructor resigned her position.

Since the AB activists among the blind often worked closely at the CB with the managers of the blindness system on a collegial basis, they were more aware than ordinary clients of organization linked self-interest in the activities of the managers. Such self-interest emerged into the public when volunteers argued among themselves, as in cases of territorial demarcation involving neighboring associations. This awareness influenced the tactics that the blind activists chose in their dealings with volunteers. One perennial bone of contention at the CB between the AB representatives and the local volunteers concerned the proceeds of the annual fundraising drive of the CB. The drive was handled locally by the volunteer associations (home canvassing by school children), and nationally by the CB (campaigning in the media and circulating receipt books). There was an agreement that one-quarter of the income should be remitted by the local volunteers to the CB, and three-quarters could be retained by them for local activities. In practice, the volunteers were remiss in remitting monies to the CB; some paid only 15% or less, others ignored the CB altogether.

The AB activists were incensed at this, because they had agreed not to engage in fundraising in return for the CB covering their needs. The local associations however, caused the CB to lack funds, and the AB held deliberations to find ways to bring the volunteers to comply. One of the concerns mitigating against the AB taking a hard line was that the local associations, if pressed for funds, might react by diminishing their material support for local sheltered-workshops, and perhaps altogether disengage from them. This would cause hardship to the workshop employees. Overwhelmingly, however, the AB activists dismissed this concern. They felt that the commitment of the local associations to their workshops was deep, and nothing the AB might do would lead the former to relinquish control. The realization of the nature of the volunteer associations, as organizations, led the AB activists to formulate their strategies in this struggle.

We proceed to the second facet of the blindness system, that of prevailing stereotypes concerning the clients. The volunteers maintained an essentially philanthropic and paternalistic stance toward their clients, and this led some of them to such beliefs as "the blind love to have people show interest in them." On a most general level such a statement would apply to all humankind, as the quest for regard by others seems to be universal. On more specific levels there are great differences between cultures, and between individuals within a given culture, as to the desire (and also tolerance) for sharing privacy. There are no grounds for assuming that blindness is a predominant factor in this. The above belief however, dovetails with many doings of volunteers vis-à-vis their clients. It constitutes an element of ideology and meaningfulness that is entailed in the relationship between sighted volunteers and blind clients. The belief permitted considerable invasion of the latter's privacy, such as we encountered in the case, in the previous chapter, of a volunteer presuming right of access to a client's personal file in the welfare office. Another instance was that of a thirty-five year-old man, Binyamin Dayan, a sheltered-workshop employee who smoked one to two packs of cigarettes a day. The man's supervisor at work, seeking to discourage the heavy smoking, went to the length of confiscating Binyamin's cigarettes.

Doings such as those of the supervisor invite moral evaluation in terms of human rights, but that would lead only to shallow insight. I suggest that such actions are ramifications of stereotypes that prevail among managers of the blindness system, moulded through the roles and the institutions that these people operate. This sociological complexity emerges well in the following incident: Mrs. Druyanov, a devoted and energetic seventy year-old volunteer, told me of an encounter she had with Rivqa Cohen who worked in the local sheltered-workshop. Late one morning she had met Rivqa on the street. Upon asking Rivqa why she was not at work, Rivqa tried to put her off, saying that materials for assembly had run out, and there was nothing left for her to do.[2] When Mrs. Druyanov pressed Rivqa for the true reason, Rivqa sheepishly admitted—she was bored and had called it a day. Mrs. Druyanov was indignant. Such a reason for not working was intolerable, she said. She could well understand why a woman working at assembling parts might want to drop a day occasionally for reasons of bodycare—the manual work harming delicate hands—but not because of boredom. This account came to me from Mrs. Druyanov and I do not have the words she used to Rivqa.

Mrs. Druyanov was a formidable, opinionated person, who usually expressed her views bluntly; it is probable that she shared them with Rivqa too. But even the reaction that she confided to me is striking. Mrs. Druyanov was able to empathize with her employee about the physical aspects of her work. Rivqa was an attractive woman, careful of her appearance, and Mrs. Druyanov, herself much older, was an elegant lady. She had understanding for a woman who might be apprehensive of damaging the skin of her hands. In that case Mrs. Druyanov could condone taking time off. But Rivqa's complaint was fundamental—the anguish of the blind work experience which relegated vigorous people to dismal work. Both women operated within that system, and neither envisaged any change. Protest was therefore futile and repression unavoidable—founded not on individual moral failing, but on constraints which the actors did not control.

But sometimes people suffered overt indignities on the part of members of the support system. Shlomo Deromi, a person of higher education in languages, recalled helping a friend in a university lobby with work on a Latin text. An employee of a local volunteer association who was unknown to him happened to be there. The man came up to Shlomo and struck a conversation.

> First he asked me if I had studied at the School for the Blind in Jerusalem, to which I replied that I had not. Then he asked me if I knew various blind people whom he named. Again I replied that I did not. The man then exclaimed, I've been working for 22 years with the blind, and I've never met a blind man who knows Latin. You want to tell me that you know Latin?!'

The felt insult was compound: the invasion of privacy, the attempted thrusting into segregation, the assumption of inferiority.

Shlomo recounted an incident that involved a blind official to whom he had applied in order to obtain assistance to purchase a newly developed typewriter, that enabled blind writers to print charts. The official initially rejected the application saying, "You need such a machine?! I have never seen a blind typist preparing charts!" Shlomo concluded bitterly, "The supporter (*ha'metapeil*, literally "caregiver") thinks he knows better than the blind person!" Strikingly, this man was oblivious to the fact that the official happened to be himself blind. Rather, Shlomo was struck by the overall inequality of the situation, and in that context the difference between sighted and blind officials lacks salience; he considered all as one in the blindness system. Though we have in the previous chapter noted significant differences between sighted operators of the blindness system and blind activists of the AB who participate in it, the client was not aware of them. From Shlomo's point of view all operators of the system are tinged by paternalism.

Besides the major branches of the blindness system that figured hereto, general voluntary associations, such as Bnei-Brith, Lions and Rotary, extend occasional assistance to blind people, when mobilized by volunteers specializing in blind welfare. More than other volunteers the activists of the general voluntary associations tend to be out of rapport with blind people. Their conceptions are founded primarily on cultural stereotypes of blind people being pitiful and inferior, so that their good will lead to retrogressive doings. The general volunteers engage in particular in arranging grand annual parties at the festivals of Purim and Hannuka, which cater to hundreds of blind clients at no cost to the latter. The parties are based on a rich program of popular noisy entertainment featuring well-known stars, and the clients are treated to cheap refreshments in generous quantities. Typically, the functions start with the organizer recalling the names

of all the organizations, institutions, sponsors, volunteers and officials who contributed to the event. Thereafter, many of the dignitar-
ies mentioned go up to the rostrum, offer greetings to the audience,
and accept applause of appreciation. These exercises in personal ag-
grandizement take place before the audience has in fact been offered
anything; the event is referred to from the outset as successful. At the
introductory greetings of one such Hannuka party, the representative
of one philanthropic organization praised an activist of another organization that had also contributed to the event. She talked of "Eli
Toledano who toiled for you (*she'tarah lema'ankhem*)." Another representative said gravely, "Bnei-Brith is at your service; whoever needs
help should apply to us!"

On another occasion, a local club for the blind that was jointly
maintained by blind activists and by sighted volunteers, arranged a
guest lecture. The speaker was an official of the National Insurance
Institute, who dealt with disability payments. The official was visibly
uncomfortable in the crowded and dreary clubroom, and he asked for
a window to be closed. Then, since the place in which he found himself gave him poor command of the audience, he moved to another
part of the room. As the official was seated when he finally started his
talk, people called out to him that they could not hear well. Whereupon he rose and commented, "Having come here, I will do everything for your comfort." The pompous style of public address, while in
poor taste, is not inappropriate in a context of perceived inequality;
the purported superiors do not bother to disguise their sentiments.

The qualities of social distance and haughtiness on the part of
supporters, evident in these incidents, are accompanied by the fact
that the supporters actually exerted themselves very little. The National Insurance lecturer hardly did "everything" for his hosts' comfort. There is also a glaring contrast between the grand gesture of
publicly inviting hundreds of people to seek succor from Bnei-Brith
and the meagerness of that organization's actual program of assistance. A local branch of another general philanthropic association
had decided to make a gift, a watch adapted for the blind, to a needy
person. The organizers desired to make the presentation in public,
and turned to the local Association for the Blind to identify a recipi-
ent. The volunteers of the association however, refused to co-operate,
because they did not consider the paltry gift commensurate to the
indignity of public acceptance. The incident neatly uncovers nuances
of difference between philanthropic organizations. Organizations that
are not part of the blindness system and are remote from the clients
are least sensitive to the latter's dignity.

Both the operators of the blindness system and their clients are
unanimous in considering the area of employment of prime impor-

tance for integration, or "rehabilitation," among the sighted. Elucidation of the role of blindness workers, in vocational training and employment, is therefore important for uncovering the extent of domination of clients as against the extent of their autonomy. Since the officials of the public branch of the system, such as the ministries of social welfare and education, play the main role in this area they, rather than the local volunteers, figure in the pertinent accounts. These officials govern primarily two occupational fields: telephone switchboard employment and training towards an academic profession. Of the two, we saw in an earlier chapter that switchboard operators are somewhat independent (although we recall the unique case of Yael Hadad whose career as a switchboard operator was virtually terminated by the officials).

In contrast to that training for the professions is fully governed by the officials. Expenses for university education in Israel must usually be met by the students, who support themselves by a combination of parental aid, income from work, and minor public grants for the gifted and the needy. The position of aspiring blind students is different. The public welfare authorities are willing to extend substantial grants to blind students. That is however subject to the proviso, that rehabilitation officers consider the aspirant's proposed studies as a reasonable rehabilitation plan. The rationale of the system is that blind students are unable to study without material assistance, that all are in need of welfare aid. The provision of public support entails limiting the options of the student in accordance with the understanding of the officials. The latter, basing themselves on evaluations of the aptitude of the student and of the employment market, will encourage studies in certain fields and discourage others. Thus, physiotherapy, psychology and music were favored fields, whereas law and the arts were not. The officials specially sought to avoid funding studies that ran on for inordinate lengths of time, and did not materialize in gainful employment for the student. The outcome of these arrangements, from the vantage point of aspiring students, was that their personal choices were closely controlled by the welfare officials, and only acceptance of such control ensured material public support. Frequently the officials rejected applications of aspiring students, because they did not consider the applicants suited for academic work. From the applicant's point of view, such a decision implied an early relegation, in one's late teens or early twenties, to a life at a telephone switchboard.

The difficulties that faced beginning blind students, coupled with the possibility of obtaining public support streamlined them to dependence and sometimes also frustration. One such case was that of a blind social science graduate, who had requested assistance for graduate International Relations studies. The official conditioned support, to the student obtaining an employment commitment from the Foreign Ministry, but the latter was not forthcoming. The student was eventually resigned to work in the public school system as a special education consultant. At a public discussion of these matters the mother of a blind student once called out emotionally,

> The blind are just like everybody else! Let them study what they please! Let them do what they want!

I suggest that in the circumstances given, the constraints of established arrangements, such clashes are virtually unavoidable.

The ways in which blindness workers conceive of their clients is usually grounded in a realistic appraisal of the overall situation, and they guide clients to the optimal alternative within constraints that no individual governs. But occasionally, the coupling of blindness workers' particular conceptions and their dominant role in the lives of clients, lead to individual discrimination. One conception of blindness workers, that blind people are naturally suspicious, is rationalized by a chain of assumptions: lack of vision obviates the possibility to scrutinize people's non-verbal communication; therefore the blind will not easily relinquish their reserve towards other people; hence the blind are inordinately suspicious. This conception is a fertile ground for prejudice against blind people in interpersonal relationships, and in particular it inhibits accepting them in superior administrative roles.

The conception was invoked in two cases that involved candidacies of blind people for employment. One was that of the position of manager of the CB for which a blind candidate was bidding. The issue was deliberated by the sighted and blind members of the CB board, and one of the considerations that weighed against the candidate, and explicitly against any blind candidate, was the stereotype of blind-functioning in interpersonal relations. But eventually this candidate did obtain the position. Another case arose in the search of one of the local clubs for a person to run its "psychology circle," a discussion group that met weekly and exchanged ideas and experiences about daily lives. The circle had been managed in the past by Liat, a personable sighted woman, but not a professional, whose sole training pertinent to the task on hand consisted of one extramural course for group counsellors. Liat had given notice that she would discontinue working, and a replacement had to be found. Nehama, one of the participants, suggested her sighted sister, Beruria, a thirty year-old graduate student in psychology. Since I was a regular member of the group I participated in the consultation and suggested three candidates who were blind. One was an experienced psychologist, another an experienced social worker, and the third a social worker who had training, but only limited practical experience and worked as a switchboard operator. These people had good reputations, and many of the participants knew them personally. Beruria, on the other hand, was completely unknown.

Significantly, the manager of the club, a visually-impaired person, dismissed my suggestions summarily. The psychologist, he stated, was unsuited because she specialized in youth, the social worker was too busy and would not accept the position, and the switchboard operator was of low professional standard. All three explanations are remarkable. About the switchboard operator I had heard favorable comments from a reliable welfare professional. The psychologist was certainly no less an expert on adults than was Beruria. Many of the participants in the circle were in their twenties, in the throes of grappling with problems of early adulthood, and the psychologist's expertise with youth might have been an asset. Finally, the social worker deemed to be so busy, was not given an opportunity to weigh his options. The manager finalized the discussion saying that a blind group leader was altogether unsuited, because he or she would not be able to react to the participants by their non-verbal facial cues (*haba'at ha'panim*). So Beruria was hired (and she performed well). Finally, it is pertinent in this context to recall the anguish of Yael Hadad, who was penalized by the severe yardstick concerning gender norms for blind people.

The exposure of people to subordination can have ramificated effects, beyond specific issues where the dominant and the dominated meet. The experience of lifelong subordination can affect many of the doings of blind clients. Such ramification is not universal among blind people, but the following case demonstrates its potential. The Dangurs were an unemployed and childless couple. Their childlessness was chosen, as was the case also with some other blind couples, since they were apprehensive of transmitting their condition to their offspring, and because they considered themselves unable to cope with child rearing. In fact, with the exception of the condition of retinitis pigmentosa (which was not the case of the Dangurs), blindness is usually not hereditary. But the Dangurs were obsessed by an ideology of voluntary childlessness which justified a major existential choice they had made in their lives. As soon as they came to know me they sought to activate me for that cause, to try to influence the blindness authorities to embark on a program to discourage blind couples from having children. My own convictions however were different, and I evaded the request. In the end, the situation became such that I had to refuse outright. This soured relations between us, and the Dangurs soon terminated them. But before finally disappointing the Dangurs I had suggested a compromise, and their response to that is illuminating in the present context.

I had no objection to assisting the Dangurs to propagate their ideas by themselves. Therefore I had suggested helping them to draft a memorandum in their own name, which I would then help to circulate, in the media and among pertinent authorities. The reaction of the Dangurs was, that although the issue was of great importance to them, they did not wish to pursue such an activist line. They were apprehensive that it might cause ill-will against them "in the institutions" (*ha'mosdot*). Israeli authorities maintain pro-natalist policies, and also blind activists of the AB, for the additional reason of disability rights, support that position. For the Dangurs, unemployed, rather detached from family and having few friends, the blindness system was the mainstay of their lives. They felt they could not permit the least chance of a mishap in goodwill from those parts. The Dangurs refrained from expressing an unpopular position over a public issue they felt strongly about, because of their feelings of dependence and insecurity toward the blindness system.

The reaction of clients to subordination on the part of the blindness system was diverse, running from respectful acquiescence, to joking dismissal, to resentment and seething anger. In general, reaction was mild toward the volunteers of the local benevolent associations, and harsh toward officials of the public branch of the system. The latter engaged in matters of livelihood that were essential to clients, while the volunteers engaged in materially peripheral matters, such as the leisure programs. The less powerful volunteers were not viewed ominously as the officials were sometimes viewed. A client attitude of the mild type is exemplified by the following case: My wife and I had visited Rivqa Cohen who worked in a sheltered-workshop. A few days later Rivqa met me, and somewhat bashfully asked about the type of perfume that my wife used. She liked it and wanted the same for herself. Rivqa went on, saying that she had once noticed that Mrs. Druyanov used a perfume she liked, but she could not ask Mrs. Druyanov about it, because "Mrs. Druyanov is very uptight and straight" (*nuqsha vi'yeshara*). Rivqa's image of the volunteer is of a positive but remote person.

Where resentment toward volunteers did arise it was phrased in terms of joking dismissal. Thus the AB held a discussion about a convenient time for meetings of the CB, which AB representatives were due to attend. Some of the AB members wished those meetings to start after 4:00 P.M., because they worked a regular working day and could not come earlier. However, the customary CB meeting time was 3:00 P.M. To conclude the discussion one of the participants quipped:

Let's settle for 3:30. By the time every one of the aunties (*dodot*) arrives, and then do their phone calls to say hello to their daughters, the time will be 4:00 P.M. anyway!

In another such discussion the issue was a case of rivalry between two volunteer associations, in which allegations of mismanagement had been made. That had been a year earlier, and the affair had petered out. One of the AB activists said:

> Last year Mrs. Even barked and all our old ladies (*zeqeinot*) took fright. Then she got out of breath, and that finished the affair.

The note is one of disregard, in which male stereotypes of sex and age figure. The blind activists are mostly men in their forties, and the volunteers mostly older women. Further, the activists are extremely busy people, working and raising young families,[3] while the volunteers are mostly ladies of leisure. Moreover, the activists are mostly Middle-Easterners while the volunteers are all Ashkenazic, and many of them of specifically German and Western European background. All this is compounded with traditional values, that make it problematic for men to accept the support of women. Derogatory expressions such as the above, and also *nooshim* (women; in Ashkenazic pronunciation which is associated with being out-of-touch, old-fashioned) are occasionally heard among the blind activists.

One of the specific complaints of the AB activists is that the volunteers are easy in giving assistance to undeserving clients. In this context they used the expression *yiddeshe mammes* and also *gevirot* (affluent ladies). The connotation of these two epithets for generous and affluent women are opposite. One is homey and the other is remote and proud; both reflect unease at the inverted gender relationship. But actual criticism of the volunteers was mild. Thus, an AB activist recounted the limitations imposed on clients using a local swimming pool, that the local volunteer association had arranged for them in order to be admitted free of charge. The volunteers had agreed to inconvenient conditions: Bathers were to be admitted only at certain times when an additional lifeguard was in attendance, because the management believed them to be at special risk. Also sighted companions had to pay full admittance, and that made it difficult for people with mobility problems to come. The man concluded with resignation, "Nothing the sighted arrange for the blind is a real success."

The general philanthropic associations in contrast to the volunteer associations for the blind, are remote from blind people, and when they turn to the latter they are the least sensitive of all those who concern themselves with supporting blind people. Inadvertently, the doings of the general associations often evince inequality and disrespect for the clients. Thus Penina Danieli recounted, she had received advance notice of a Purim party, but she did not plan to attend. On the evening of the party, a volunteer whom Penina did not know came to her apartment unannounced, to take her to the function, and called out, "Come to the party!" Penina felt slighted, because being vigorous and mobile she felt able to go places by herself. But more than that, she objected to the volunteer's assumption that she would want as a matter of course to go to a function organized for blind people.

Similarly, the public schools seek to encourage children to engage in charitable deeds. However, the teachers do not offer the children detailed guidance how to go about this, and that causes good will to be channelled into stereotyped inequality and disrespect. Nehama Gadol was involved in such an incident. Late one afternoon as she was relaxing after work, Nehama was aroused by loud pounding on her apartment door, "hysterical banging" in her words.[4] Three schoolgirls, aged about eleven, poured into her home, breathless and without explanation or personal introduction, burst out, "We came to help!" Nehama, shocked by the uncouthness and bluntness, told the children that she required no help. In fact, this woman manages poorly in home care, and could well have used the assistance, but she was put off by the approach.

Stereotypic attitudes toward blind people are not limited to particular categories of people, thoughtless philanthropists, ineffective teachers, immature children. We encounter them at all stages of the social ladder. Complaints about physicians were legion. An adult woman was incensed when a physician told her to come with her mother. Another woman complained that physicians spent an inordinate amount of time speaking about irrelevancies, asking how she managed housekeeping, child care, but were curt in medical explanations. Also a consultation with a rabbi elicited this pattern. Ya'aqov Megidish, who was very observant, had gone to consult how he should observe the yearly Tishe'a be'Av day of mourning (held in commemoration of the destruction of the Jerusalem Temple in antiquity). It is customary to fast on that day, and also to refrain from wearing ordinary shoes. The latter was irksome to Ya'aqov because it interfered with his normal mobility, which required sensitive treading. The rabbi summarily absolved Ya'aqov from the customary practice saying, in Ya'aqov's words, "that I suffer enough anyway, and that I may wear whatever I please." The argumentation is obviously stereotypic, but remarkably, the rabbi's innate attitude led him to a solution that is dubious in the terms of halakha (religious law) that normally governs such decisions. The rabbi could have made the point more soundly by arguing, that interference with the normal footwear of a blind person might make mobility unsafe, and to absolve on that base. Such a halakhic argument would also have obviated the diffuse and pitying inequality that was embedded in the rabbi's statement.

Remarkably, even a group of disabled people evinced stereotypes toward blind people. During the 1984 general election campaign a group of disabled people sought to gain political representation in the Knesset, and they came to present their case at a meeting of the AB, in a bid to gain support. These activists were mainly motor disabled people of various kinds, and did not include any blind person. At the meeting, the disabled activists briefly described their program, but since time was short, the AB board members asked for copies of their platform to study at leisure (with the assistance of sighted readers). The political hopefuls were taken aback. They did not have any material on hand, because, they admitted sheepishly, they thought such material would be useless for blind people.[5] The consistent factor that runs through these incidents is lack of familiarity with blind people that leads variegated individuals—able-bodied and disabled, educated and uneducated—to conceptualize stereotypically.

The AB activists who participate in the management of the CB jointly with sighted volunteers are in a unique position, being both clients and operators of the blindness system. While they do express reserve toward their sighted colleagues as we saw above, this is anything but harsh. Sometimes the AB activists participate in their paternalistic doings, and express themselves in terms that are tinged with nuances of segregation and inferiority. At one function, a local AB representative made appreciative remarks thanking "in the name of the blind" those who had sponsored the event, and concluded by calling upon them to "continue to help as much as you can." Stereotypical attitudes do not pit blind people against the sighted. Many sighted people do not share those stereotypes and many blind people do, to the extent of even being judgmental in a discriminatory way, as in the sad case of Yael Hadad. Some blind people condemned her as being "a little degenerated," while others said she was being victimized.

Of the two main categories of sighted operators of the blindness system, the public officials and the local volunteers, the former were viewed much more negatively, both by AB activists and by ordinary clients. I encountered expressions of bitter antipathy toward the officials. Shula Bergman, who worked as a switchboard operator, summarized her views of officials as follows:

> Although I was already married they wanted to dump me
> for a year into Migdalor.[6] One of the bastards had decided
> that otherwise they would send me to a sheltered-
> workshop . . . They're not dedicated to their job. For them

it's easiest to send people to Migdalor, instead of making greater efforts for them . . . Those who work in the welfare ministry are bastards of the worst sort!

Eventually, this woman claimed, she was trained informally by a friend, and evaded extended formal training and the separation from her husband this would have entailed. Later she found a switchboard job for herself, and persuaded the officials to subsidize the necessary adaptation of equipment she needed. In the opinion of Hava Dangur, who lost her position in competition with another switchboard operator in her vicinity, the officials are "human offal who torment and victimize us." Miriam Aflalu recounted that an official had decided in two different cases, that the individuals concerned were unsuited for switchboard work. She however, took these people under her wing, and trained them by herself at her job. "I devote myself to the blind," she said proudly. Whether those people eventually managed to cope as operators I do not know; the significant point is the triumphal note of the woman who conceives of herself as battling against a cold-hearted bureaucrat. However, many officials have exerted themselves to find work for people, and some of those who were assisted remain appreciative.

In this and the previous chapter we described how blindness workers impinged on the lives of blind people. We also saw how the latter's experience of support, from both blind and able-bodied blindness workers, was shaped. In part four of the study we shall follow people as they reach out, beyond attainment of the fundamentals of life, growing to maturity and making a living. We focus on the steps that people take toward broader self-assertion and independence.

Part IV

Reaching for Fulfillment:
Friendship, Dignity, Integration

Chapter Ten

The Dilemma of Association among Blind People

One of the virtually universal features of culture is the conceptualizing of people into stratified categories. A common and extreme form of this is the subjection of people in inferior social categories to diffuse discredit, or stigma. The latter entails a continuum of practices, from mild discrimination to radical exclusion and persecution. Mainline sociology has shed much light on one particular aspect of these phenomena, namely the interstices of ethnic and racial relations. Hence, for instance, the voluminous literature extant on Blacks and Jews in Western countries. However, the extension of the sociological perspective to other categories of people who have been historically discredited by the larger society—women, homosexuals, the young and the aged, the disabled—is recent and much less developed.

There are salient differences between the various categories of discredited people. So-called ethnic minority people might be channelled into low-class socio-economic positions, but at the same time they often develop rich symbolic systems and sub-cultures, and sometimes full-fledged communities. Similarly, people who engage in specific behavior defined as illicit by the dominant groups of society, the so-called deviants, although inhibited from associating openly with each other, often do so covertly. Such social deviants tend to develop symbols and sub-cultures, sometimes even secret societies, though usually not fully institutionalized communities (see for instance, Sagarin 1969 and Pfuhl 1986, ch. 7). The presence of positive symbols encourages mutual reinforcement within communities of the discredited; discredited people are then able to evaluate themselves more positively than do those who dominate them.

People who are physically disabled do not evince this pattern; with the possible exception of the deaf, they do not usually construct sub-cultures of their own. The associations and friendship networks of disabled people have not been documented as being institutionalized societies to an extent similar to that of minority ethnic groups, and groups based on moral deviation.[1] The able-bodied in society

115

commonly evaluate the condition of disabled people negatively and channel them into segregated social niches. But disabled people, while basically acquiescing to this evaluation, do not usually cultivate symbols of their own to challenge it. Ethnic minorities can, through the creation of evocative slogans such as "Black is Beautiful!", legitimize themselves and counteract racism, but this course is, on the whole, not open to the disabled minorities. Despite the efforts of activists of the disability-rights movements, to develop positive sub-cultural symbols and organizations (such as described in Goldin 1984), it is a moot question how widely these activities are accepted among the masses of disabled people. Disabled people often seek to escape associating with other disabled people, in addition to being themselves rejected by the able-bodied. These actions of disabled people are pertinent to the broad issue of mutual rejection and association among the discredited: When and how do people express the situation of being discredited in terms of separate community formation? When do they refrain from associating with each other?

Among people who are discredited in terms of ethnic and religious categories we encounter both proud, mutually supportive community building, and radical mutual rejection. I cite some examples from the field of Jewish sociology to indicate the broad spectrum of expression of the situation of discredit, even within a relatively narrow social field. Traditional Jewish communities in pre-modern societies were usually characterized by tight grouping, vigorous internal institutions and a rich sub-culture (Sharot 1976, ch. 1). On the other hand, among Central-European Jews, in the generations following the dissolution of the traditional communities, there emerged the phenomenon of "self-hatred" (Lewin 1948: 186–200). Between these poles, Shuval (1966) has quantified the phenomenon of mutual rejection among Jewish Moroccan immigrants in Israel who, upon arrival, found themselves near the bottom of the socio-economic ladder. And in a recent ethnography of Jewish emigrants from Israel in a New York borough, Shokeid (1988) has documented ambivalence in social relationships, that is linked with the emigrants' discredited position, both among American Jews and among their former countrymen. Mutual rejection among the discredited, as the case of the Jews shows, is highly variegated and sometimes absent.

Also within the category of discredited people, among the particular category of the physically disabled, mutual rejection is not uniform. There are notable differences between various conditions. Thus, the condition of epilepsy, due to the particularly harsh stigma that it carries, leads to the extreme of mutual shunning. Support groups among people who have epilepsy are uncommon. Most people who have epilepsy are reported to be unacquainted with even a single other person having that condition (Schneider and Conrad 1983: 237). On the other hand, deafness leads to the extreme of sociability, due to the particular situation of communicative impairment and to the peculiarity of linguistic interactions among deaf people (Higgins 1980; Becker 1980; Sacks 1989; and also literary presentations such as Walker 1986: 22, 117–118; Greenberg 1970).[2] Dwarfism also, due to the particular problem of marital compatibility in terms of stature, leads to notable sociability, though clearly less than among deaf people (Ablon 1984). The condition of blindness is in an intermediate situation. It is less sociable than deafness, but much more so than epilepsy (see Musgrove 1977, ch. 6, for some further preliminary comparative comments).

I suggest that a major element in these differences among various categories of discredited people is the variable of cultural construction, or symbolization, of their various conditions. Where the discredited are culturally creative and evolve positive symbols of their condition, they enable the development of mutual respect which can lead to association. On the other hand, where such positive symbolization is absent, there lacks a basic premise for association. Consequently, the negative stereotypes of the dominant strata prevail, discredited people react to each other much as the dominant people do to them, and mutual rejection ensues. Mutual rejection and the converse, community formation, among disabled people and among the discredited in general, constitutes a topic of major sociological relevance, in terms of both theory and practice. The conditions of physical exception pose such questions as: When do disabled people distance themselves from each other, along with the general stigmatization of their condition in society? When do they voluntarily draw together, associate, and build communities? And when disabled people do draw together, what kinds of social bonds do they develop?

This chapter aims at contributing towards elucidation of some of the social factors that pertain to mutual rejection and association. In the next section we dwell on the way derogatory stereotypes of blind people are perpetuated by blind Israelis. Thereafter we proceed to social formations of blind people, in which the convolution of association and rejection can be seen to operate.

I. Stereotypes and Rejection Among Blind People

One of the expressions of the general culture within which blind people operate is the tendency of the sighted to reject and to segregate the blind.[3] These practices also spill over into doings among blind people themselves. In this section we consider stereotypes of the general culture, which bolster rejection of the blind, on the part of both the sighted and the blind.

In the course of my observations many blind people voiced the slogan, "The blind are like anyone else, only they can't see." But the slogan was hollow, because these same people also entertained prejudices about blind people, thus demonstrating their feeling that there was more to blindness than just lack of sight. A discussion at an encounter group of blind people which figured heated expressions of the aforementioned slogan, exemplifies this. The discussants, mostly young and immature, were uninformed about occupational possibilities beyond their personal doings, and unable to mention a single additional occupation that they felt might suit blind people. Consequently, as the discussion got onto specifics, it fizzled out. Nehama, one of the participants, later commented to me negatively about Yehezqel Mazuz, a blind man whom she had heard over the radio participating in a quiz, and answering questions about vehicle maintenance and driving. "Yehezqel presented himself as if he knew everything," Nehama said, "but how can that be? A blind person can't drive a vehicle!" In fact, Yehezqel was very knowledgeable about cars; even manually, short of actually driving a vehicle, he was very adept. But that was beyond the scope of Nehama's imagination.

While none of the people who participated in this discussion were active in the public affairs of blind people, nor very knowledgeable in these matters, it is notable that I encountered the same attitude in a radically different group, the members of the committee of the Association of the Blind (AB). These were mostly older, mature people, heads of families, stably employed, and involved and knowledgeable in matters of concern to blind people. One of the issues that the AB committee raised in many consecutive meetings, and always rejected, was a proposal that the Association engage in public fundraising, without the assistance of sighted volunteers. The proposal was repeatedly raised by someone or other, as the committee reached a point of exasperation when discussing a particularly thorny problem of fundraising and relationships with the sighted volunteers. Consistently, whenever the idea of independent fund-raising was raised, the discussants would not explore it. People snickered and giggled and left the matter at that. They evidently felt that such a project was beyond the abilities of sightless people, and that the assistance of sighted volunteers was indispensable. Like the members of the encounter group, the activists had a low-level view of the abilities of blind people.

Moreover, among various blind people, both mature and inexperienced, I encountered stereotypes that stigmatized blind people morally. Some expressed distaste at working together with blind colleagues. "Heaven forbid," said Pamela Samukha, "that blind people work together! Then you have jealousy and gossip!" This woman was an assembler in an industrial plant; besides herself, there was only one other blind employee there, Mazal Eini, the switchboard operator. Pamela continued: "Mazal and I are friends, because we're the only blind people there, and also because we don't live in the same neighborhood". Had there been more blind employees, Pamela implied, there would have developed friction among them, and she and Mazal might not have been friends. Another worker at an industrial plant, where he was the sole blind person, well integrated among sighted workers, believed that where blind people are colleagues at work they are suspicious that one of them gain better treatment than the other (for instance in obtaining components that are easier to assemble). An employee at a sheltered workshop for blind people complained:

> At our place we have jealousy and hatred, although people have worked together for decades. But the switchboard-operators are fortunate; they are by themselves among the sighted. They are respected. But amongst us—God help us!

Another negative stereotype, volunteered by a switchboard-operator, concerned the scope of interests of blind people:

> The scope of interests of blind people is limited. They have nothing to converse about, because they do not see things! In particular, those who work in the company of other blind people only, gossip about people, what they do, how much they earn.

I witnessed a discussion in a group of rather sophisticated people, the activists of the AB in one of the localities, who had arranged that blind people and their sighted companions could, at certain specified times, have free access to a public swimming pool. Some people, these activists complained, exploited the arrangement unfairly. Instead of coming accompanied by just one of their sighted children, they came with several. One man came at wrong times, and when denied free access, behaved insolently. "They will yet spoil the arrangement for all of us!" moaned one activist. Another concluded on a resigned note, "The blind only take, but do not give". What these statements, originating from diverse individuals, simple and sophisticated, segregated and integrated among the sighted, have in common, is disparagement of blind people.[4]

Disparagement, I suggest, is linked to the physical condition of blindness, and to the way society, composed of both sighted and blind people evaluates this condition. An important element of sightlessness is the dearth of information that reaches the blind person, due to the lack of visual stimuli. One way of coping with the dearth of information is for blind persons to engage in egregious behavior, so as to elicit verbal responses, and thereby ascertain their surroundings. The awareness of blind people of this technique, emerged in a discussion of the AB board, planning a public demonstration. The program called for a countrywide gathering of blind people at the offices of the Treasury in Jerusalem, to air grievances against the authorities. The activists were concerned that too few people might come. But finally one of the discussants quipped that the worry was groundless, "For every blind demonstrator is like two sighted ones, considering the amount of noise they'll make!"

Another element of sightlessness is the accompanying mobility, particularly when cane-aided, which is both audible and visible. The audibility is objectionable to many blind people, and though cane-usage is by far the most accepted mobility aid among Israeli blind people, there is evidence of ambivalence toward it (see chapter 3). Many blind people cannot resign themselves to adopt practices that cause them to stand out among the sighted, no matter how well these are suited to their physical condition. Such a person was Ruth Gabay, a homemaker who would not use the long cane, although she lacked any other mobility aid. This childless woman, married to a working husband, spent most of her time isolated at home. She spoke of people such as herself as being *regishim*, bashful (literally, "sensitive"). Of others who use the long cane and are outgoing and talkative, Ruth spoke wistfully as "having courage" (*yesh lahem ometz*). "But I don't have courage," she said of herself.

Many people overcome such inhibitions, some of them with charm and finesse. For instance, a blind man entered a club hall where a group of blind players were quietly engrossed in a corner in a game of domino. He called out loudly, "What's all this noise here today?" The players laughed and promptly responded, identifying themselves. However, not everyone is endowed with such social graces. Their behavior, when it confronts the inhibitions and ambivalences of other blind people, such as Ruth, can lead to mutual rejection. Thus, one woman volunteered the following comment:

> It is unpleasant to hear a blind man tick-tacking (*le'taqteiq*) with his cane. Take Shalom Mashiah, for instance. He is a typical blind man: noisy, undiplomatic, unreserved.

Shalom was a markedly independent person, adept at cane-aided mobility who evinced egregious behavior, initiating obtrusive, noisy exchanges. The speaker, Miriam, was also an outgoing able person, but, having command of the assistance of sighted companions, she had never mastered the art of cane-aided mobility. Miriam linked audible mobility and egregious socializing with the physical condition of blindness. Though both practices are functional in terms of the condition of sightlessness, Miriam evaluated them negatively. Whereas Ruth, lacking alternate resources, expressed only inhibition and reserve, Miriam who does have such resources, is secure and explicit in her rejection. For both these very different women, the aforementioned practices were sources of embarrassment.

Of all the negative stereotypes of blind people, that of being mendicants, evoked the strongest emotions. In recounting tales of people whose income derived from begging, the informants sometimes used such vivid images as "Begging is a disease," "A living worm in the fruit". Even for Shlomo Deromi, a blind graduate student, commuting to the university, and launched on to a respectable status, the image of the blind beggar evoked strong feelings. He expressed himself harshly about a blind beggar whom he passed regularly at the bus terminal. Shlomo had hardly any contacts with blind people, and certainly not with blind people near mendicancy, yet his attitude was akin to that of Meir Nagar who may have brushed with mendicants in the course of his life. The attitude to beggars was common to people of varied statuses.

Nagar, an elderly man of Baghdadi background, was employed in a sheltered-workshop. He lived near several blind people of his age and background, and socialized with them after work. In talking of his social life, Meir once burst out spontaneously, "I would never invite to my home anyone who opens his hand (*poteah yad*)!" The usage of this idiom expresses revulsion at begging more powerfully than any verbose explanation. In traditional Jewish culture, which is part of Meir's background, one avoids mentioning unpleasant matters, for fear of having something unpleasant brush off onto oneself. The positive phrase that Meir intuitively chose appears in familiar liturgical passages, that refer to God "who opens His hand" to give to the needy and to accept the penitent. Meir thus avoided the straightforward but negative term "begging", and expressed the act with an ambiguous idiom that serves both giving and taking, a code that is reserved for grave matters.[5]

Many of my blind acquaintances greatly exaggerated the weight and incidence of begging among blind people.[6] Even in the following thoughtful comment of one of the men in Meir Nagar's circle of friends, there is the implicit notion that begging by blind people at bus terminals is common:

Whoever begs at the Central Bus Station makes four times more money than anyone else, but he loses honor. Begging is avoidable now because the Government does not leave anyone without food. God be praised!

In fact very few blind people engage now in public begging in Israel. However, those individuals are highly visible due to their operation at crowded bus terminals in the major cities. Their presence deeply disturbs the numerous blind people who, having occasion to pass them, hear their rattling tin cups and plaintive calls. A few more blind beggars operate at the gates of some of the cemeteries in major cities. Altogether, I estimate that their number throughout the country, does not exceed ten.

Self-negating stereotypes are common among the people studied. But at the same time many were not knowledgeable of the heroes among local blind people, the outstanding artists, academics, businessmen and professionals. These, I suggest, are facets of a situation where people are discredited by the dominant strata of society, and themselves do not engage creatively in positive symbolization of their condition.

II. Varieties of Social Circles

The prevalence of negative stereotyping among blind people acts as a centrifugal force among them: they are eager to integrate, or at least associate with sighted people. That desire however, is hampered and sometimes stultified, by the attitudes and doings of sighted people.[7] The outcome is that blind people often move into avenues for fellowship that are characteristic of lonely people. At some point in their lives many blind people explored using the radio to establish human contact. This impersonal but accessible medium offers programs that permit participation by telephone: programs for people seeking solutions to personal problems, redress from bureaucratic indifference, general knowledge quizzes, etc. No long-term relationship was, to my knowledge, ever established by a blind person as a result of participating in these programs, but the existence of the possibility was important to people. And some particularly egregious people claimed that they made "friends" through casual meetings on the street and on the bus.

Failing to integrate to their satisfaction into the company of sighted people, and despite the reservations they have about blind people, many of them congregate in the company of their own kind. However, blindness was not usually a sufficient base for fellowship. This was so only when blindness was delimited by additional social factors. The drive for companionship among blind people was generally not strong enough to overcome great social differences among them. The case of Yoram Peres, thirty-five year-old and single, exemplifies this. Verbally, he was emphatic about distancing himself from blind people, nurturing negative stereotypes about them. Yoram was also scornful of the AB and of the blindness system as a whole. Working in an office with a hierarchic structure, Yoram had succeeded in ingratiating himself with sighted people well above his own low position in the hierarchy. He used to go out to musical events and to the theatre in the company of high-ranking officials and their spouses. Yoram managed this by arranging joint purchase of the tickets and co-ordinating schedules, all through his convenient position at the switchboard. Such doings were appreciated and afforded Yoram a measure of social acceptance among people at his place of employment. When going out with his colleagues, Yoram did not use the long cane, but was guided by them. Moreover, Yoram insisted that he be not led by a sighted companion, but rather that both walk abreast. Yoram thus sought to divest himself of the most visible sign of his condition, impaired mobility, and to blend into general society.

However, the people with whom Yoram spent long hours over the telephone were primarily blind switchboard operators, scattered throughout the country. When he went on yearly vacation, he used to travel far to visit these friends. Yoram was discriminating in his friendships, snobbish in fact. The blind friends whom he sought out were outgoing, vital and independent people like himself, and of identical occupation. Yoram would have preferred having only sighted friends, but reality was different. Despite his assertions that he had many sighted friends, Yoram's experience of a working-life as a blind switchboard operator circumscribed his social relationships.

A similar pattern is evinced by another person of very different personality and situation in life. Hava Shmuel was a sickly and harassed housebound mother, married to a switchboard operator, who in contrast to Yoram was resigned to the company of blind people. Recounting how she had moved away from her hometown to the town where she had married, Hava said that she did not wish to live in her hometown because there were no hevre there, and also because employment for blind people was limited there. But in her new city of residence, she said, there are lots of hevre who visit each other. Hava went on to elaborate the nature of her hevre: blind people employed as switchboard operators, of about her own age, who had been her contemporaries at the Jerusalem School for the Blind. Hava's circle was delimited by blindness and additional social factors, being old schoolmates of similar age and occupation.

The pattern of association that these individuals evince recurs in several formally structured social groups. One group of blind people was active in a city area I call Sifriya, where many blind people who stemmed from Baghdad, lived and worked as switchboard operators. About thirty-five of them, some now retired, associated in a local club for the blind. The pattern of their meetings was reminiscent of the atmosphere in coffee houses patronized by other elderly Baghdadi immigrants. The club regulars were aged about sixty, predominantly men. Although most of them had a perfect command of Hebrew, the language mainly heard on the premises was Iraqi Arabic, and the popular activity was playing domino once or twice weekly, in a cloud of cheap cigarette smoke.[8] People evidently enjoyed each other's company, and regularly travelled a distance in order to meet. However, their mutual attraction did not cut across any major sociological distinctions in terms of sex, age, ethnicity, culture, and socio-economic status.

Another group of blind associates, numbering around twelve, was a kind of encounter group that met weekly in another section of the city. Termed by themselves and by outsiders "the psychology circle", this was a special interest group that brought together people who wished to talk about personal matters. The group started out being socially heterogeneous, the participants coming from various sub-ethnic backgrounds, ages, family statuses, education and occupations. Their common denominator was their physical condition. However, during the period of about seventeen months in which I participated, a continuous process of homogenization took place. Young unmarried people became the core participants; older and married people dropped out. Also, young people of superior ability or imagination lost interest, and a common, low standard came to prevail in the discussions. Thus, in time, the people of the circle shared a great deal more than their physical condition.[9]

A third social group comprising about fifteen people, was a sports group that met in a third section of the city. Here again, it was not blindness alone that brought these people together, but rather their interest in engaging in physical exercise. Those who lived close to each other also met regularly to play domino at a local club. The sports group was socially more heterogeneous than the other two. There were men and women of variegated ethnic backgrounds and ages, ranging from the teens to mid-forties. Diverse marital statuses were represented among them: single and widowed, married and separated. Most of the participants were totally blind, but some had residual sight, a matter of particular relevance in competitive sports. There was also much socio-economic heterogeneity: there were high school students, switchboard operators, sheltered-workshop people, and an academically trained professional. In terms of behavior too, people were very different. Some were charmingly articulate, others bashful and subdued.

People in the sports group frequently related to each other jokingly. Bantering exchanges were common when the participants formed competitive teams and engaged in the aggressive and exhausting game of gateball. Thus, as Avraham San'ani, who was a highly educated professional, hurled the heavy gateball at Nissim Trabelsi, a rather uncouth switchboard operator, he would call out, "For you Amaleiq!". Nissim would respond similarly as he thrust the ball back to him. The name "Amaleiq" is biblical and figures in the story of Esther and Haman and in the annual Purim celebration. In popular usage the name "Amaleiq" is commonly used to refer to cruel enemies of the Jewish people. The expression, ridiculous in the context of the game, is bandied between partners for whom association in aggressive playful competition is problematic, because they actually are divided in significant ways. The aforementioned differences, of status and so forth, raise barriers to playfulness and closeness. The differences were, however, jokingly expressed by a term so exaggerated, that the actual differences between the players were bracketed off. The gateball match could proceed.

The sports circle is heterogeneous also in so far as some members have spouses who are sighted or visually-impaired and others have blind spouses. Sighted spouses, even if they were so inclined, cannot participate in the group's activities because these are designed around the limitations of blindness. The blind husband of a sighted woman will therefore participate alone, and several couples where both members were blind, participated jointly. Thus Danny and Pirhiya Akram, both of whom were blind, came together, while their friend Avraham Sanani left his sighted wife at home. At one point Pirhiya failed to thrust the gateball properly. Avraham who played on the same team called out to her, "Vashti! It's a good thing I never married you!" Pirhiya laughingly called back, "But last week you said the opposite!" Of a nature similar as the previous appellation, the name "Vashti" is sometimes used as a derogatory female epithet. In this case it figures in a context of social asymmetry. The joking relationship permits people to co-operate in play after differences between them are recognized and bracketed off from the ongoing activity. In the anthropological study of joking it has long been recognized, that where people of markedly differing status are thrown together, joking relationships often stymie potential abrasion.[10] The sports group is notable for the joking relationships that emerge precisely at those points in its structure where heterogeneity is salient. I suggest that this group's success in maintaining itself, despite the heterogeneity, is linked to its ability to avert potential friction by the joking relationships practiced by its members.

The three social groups—the sports group, that of the domino players and the encounter group—are comprised of blind people. Formally any blind person was welcome to join, but informally two of the groups developed selective practices that, for all practical purposes, resulted in their becoming homogeneous. In the third group, where selectivity was not rigorous, joking relationships emerged.

III. Conclusion

The stereotypes and cultural images that we saw point to the existence of impulses for mutual rejection among blind Israelis. Blind people lack the specific social problems of certain other categories of disabled people, deaf and small-statured people in particular, which encourage those people to associate.[11] Thus deaf people interacting can overcome unique problems of communication; small-statured people can overcome unique problems of intimacy and bonding. Blind people are able to gain some empathy and understanding from people of similar physical conditions, but they have relatively less to gain from such interaction than people of the aforementioned categories. In the case of blind people, therefore, the stigmatizing discreditory impulses of the able-bodied vis-à-vis the disabled generally dovetail to a considerable extent with similar impulses of the blind people toward each other. In the case of conditions such as deafness, there is much less dovetailing of discreditory impulses of the able-bodied and of attitudes of deaf people towards each other.[12]

Attitudes towards disabled people, both on the part of able-bodied and of disabled people, are socio-culturally learned. Both categories of people, able-bodied and disabled, live in a common social world, and it is only to be expected that they will have much in common in their social practices. There are secondary differences in the attitudes of various categories of people toward the disabled, which are rooted in the peculiarities of specific conditions, such as those I have indicated. The learning process of the general attitude and the details of the differences are major topics of disability studies, which invite more research.

The blind Israelis did maintain several social groups of their own. Our overview of some of these groups, in the context of the negative stereotypes, permits us to assess the nature of the process of association among them. The groups were not randomly heterogeneous in terms of general sociological categories, such as age and socio-economic status. The groups were founded on the special cultures or interests of individuals, in addition to disability: in the Sifriya group—on ethnicity, in the encounter group—on the desire for personal expression, and in the sports group—on physical activities and neighborliness.

In conclusion: the participants did not consider the physical condition to be of pivotal importance. This conclusion derives from the fact that in one of the groups, the encounter group, several adult mature and married blind people, left the group. In another group, the sports people, despite its heterogeneity, membership remained stable for the particular reason indicated above. In summary, the segregatory force of able-bodied society on blind people may drive some into social niches of their own. But it does not overcome internal categorical differences among blind people. Blindness is not commonly an attribute that leads blind people to associate, but in conjunction with other attributes, it may be.

Chapter Eleven

The Alternative of Ethnicity

Jewish ethnicity in Israel is a favorite topic for students of Israeli society, and a bibliographic review (Smooha 1987) includes over six hundred major items, full-length books and articles in scientific journals. In view of this, it is striking, as Smooha notes, how sketchy our knowledge of the topic remains. Even to such a basic question as the extent of social and cultural pluralism among Israeli Jews, we have no clear answer beyond superficial generalities on the one hand, and highly specific local information on the other. However, some generalizations recur independently in various studies. One is that there is little interest in preserving Middle-Eastern Jewish ethnic cultures as separate cultures, nor of mobilizing them for political ends. At the same time political parties have been shown promoting ethnicity for their own ends. This is evident in as early a study as Deshen 1970, chapter 8 (which is based on 1965 data), through Deshen 1974 based on 1969 data), to Herzog 1990[1] (based on 1984 data). Ethnicity in Israel is, therefore, a convoluted phenomenon; it exists—hedged with apologies and camouflage. Only in the past fifteen years, have some elements of cultural ethnic practice, such as the spring festivities of Middle-Eastern Israelis, attained wide societal acceptance in the context of the political emergence and assertion of the Middle-Easterners.[2]

The ethnographic study of Israeli ethnicity, in line with the ethnography of ethnicity in general, falls into two main grooves. The most common one is that of uncovering the patterns of ethnic activity that various discrete groups follow. The less common one is that of uncovering the changing, situational conditions that lead people, even within given groups, to adopt varying ethnic strategies. Thus, to take one instance in Israeli ethnography, Yemenite immigrants and their offspring have been shown repeatedly to exhibit relative tenacity in adherence to their sub-culture of origin, more than other Israelis (Berdichevsky 1977, Lewis 1985, Loeb 1985, also Ben-Rafael 1982).

129

At the other extreme, Israelis of Bulgarian background seem to evince the least interest in their sub-culture. Groups such as the Israeli Bulgarians, however, because of their lack of cultural distinctiveness, have attracted very little research on the part of anthropologists, given the latter's predilection for the exotic. Hence, our knowledge is particularly lacking in respect of patterns of disaffection and rejection of ethnicity.

The study of blind people affords an insight into this relatively uncharted corner of ethnic studies. I observed and learned of activities among blind people that pertained to ethnicity, but which reflect rejection of ethnic alternatives. Ethnicity and ethnic activities in particular, constituted for the people of the study one of several alternative avenues whereby they could seek social fulfillment, in terms of establishing friendship ties and integrating with able-bodied people. The study of these activities among the blind Israelis, permits us to approach a question for which data are relatively sparse. Namely, why do some people, in contrast to others, detach themselves from their background culture, and what are the dilemmas they face in doing so? By no means do I imply in posing this question, that the opposite phenomenon, that of people exhibiting ethnic attachment, does not set a sociological problem. Indeed it does. Hardly any human action can be taken for granted sociologically. It just so happens that students of ethnicity have devoted relatively few efforts to the question raised.

The individuals whose doings are presented in this chapter were not directly involved in ethnic matters, and only on rare occasions were their activities at all pertinent to ethnicity. It is notable however that in the course of observations and interaction with these people, they were negative, and sometimes harsh, in their expressions concerning ethnicity. There was indeed the Sifrya group which was composed primarily of people of similar ethnic, sex and age categories. I did not study those people closely, and it is possible that they evinced positive attitudes toward their Baghdadi sociocultural background. Be that as it may, even among non-affiliated, alienated people, such as those I did study (and they are the most representative of blind Israelis generally) the attitude to ethnicity warrants our attention. It is not a natural given that people should reject ethnicity if they happen not to attend a club such as the one mentioned.

The expressions of the beliefs of people in matters of ethnicity are presented in the first section of this chapter. Section two consists of observations of incidents where people interact, in which beliefs in matters of ethnicity can be seen in more dynamic contexts. The basic data are accounts of actions in which ethnicity figures, where people establish positions that pertain to ethnicity. Although the weight of the disability of blindness is not such as to determine the social actions of people, it is a matter of importance. The thrust of the argument is, that blindness has the potential to lead people to the particular actions described. This potential, however, emerges in actual life most differentially, and to account for that variety idiosyncratic factors other than disability must be uncovered.

I. Ethnic Beliefs

The people of the study were emphatic in their spontaneous expressions of ethnicity. Consistently they evaluated Ashkenazic (Northern European) origins favorably while depreciating Middle-Eastern[3] origins. Facets of the environment that they conceived of positively they linked with Ashkenazic origins, and the converse they linked with Middle-Eastern origins. Thus, I once complimented Asher Dalal, from Baghdad who was in his early fifties, on the good looks of his wife to whom he had been married for over thirty years. His pleased reaction was, "Yes, and at the time we married she looked just like an Ashkenazi!" Asher might have conceptualized his wife's attractive appearance in various terms, but he chose to do so precisely in terms of an Ashkenazic frame of reference.

The incident that follows also demonstrates the evaluation of experience in ethnic terms, but in reference to a situation that is part of the condition of disability. Tirsa Hakham, a single woman in her fifties, also from Baghdad, had difficulties running her home, and was sometimes assisted by volunteer high school girls, who helped her with shopping. Talking about them Tirsa was effusive in praising those of Ashkenazic background, and in complaining about the others. "With Sephardic girls it is difficult to manage. The Ashkenazic girls are nicer", she said. Some of the Sephardic girls, Tirsa stated, had stolen objects from her. To one of them, she claimed, she once gave money to make a purchase, and the girl had disappeared. Tirsa's volunteer girls all came through a social activities program of the local religious high school. I do not conceive of great differences among the students. The categorization of whatever differences there were among them in clear-cut ethnic terms is a reflection of Tirsa's conceptual universe. In that universe Middle-Eastern origins are depreciated, even in the context of well-meaning young volunteers.

The segregated institutional arrangements of education for blind children in the recent past, away from home in dormitories, often led to poor rapport between sighted parents and their blind offspring (see chapter 4), but Rivqa Cohen, a widow in her mid-forties, maintained

warm relations with her Yemenite natal family. In her own home the
relations between Rivqa and her sighted teenage children were ridden with conflict, which was partly linked to Rivqa's condition as a
disabled person (see chapter 5). When Rivqa talked about the problems she had with her children, she interpreted them in blanket
ethnic terms, "Among Sephardim there is no rapport between parents and children". But Rivqa's relations with her natal family were
positive; her own experience did not support the ethnic stereotype. As
in the previous cases, Rivqa's conceptualization is grounded in her
idiosyncratic conceptual universe, and not in any positive reality beyond her.

Another variant of the ethnic interpretation of poor family relationships, was volunteered by Yael Hadad. Unmarried and unemployed, in her mid-forties and of Baghdadi origin, Yael recalled that
when, as a child, she became aware of her blindness and required
support, her mother failed to provide explanations and relieve her
anxieties. "My mother went into a panic," summarized Yael. Then she
went on to generalize:

> Amongst us Middle-Easterners (*adot ha'mizrah*), people do
> not know how to explain things. People are afraid of hurt-
> ing each other. So they don't talk.

This comment captures a feature of hierarchical human relationships
which are sometimes present in traditional families. But again, the
generalized linking of this feature to the Middle-Eastern background
does not capture reality. Rather it reflects Yael's conceptual world.

Ethnic stereotyping also figured in the conceptualizing of relationships between men and women. Two single people, David Levy
and Nehama Gadol, had established contact through "a lonely hearts"
radio program. Both were of Baghdadi background, employed as telephone switchboard operators, he in his forties and she in her early
thirties. In Nehama's account of their relationship there figured primarily the nature of David's personal habits, which she found objectionable. According to her account, David had explained that he required much sleep both at night and during the day after work.
Therefore, David was available for socializing for limited periods only.
The salient point in this account is Nehama's reaction: David was a
recluse, she said, apprehensive of going out into the world and meeting people, whereas she herself was friendly and outgoing. Nehama
went on and linked David's idiosyncrasy to the fact that in contrast to
herself, he had grown up in Baghdad and had received only part of
his education in Israel. However, there were people of similar background, age and education as David, who behaved very differently,
and Nehama was well acquainted with some of them.[4] Clearly, she

selected the ethnic factor out of a reservoir of available knowledge, in order to conceptualize an experience.

A common type of negative experience of the people of the study hinged on the patronizing attitude of many sighted towards blind people. The informants recounted incidents in which well-meaning people had unwittingly embarrassed them. These incidents ranged from mild incivilities to the ultimate insult of having a stranger press cash into one's hands in the street or on a bus. The informants conceived that as a grave humiliation, because it imposed upon them the role of blind beggar. In the context of the present discussion the significant point is, that many informants linked such negative behavior to the often putative Middle-Eastern background of the actors.

Moshe Danino, a handsome young teacher of Moroccan background, reported an encounter he had with a new class of ninth grade girls in his hometown, which was populated mainly by people of Middle-Eastern background. At his first session with the class, Moshe reported, he discerned sounds of sobbing from all corners of the classroom. Disturbed, he interrupted himself and asked the girls what was the matter. They answered haltingly, in tears, "It's . . . it's . . . because of . . . you!" Moshe explained that the girls' reaction to his blindness was linked to their Middle-Eastern background. That background prevented the girls from accepting him as a teacher, but rather to view him as a pitiable blind man. Moshe went on, recounting that he frequently encounters pitying and patronizing behavior in his town. He hears people calling out to each other as he goes about in the street, "Take him home!", "Help him!"

The conceptualization of negative experiences in terms of Middle-Eastern origins can lead to a general negation of Middle-Eastern culture. An indication of this was volunteered by Nehama Gadol who, upon returning from her annual vacation on the campus of the Jerusalem School for the Blind, complained that she had been annoyed there by the loud playing of "Oriental music" on transistor radios, by some other vacationers. That, she said, she "hated". Nahama was an extremely soft-spoken mild person; coming from her the word "hate" was extraordinary. She evidently had very strong negative feelings about "Oriental music".

Emphatic rejections of the Middle-Eastern background were also expressed by Hava Dangur. In her early fifties, born in Baghdad and partly educated in Israel, Hava recalled the epithet "Iraqi pyjama", that used to be thrown at immigrants from Iraq in the early years of immigration. At that time Iraqi men in their leisure time liked to lounge around, and sometimes walked the streets, dressed in pyjamas. Though decades have since passed and the practice is long gone, Hava still smarts from the sting of the old insult. But Hava has

internalized the negative evaluation of her background culture. She
consciously distances herself from the language, manners, even the
people of her immediate family .

This kind of rejection, close to self-hatred, sometimes expresses
itself, in crude insults. The Nagar couple were in their late fifties, he
blind from infancy in Baghdad, worked in a sheltered workshop,
while she, visually-impaired from Tripolitania, had raised their several children. One evening the Nagars were talking of the hard times
they had gone through, and of their successful sons. As the conversation moved on to the value of self-support, demeaning references to
"Iraqi shopkeepers who work in pyjamas" cropped up. The image, a
figment of the imagination, illustrates how the speakers link
slovenliness with the Iraqi background. Speaking of medical treatment, Yael Hadad once referred scathingly to physicians at the time
of her infancy in Baghdad, "Where I was born—there were asses, not
doctors! " Yael was a knowledgeable person, aware that medical knowledge everywhere had advanced since her childhood. But in conceptualizing the medical treatment given to her many decades ago, she
focused upon the element of locality, depreciating her background.

While people hardly ever volunteered positive statements or evaluations of matters related to the Middle-Eastern background, blanket
positive evaluations of the Ashkenazic background were common. Hava
Dangur, rambling on about her ethnic likes and dislikes, said, "Should
I meet someone from England I would certainly prefer him to someone from Tripolitania". Iraqis she disliked too: "Iraqis will insist that
you eat with them, but when they come to you, they won't eat!". She
was referring to the complex of Middle-Eastern practice concerning
hosting. Like most human doings, the practice has attractive and
unattractive aspects; but to Hava it was wholly abominable. Another
blind homemaker, Yokheved Megidish originating from Tripolitania,
had raised six fine children (see chapter 5). She had Ashkenazic
neighbors, who besides being sighted, had much smaller families. Yet
Yokheved was full of admiration for the putative abilities of neighbors, for whom homemaking was immeasurably easier. Yokheved concluded her account with an emphatic ethnic evaluation, "I admire the
Ashkenazim! " A cognitive, virtually ideological rejection of Middle-
Eastern identity runs through these statements.

II. Existential Grappling

Many blind Israelis are relatively poor, live in crowded neighbor-
hoods, and belong to strata that are politically weak. Though many of
them are of Middle-Eastern, and particularly of Baghdadi origin, Is-

raeli blind people do not evince any trend towards manipulating ethnic symbols. There have, over the years, been many cases of ethnic assertion in Israel by people struggling for material and political benefits. But the statements of the people of this study, point resolutely away from that possibility. The cases that follow demonstrate the position of people over ethnic issues in dynamic contexts.

Yael Hadad was a telephone switchboard operator who fell foul of employers and rehabilitation officials, because of what they considered to be her inordinate familiarity with co-workers. In time Yael lost two jobs. Her relations with the rehabilitation staff deteriorated to a point where she expressed her frustration at Mr. Kravitz, the official responsible for her case, by verbal abuse and a mild physical assault. Thereupon the official refrained from investing further work into her case, and in effect destined Yael to a life of permanent unemployment. In talking of her lot, Yael was always vehement in her wrath at Mr. Kravitz. On one occasion, after she had poured out her heart to me in her usual monologue of bitterness, Yael trailed off wistfully,

> ... I don't want to say that Kravitz the Pole, discriminates against me because of ethnicity. It's not nice to say that. I know that he really got jobs for many Orientals too ...

Unlike many other blind people, Yael undergoes a unique ordeal. She nagged herself, she told me, with the question, "Why?! Why do just I have to suffer like that?! Wasting my years!" The possibility of interpreting her anguish in ethnic terms was evidently on Yael's mind. But she refrained from resolving her existential cognitive problem through this readily available channel.

The repugnance for Middle-Eastern origins also surfaced at meetings of the board of the Association of the Blind (AB). During the discussions of the AB board there recurred mention of Avia Degani, a blind activist who had run foul of the Association, and was intensely disliked by the AB activists. Like many Israelis of all backgrounds, who have Hebraized their surnames which were mostly Arabic, German and Slavic, Avia had discarded her original surname which was Middle-Eastern, and also her given name which, though Hebrew, was carried exclusively by Middle-Easterners. But when Avia's name came up in deliberations, the discussants referred to her by the old name that their opponent had discarded many years before. By changing her name, Avia had sought to shed an old Middle-Eastern identity, but her AB opponents kept the memory of that identity alive in the context of negative depictions, thereby degrading her.

However, many blind people retain their old foreign names, like most Israelis. Here too, considerations linked to the issue of ethnic identity sometimes came to the fore. Pamela Samukha's given name conveyed a typically Levantine identity. Born in Baghdad, in the early 1930s, her parents had given her a then popular English Levantine name; no less than four girls in her class at school were named Pamela. Later in Israel Pamela Samukha did not change her name, but in talking about this she linked the matter directly to the issue of patriotism. Pamela regretted, she said, not having Hebraized her given name in the past, for she "loved the country".

Like the opponents of Avia Degani, Pamela felt negatively about her original given Levantine name. But Avia had changed her name and Pamela had not done so. In her broodings over the matter, Pamela confided what disturbed her: she was apprehensive that her negligence to Hebraize her name might mistakenly reflect on her overall attachment to the country. For Pamela, as for Yael Hadad, reflection on Middle-Eastern origins was a cause for anguish. And when, as in the case of Avia at the AB meeting, those origins were alluded to in a context of conflict, the outcome was abrasive.

The cognitive depreciation of Middle-Eastern identity sometimes goes hand-in-hand with gut feelings of human warmth towards people of common background. The aforementioned Rivqa Cohen, who was of Yemenite background, had spent a pleasant evening at my home with my family. As she was taking leave, she expressed her pleasure, "I feel with you just like among Yemenites!" Earlier we saw this same person expressing crude prejudices about Middle-Easterners when talking about specific matters. The informants sometimes expressed the feeling that people of the same particular background ought to be loyal and supportive. But the presumption of trust was thwarted by the cognitive belief that minimized the salience of common origin. The clash between feeling and cognition can be painful as evident in the following exchange between two actors, both of whom we saw in other contexts verbalizing vigorously against Middle-Eastern origins: Nehama Gadol and Yael Hadad, both of Iraqi background, were talking about an electronics technician. One of the women had given him a watch to repair, but it had broken down again. She said that she suspected the man had not replaced the old battery with a new one, as he ought to have done, but had inserted a used battery. The other woman agreed, saying sadly, "Yes, that is possible, even though the man is Iraqi". For these women the fact of common origin is linked to a presumption of trust, but the trust is flawed.

Some individuals however, in certain situations, exhibit the personal resilience to dismiss the clash between reasoned attitudes and gut feelings, by joking. Such an incident evolved at one of the AB meetings where Middle-Eastern origins were confronted by humorous exaggeration, and dismissed painlessly. The AB board members were discussing a recent increase in domestic electricity rates. This posed a problem for blind homemakers who avoided the use of gas cooking ranges for reasons of safety. Someone raised the possibility of appealing to the Iraqi-born minister of energy in person. Thereupon a Yemenite member of the group quipped to one of the activists, Reuven Ovadia, who was born in Baghdad, "Reuven, you should call on the minister! He's an Iraqi!" Reuven retorted, "No, I can't; the minister is Kurdish!" Everybody laughed, and the discussion continued seriously as before. In jokingly raising the possibility of ethnic mobilization over the problem of electricity rates, and just as quickly dismissing it, the AB people exaggerated the salience of particular places of origin. They playfully revealed that manipulating the ethnic factor was on their minds, but rejected it outright. The minister in fact was a native of Baghdad just like Reuven.

III. Conclusion

Our point of departure in the investigation of ethnicity among blind people was the fact that people of certain backgrounds are more attached to it than others. In focusing upon blind people, the pertinent information chanced upon in the course of fieldwork is notably uniform. To the extent that the people I studied made me privy to this aspect of their lives, they suppressed and rejected the ethnic alternative.

This finding necessitates a methodological aside. Ethnographic data generally are informed by the field situation and the person of the ethnographer. That is certainly the case here too. We must, therefore, consider the effect of the field situation: the researcher and his wife were different from most of the people studied, in terms of being able-bodied, of high socioeconomic status and of Ashkenazic ethnic background. The effect of these differences did not inhibit people in the field from expressing themselves critically in my presence, sometimes bitterly, about people of my own category of able-bodied. To this I would add that I took care to try and impress upon people in the field the fact that I felt close to Middle-Eastern Israelis, as a result of various personal and professional circumstances, and that I respect Middle-Eastern Jewish cultures. There is little reason, therefore, to assume, that the attraction to Ashkenazim and disaffection for Middle-Easterners, that was so often expressed in my presence, is just an artifact of the field situation. It is more plausible that the source for the consistent disaffection for Middle-Eastern origins that people exhibited lies elsewhere.

To uncover this we must consider one of the social ramifications of the condition of blindness, namely, that it hinders communication between people and can therefore lead to social isolation and profound loneliness. Even when blind people manage their lives in such ways that they do not become isolated, the potential remains. This hazard is part of the fundamental existential condition of blind people, and they try to act so as to obviate it. In Israeli culture, the Middle-Eastern ethnic identity has, ever since the foundation of the State, been considered a marginal option relative to the Israeli-Ashkenazic identity. Matters in this respect have changed over the years, but essentially Middle-Eastern ethnicity is still viewed by dominant sectors of society as a minority alternative.

The rejection of Middle-Eastern ethnicity by blind people should be considered in that context. Middle-Eastern ethnicity constitutes a threat to the hard won social niche and acceptance that blind individuals have carved for themselves. It constitutes an ominous potential for shunting people onto the sidelines of social life. This facet of the existential experience of blind people should also be seen in connection with the findings of the previous chapter of this study. Namely, that blind people in Israel tend to shun the company of other blind people; they generally associate with each other only when there are specific reasons for doing so, such as common interests. Mutual rejection is thus an additional element in the social situation of blind people, that bolsters the fundamental hazard of isolation. All this predisposes blind people to avoid ideological positions that are not accepted by the dominant strata, and which might actualize the hazard.

The positions that individuals held on the question of ethnicity, extended only over a very limited continuum. At the extreme, we encountered crude prejudices, harshness and hostility toward Middle-Eastern origins. Dovetailing this, we encountered reluctance to embrace positions inimical towards Ashkenazim. At a more balanced point on the continuum we encountered references to Middle-Eastern origins that were weakly positive, expressing the frailty of ethnic bonds. We also encountered joking dismissal of ethnicity. And that was the furthest extent to which people moved on the continuum away from radical expressions of rejection of Middle-Eastern origins.

Reuven Ovadia, the person who figured in the bantering exchange about activating ethnic ties, exemplified that position. He was the only one of the people in the field who confided to me that he had voted in the 1984 elections for one of the new religious Middle-Eastern ethnic parties. Whereas many others, of similar background, continued to vote for the increasingly discredited Labor party, that had been the mainstay of the veteran Ashkenazic establishment. But even Reuven was not solely motivated by ethnicity. He was at the time undergoing a process of religious revival, adopting orthodox observance in his daily life.

Significantly, my data include no incidents reflecting anything approaching an actual Middle-Eastern ethnic stand, in the guise of acting to preserve one's background heritage or of mobilizing people of one's own background for common action. Those who moved in the direction of such a position, bantering with ethnicity, were markedly successful and outgoing people. In terms of social practice they "coped" with disability. This suggests an important conclusion, that with increasing security in their social status, blind people are less haunted by the existential problem of potential isolation. Hence they permit themselves to adopt controversial ideological and political positions, away from the main road of the establishment.

Chapter Twelve

The Alternative of Citizenship

In forging social niches and associating, people must choose between alternatives, some of which are more acceptable than others. We have observed blind Israelis selecting between alternative ways of association. Since Israel is a society of immigrants, one route readily on hand is for people to associate on the base of common ethnic background, but that possibility was dismissed resolutely by the people of our study. Another possibility was that of associating with people of similar physical condition. Here we also found marked aversion; people avoided associating on the base of common blindness only. However, the people of our study were less deliberate whenever there were common social factors besides physical disability. Then blind people did not reject each other's company (see chapter 10).

The fact that blind Israelis view certain alternatives for association less negatively than others leads to raise the question: What are the desired, positive, social alternatives of blind people? Where actually do they seek to strike social roots? The thrust of the observations that follow in this chapter is, that in terms of positive aims, blind Israelis desire to be considered by others as citizens. The vehemence of patriotic sentiments that blind people verbalized was notable. Such sentiments, we shall see, are a moving force in many blind peoples' actions.

Due to the overall political situation in Israel the military effort is central in the concerns of ordinary citizens. The able-bodied are required to serve extended periods in the armed forces.[1] Only two significant categories of people tend to evade military service, the extreme orthodox and the criminal fringe. Both these categories of people are, in different ways, marginal and detached from most other Israelis. Military service is part of all other people's routine. The situation is different from that of countries that maintain less extensive conscription, and where as a consequence, military affairs concern only a professional stratum which is often peripheral to society at large. In Israel it is lack of participation in the military that relegates to the periphery.

Blind people are poignantly aware, that release from military service is an element of segregation from the able-bodied. Thus, in talking about himself one informant, Shlomo Mashiah recounted his tribulations carving out a suitable economic niche for himself. He eventually wound up as a switchboard operator, profoundly bored and dissatisfied with his work. He once blurted out,

> But what pains me most, is the fact that I cannot serve in the army or in the police force!

In Israel one encounters the phenomenon of physically disabled young people, who clamor to be enlisted in the army.[2] Such a person, Yoram Peres, reported that when he came of age he tried to volunteer for military service, but failed, being totally blind. The pain of that experience has remained a potent force in Yoram's life. Now in his mid-thirties, he has developed into a workaholic switchboard operator; who channels much of his energy into his work. One of Yoram's practices is to work many hours overtime, and at hours that most workers consider undesirable (such as festival-eves when traditionally families get together). Thus, he works regularly on Passover-eve, the high point of the family ritual cycle. The only times that Yoram does not agree to work overtime is on the civic festivals of Independence Day and on the preceding eve of Memorial Day for fallen soldiers. Yoram is not a deliberately irreligious person; he enjoys listening to certain religious programs on the radio. But civic events linked to army service are more meaningful to him than any other ritual events.

Prior to his present place of work, the Manpower office that has links with a military installation, Yoram worked several years as a switchboard operator in a small factory in Yeruka, at some distance from his home. Over the years he made efforts to move to the Manpower office, which was closer to his home. In spontaneously recounting the events of his job shift Yoram explained:

> It was the October 1973 War that really clinched it with me (*she'gamra oti*). Here I was in Yeruka, transferring calls for people who were packing biscuits, while a war was being fought. In the Manpower office on the other hand, they were engaged in matters linked to army needs, and also many army employees worked on the spot.

Yoram recounted that he exerted himself over the next six years, to secure the Manpower position. Before finally succeeding, he moonlighted at Manpower after the hours of his regular job, working with inconvenient equipment that was not properly adapted for the needs of a blind switchboard operator. After a year and a-half of working under such conditions, the Manpower management finally completed the adaptation of the equipment and offered Yoram a regular position, which he has held ever since. The choice of a patriotic rationale in Yoram's account reflects the salience of national service in the self-presentation of this person. Moreover, it possibly reflects also Yoram's actual feelings about the weight of military service; in his efforts to shift jobs he may have been actually motivated the way he described.

Another way of participating in the military effort was that of Margalit Yemini. She was a popular labor organizer at the factory where she worked as switchboard operator, and a respected matriarch among her six teenage and adult children. But not always had things been so, she recounted. When Margalit's elder son, now a career army officer, was a child, he had been ashamed of his blind mother. When she occasionally came to the child's school he would avoid her and not go out together with her. This went on for many years, and changed only when the boy was in the eighth grade. Margalit recalled how that came about: At the end of the school year, there was a joint party for parents, pupils and teachers, and Margalit participated by reading a poem she had written for the occasion. The theme was a prayer, that when time came for the youngsters to join the army, they should all be successful and complete their service safely. That Margalit claimed, triggered the change in the boy's attitude, and since then, in her view, her other children have accepted her also.

The typical way for parents to participate in the military effort is vicariously, through the service of their able-bodied children. People who have sons who engaged in combat duty were routinely proud of them. Yemima Kagan, the mother of an air force pilot, believed that she could have influenced the army authorities to station her son at a desk job, but, she claimed she refrained from doing so. Not all parents however, were equally successful in raising their children. Rivqa's Cohen's children had dropped out of school and loafed around, working only irregularly. Already a year before her elder son was due for conscription, Rivqa was worrying that the army might reject him because of his poor record. She told of arguments she had at home concerning work and civic duties. Her other teenage children used to scoff at her, she said, because of her working in a sheltered-workshop for poor wages, virtually token payment, and the boy wanted to shirk army service. Rivqa reported that she would say to her children:

> I did not serve in the Army, therefore I must contribute by my work! A person ought to give to society and not just take!

In this presentation of self the civic theme encompassed both a patriotic impulse and a labor ethos.

This combination is typical, for in Israeli ideology generally, there is a link between labor ethos, patriotism and military service. Meir Nagar, proud of his soldier-son, was emphatic in expressing revulsion at labor agitation,

> Strikes, destroy the country! A Jew should not destroy the country! In the time of Ben-Gurion, may his memory be blessed, people used to build the country, not to destroy it. Now, agriculturalists destroy fruit and vegetables![3]

Pamela Samukha linked patriotism with the labor ethos in a more personal way. A frail lady in her fifties, she worked arduously in an industrial plant. She said,

> When I think of sighted people who live on relief, I feel superior. When I go out to work, in a flood of rain and winds blowing, I feel wonderful. Why exploit the State?

Pamela went on saying that she would like to do volunteer work. "... Perhaps when I'm retired ... ", she trailed off wistfully. But the potential of such people to develop a marked labor ethos may sour relationships with the sighted in their environment. That happened in the case of Yael Hadad who said,

> When I work and see everyone around me loafing about (*kulam mitparperim*) that angers me! I remain silent and that eats me up![4]

The expression of civic sentiments in Israel is to be expected in discussions focussed on work and military service. But remarkably it emerged also in other contexts. People just erupted into expressions of civic sentiments, that were not called for by the topic under discussion. When Rahel Bogen, a single woman in her fifties, recounted her childhood, she described a comfortable Levantine middle-class background in Cairo. She had enjoyed the services of private teachers whom her father hired to come home to Rahel, and teach her Braille, piano playing and French. In the early 1950s, talk began in the family of emigrating to Israel, Rahel recalled, and she alone was opposed to the move. She went on detailing the comfortable routine into which her life had set, and that she had been apprehensive at the proposed upheaval. Unsure of having clarified herself to me, Rahel went on spontaneously with emotion, "Don't think that I don't like living with Jews! I was afraid!!" Rahel had described her childhood circumstances very reasonably, but she felt her position required bolstering. Hence the emphasis that her reluctance was not rooted, Heaven forbid, in a weakness of national sentiment, a point that had not come up earlier in our conversation.

Sometimes these sentiments of people emerge in more subtle ways. In recounting their life experiences people sometimes interpreted them in terms of national service. They made their lives meaningful thereby, and incidentally exposed the crucial hold of the value of patriotism in their lives. Such an interpretation erupted in the life history of Zekharia Dayan, one of few people who seemed to be content living off relief. Shortly after immigrating to Israel in the early 1960s, the rehabilitation officers began to channel him along the path of the local blindness system. Zekharia was directed to a vocational center for training as a switchboard operator. In describing that junction in his career he used the expression, "I was mobilized (*guyasti*) for Migdalor".[5] Zekharia chose a specifically military term, in describing a point in his life for which he might have used another one of many appropriate terms.

The involuntary element in being ordered to study in a residential school can lead to a military association. Zekharia found himself at Migdalor, at about the same age that able-bodied Israelis do their compulsory army service. Zekharia's viewing his Migdalor experience in a military light is not only realistic to an extent, but more crucially, it is consistent with a profound existential concern, that of overcoming segregation. The man thereby linked himself to a core experience of his able-bodied peers, that of national service. In expressing himself the way he did, Zekharia evinced an interpretation of the Migdalor chapter of his biography, not as one in which he was shunted to the margins of the activities of his peers, but on the contrary, as one that was analogous to their activities—mobilization of a kind.

A similar case of interpretation arose in a remarkable incident at the psychology circle. This requires a word of introduction about the people involved, Amos Schreiber and Kalman Barukhi. Amos was a burly married man in his fifties, who presented himself as a happy person who had found his place in life. Amos was employed at a sheltered-workshop where he operated the more complex machinery, and like all workers in his situation his salary was hardly more than a token one. But he was emphatic about his success at work and also about the beautiful family life he lived. However, Amos had a short temper and a sharp tongue.

Kalman was a very different person, a young man in his twenties, immature and much involved in the throes of late adolescence. Single and without a stable occupation, Kalman sometimes hung around the family store and sometimes worked in a sheltered-workshop. Kalman's fairly affluent family gave him comfort and the leisure to try and find a role for himself. He pompously claimed to have many skills and much experience, but his insecurity was obvious. Lacking in charm and assertiveness Kalman cut a poor figure next to

Amos. While the latter was pleasant to one and all in the group, he had a violent antipathy for Kalman. Amos's verbal abuse often left the hapless Kalman speechless, and on one occasion he physically struck him. In view of the glaring discrepancy in personality resources between the two men, all this is puzzling.

The clue lies in their working sometimes in the same sheltered-workshop. In Amos's presentation of self among strangers at the psychology club, he emphasized the high quality of his work. But the fact that at the same time there was with him a much inferior person, in terms of skill and personality, cast doubt on Amos's claims. For it would seem dubious that a place of work of high quality should employ such contrasting workers as equals. In the workshop the presence of persons such as Kalman is forced upon Amos. But in the psychology circle that was not rigidly structured, and where Amos was building up his public image, Kalman's presence was intolerable, perhaps even threatening, to him.

On one occasion at the psychology circle, Kalman explained why he had at one time stopped working at the sheltered-workshop,

> I actually wanted to work, but the manager did not accept me nicely. He demanded that I arrive at work at 7:30 A.M. But it's difficult for me to get there so early. That's no good (*lo beseider*)."

The hour that Kalman quoted is the regular beginning of the working-day in most offices and workshops in Israel, and that is when masses of employees, blind people included, get to work. A bland statement such as Kalman's, would usually have been passed over by the participants in the circle with little comment. But Amos exploded. He boomed at Kalman vehemently,

> Don't you dare throw mud (*le'lakhleikh*) at a factory that employs 40 workersl!! How dare you smear (*le'hashmitz*) a veteran workshop (*mif'al vatiq*)!!!

The tone and content of the exchange was grotesque, out of all proportion. It is Amos's choice of image, in attacking Kalman, that is remarkable in the present context. The term *vatiq* (veteran) is richly symbolic, and figures in accounts of pioneering and building of the country. There, one encounters references to "veterans" as against "recent immigrants", and the former are always in the vanguard, blazing the way in the face of adversity. One also encounters usage of the term "vatiq" in reference to derivatives of the pioneering effort, such as in the distinction between settlements founded by more and less recent immigrants. In Israeli culture, the pioneer ethos has a rural stamp, while doings in the industrial and urban sector are not usually endowed with images and symbols of pioneering. Hence Amos's term "mif'al vatiq" is innovative, not a routine cliché. Amos chose to combine "veteran" as an adjective to "workshop", attributing to his place of work an association of grand qualities, rooted in the national ethos of the country. Kalman's innocent complaint about the trouble of getting to work on time is here dramatically linked to national myth.

Often in talking about their lives, people spontaneously expressed patriotic sentiments. Thus, in talking about the economy Yafa Makhluf said, "I love the State. It's only a shame that now it is slipping (*midarderet*)." Then she went on, referring to a stereotype of life in New York City, "In America if someone gets injured on the street, no one will help; people will just pass by." The implication is that in Israel people do extend assistance, and that is a motivation for her patriotic sentiments. This motive recurred, more explicitly a number of times, as people talked of their civic values. Asher Dalal, employed in a sheltered workshop, explained his patriotism because, "Nowadays there are hardly any blind people who just sit at home; the authorities rehabilitate everyone." But not just people who were satisfied with existing conditions, expressed a realization that they were beneficiaries of society. There were also people close to the small disability rights movement (see chapter 13), highly sensitive of their rights to dignity and independence, who vented this trend of thought. Shime'on, an activist, told me that he felt he "must contribute to society, because I receive so much."

Remarkably, the impulse toward civic values is sometimes so powerful that people are inclined to pay a price for its expression. Earlier we saw Rivqa, who contended in her home with friction that hinged on differing values of labor. Rivqa might have attempted to adapt her style of living to that of her children, loafing about for much of the day, and from the aspect of income the difference would have been minimal. But from the aspect of self-respect the difference to her would have been immense. "One must also know how to give," Rivqa used to argue to her children. Thereby she thrust at them a value that was foreign to them, and marked the gulf that cleaved the family.

Also Yael Hadad reported of domestic stress, linked to differing kinds of patriotism. She recounted, that despite the fact that she suffered greatly from the attitude of government officials towards her and was deprived of work because of them, she nevertheless resented that her brother who was disillusioned with the country, spoke of it critically. Whenever he does so she said, she "fights with him (*rava ito*)," because she "loves the State." Yael went on recounting that her extended family had suffered several war casualties over the years. Paradoxically she linked this to her behavior vis-à-vis her brother. The tragedies bolstered Yael's patriotism. Lacking a family of her own, poor and disgraced, devotion to the country was for Yael an important hold on to a conception of order and meaning. Lacking such patriotism the death of kinsmen at war becomes meaningless. When the anchor on reality is more tangible (having health, family, social status, income, etc.), people can sometimes permit himself to question the value of patriotism, even in connection with death in battle. But for someone as poor in existential resources as Yael, that was intolerable.

Both Yael and Rivqa lived in painful circumstances and readily admitted to being unhappy people. Yoram Peres was a different person; he did not complain, and managed his life successfully, enjoying higher income and status. But Yoram too exhibited the same kind of readiness to pay a price for his patriotic convictions as Rivqa and Yael. Yoram used to volunteer to work overtime on major religious festivals. The Purim festival Yoram disliked, specifically because it is traditionally noisy; in the streets one encounters youths, equipped with toy plastic cracker-hammers, striking each other on the head. Sometimes also passersby are rudely assaulted. The Day of Independence however is noisier than Purim, yet Yoram waxed eloquent when talking about it. Using language free of clichés, Yoram said,

> I love Independence Day. It is a festival that means everything to me (*hag she'omeir li hakol*).

He followed the Independence Day celebrations on the radio, the distribution of the Israel Prizes, the kindling of the festival flares, and the Bible quiz. In contrast to most Israelis, Yoram did not go outing that day. "I sit at home—like Job," he said.

Yoram's contrasting attitudes to Purim and to Independence Day are remarkable. On Purim too he listens to the program of the day, the reading of the Book of Esther, and on both days he avoids the streets. But Purim he shuns and Independence Day is meaningful to him. He evoked in this context the powerful Biblical image of the solitary Job.[6] Yoram accepted Independence Day although some of its features are objectionable to a blind person. The assault on the hearing sense, with radios and specially installed loudspeakers on the streets, all blaring, makes orientation difficult. Also the unfamiliarly crowded streets hamper navigation. But the vitality of Yoram's patriotism lead him to overlook all this, and celebrate—in solitude.

The quest for civic status among blind people can also be observed at the public level, in overt politics. Blind people could, in theory, coalesce as a political pressure group, to advance their particular interests. But in common with disabled people generally, the blind have usually been inhibited from doing so. Other categories of people in various societies, whose interests have often been just as highly circumscribed as those of the disabled, such as people of particular religion or occupation, have routinely coalesced as political groups. Therefore far from being a matter of nature, the quiescence of blind people in politics warrants the attention of the sociologist.

At the time of fieldwork the general elections of 1984 took place. The generally aroused political awareness caused blind people to confront the question of their politicization. One occasion, where the possibility was raised occurred among workers of a sheltered-workshop. These workers had grievances of an occupational nature. They felt that they were being underpaid, and grumbled that the sighted staff looked after their own interests rather than those of the disabled workers. In this context one of the articulate among the workers declared to me, that there ought to be a blind member of Knesset (the Israeli Parliament), who would see to the interests of blind people. The statement was however made in private and to me, an outsider, it was not raised publicly among the workers, and did not reach a stage where it could be discussed. A slightly less fleeting confrontation with the question of politicization occurred at a meeting of the Association of the Blind (AB). A group of people with a variety of disabilities, had organized to participate in the elections under the label of "The Invalids' List", and their representatives came to a meeting of the AB board to solicit the latter's support. The Invalids' List activists had originally included one young blind man, Nehemia, but he had eventually lost interest and he did not come to the meeting with the AB. The reception of the Invalids' List representatives was cold. The latter presented their platform, but the AB hosts— normally vociferous at meetings—listened quietly and reacted merely by saying that no representative of the Israeli blind was in a position to promise their votes.

After the visitors left the AB activists scoffed about Nehemia, "He thinks that he'll command the blind (sheyishlot 'al ha'ivrim)!" They went on recalling that some years earlier the Center for the Blind (CB) had for a while employed a sighted official who was a member of Ma'arakh, the labor party, and that official had explored making an arrangement with the party whereby the blind would support it at the polls. The AB activists were amused as they now recalled that attempt at mobilizing the blind vote en bloc. Blind people, they scoffed, are not a homogeneous group that could be brought to support one particular party.

Disdain of the Invalids' List was widespread among the people of the study. All were scornful at the notion of abdicating their rights as citizens to express themselves at the polls over general issues, and to concentrate just on their special grievances as disabled people. Eventually the Invalids' List failed at the polls and lost its deposit. However it did gain 0.6% of the total number of valid votes cast, which in absolute numbers was close to 10,000 votes.[7] We have no way of knowing who voted for the List, but judging from the dismissing way in which the people of the study referred to it, it is improbable that many blind people were among them.

Conclusion

The people of the study evinced vehement sentiments of bedrock patriotism. Their civic identification had a pristine stamp, which was more characteristic of Israelis in the 1950s and 60s than it is of present times. During the early years of the State Israeli political culture was marked by consensus, whereas after the 1960s new problems and cleavages emerged. Various solutions to these problems have been proposed by successive governments, but the solutions have been objectionable to varying sections of the population. Consequently, ever since the early 1970s some of the old patriotic identification of people with the State has dissolved. But among the people of the study there are indications of the continuing vitality of political innocence. Such vitality is certainly not unknown among able-bodied Israelis, but it is not universal. Among blind Israelis, this study suggests, there is considerable unanimity. The trend among them is to avoid positions that are removed from the political center. It is probable that some individual blind Israelis hold positions that are critical of the polity, but the data to which people made me privy in the context of the present study is unequivocal in the direction that I have indicated—bland, uncritical, conventional.

This political culture dovetails with the condition of blindness. The latter includes a potent element of impaired communication and hence of social isolation. The adoption of marginal political stances is hazardous for people whose social attainments were gained through unusual effort, and whose social standing often remains insecure. This also is the context of the rejection of the idea of blind people supporting one particular party. Such was the practice decades ago, when most of the population were new immigrants manipulated by party machines. The notion that blind people might vote en bloc is linked to a view of them as old-fashioned, unfamiliar with the proper way of playing politics, and that is objectionable to most activists for the dignity of disabled people. Striving for involvement in patriotic matters is consistent with blind people's activities in the area of work, and both are consistent with the overall struggle against relegation to the periphery of society. In their anxiety not to be so relegated some blind people formulated an ideology against making any demands of society, or formulating any rights for the disabled. But hardly anyone lived by these heroic beliefs in my observations; assistance of various kinds was extended by public bodies to blind people, to greater or lesser extents, and accepted to greater or lesser extents.

It is significant that we encountered the heroic ideology in connection with the Invalids' List. The AB people explained their lack of interest in the List in terms of what they considered the illegitimacy of raising particular demands for themselves as disabled people. The repugnance for blind particularism runs deep. The source of the sentiments of citizenship and patriotism that we have seen lies in the hazard of isolation, that is part of the condition of blindness. The ensuing political culture is one of people who stand at an indeterminate point, between old-time segregation and subjection to philanthropy on the one hand, and full rights for the disabled, as part of general human rights, on the other. Blind Israelis have rejected the paternalistic position, but still grope for a mature formulation of a human rights position. The political culture that we have uncovered is an element of that unfinished business.

Chapter Thirteen

The Dilemma of Integration Among the Sighted

As in many other societies, blind people in Israel were in the past often relegated to passive, charity-eliciting roles. When gainfully occupied they were engaged in a small number of occupations, tended to be segregated, and subjected to considerable custodialism. Increasingly over the years this has become objectionable. With the advent of occupations (and leisure activities) in which blind people did not engage in the past, such as telephone switchboard operating and the computer industry, many blind Israelis have become critical of their traditional position in society. This restlessness is also rooted in the emergence, however modest, of the disability rights movement on the Israeli scene. But no linear causal relationship can be established for these developments. One cannot reasonably claim that because of the opening of new occupations, people have become more vocal in demanding their rights; nor can one argue the opposite, that awareness of rights led to new occupational possibilities. Rather, I suggest the relationship to be a multilineal one, with the various developments reinforcing each other.

The main organizational outcome of this has been the emergence of the Center for the Blind (CB), as we saw it in operation previously (in chapters 8 and 9). Currently, as we have seen throughout this monograph, the social status of blind Israelis is generally indeterminate and transitional. It is removed from the pole of subordination and lack of rights, but it also is away from the pole of fully attained rights and emancipation as envisioned by disability rights activists. In this final chapter, the focus is on a prime aspect of the activities of the CB—its effect on the integration of the blind among the able-bodied. The doings of the CB are juxtaposed with those of a small rival organization, the Association of Blind University Graduates (ABUG). Analyzing some of the doings of the CB and ABUG, this chapter will uncover the positions of blind Israelis on the issue of autonomy as against acceptance of assistance from the sighted. Concretely, we are concerned with the questions: When do blind people struggle for self-sufficiency? What is the limit of the readiness to accept assistance? When do blind people exhibit an extroverted position for integration among the sighted, and when do they exhibit an introverted position that is segregationist?

The thesis of the chapter is that different attitudes and positions among blind people on these matters are rooted largely in the overall predicament of being a blind person and not merely in idiosyncracies of personalities. The predicament of blind people in Israel entails being torn between traditional discredited, passive roles, and new roles of emancipated disabled persons integrated into mainline society. The social role of blind people, in transition from traditional dependence to indeterminate emancipation, entails contradictions. The dilemma concerning accepting help from the public is part of the broad issue of segregation as against integration of blind people. Much has changed since the days when blind beggars were a common sight and those blind people who did work were segregated mainly in basketry workshops. Modern sensitivities and new material possibilities have brought the integrationist stance to the fore. Simultaneously however, the segregative stance remains in evidence and vital, and the conflicting positions fuse.

The traditional segregative stance is articulated in the following flysheet:

> To all of you we appeal! The Jerusalem School for the Blind requests the help of all of you! We say [at this time in our prayers] "These lights we kindle," but who will lighten up the eyes of the inmates of the School for the Blind? Who will help them? Who will teach them a craft to make a living? On the Sabbath of Hannuka, when the candles spread a precious light in every Jewish home, please forget not those whose lot is darkness. Commit yourselves generously in the synagogue at the time of Torah-reading, and give before and after the Sabbath of Hannuka! On the Festival of Lights, take to your heart those who have no light and remember them!

This message stems from the 1940s, and was used in the annual public appeal of the Jerusalem School for the Blind during the week of the Hannuka festival, requesting monetary support. The Jerusalem School is under religious administration and in the appeal sighted volunteers, supporters of the school, latch onto the religious symbolism of the festival of Hannuka, "the Festival of Lights". The Hannuka candles are juxtaposed with the presumed "darkness" of the blind who are presented as inmates, not just as pupils; and their needs are elemental, not just specific training. The lot of the blind is "darkness", not lack of the specific faculty of sight. Blindness is presented here in the traditional diffuse way. Thereby blind people are conceived as radically different from the sighted.

Such presentation of blind people is acceptable, among both blind and sighted, to the extent that blind people fill segregated positions in society. Needless to say, this presentation is objectionable where sensitivity for the dignity of disabled people is developed. It is abominable among people of disability rights convictions. But such old-fashioned leaflets still circulated in the early 1980s in some Jerusalem synagogues.

At one time the publicity practice of the Jerusalem School for the Blind came up at a meeting of the activists of the Association of the Blind (AB), that preceded a meeting of the CB board. In the context of critical comments about the school, one participant mildly suggested that perhaps something ought to be done about the objectionable publicity. But the others dismissed the idea. They said that the fact that such objectionable material circulated in synagogues did not matter, since it was not widely distributed. The activists implied that projecting an undesired image of blind people in synagogues was immaterial, and controlling the doings there was, in any event, beyond their ability. But the grumbling of the AB activists, subdued and low-keyed, was not totally ineffective. In the 1985 yearly campaign, the Jerusalem School modified its appeal. The handbill still included the diffuse term "those whose lot is darkness," but most of the other objectionable expressions were eliminated.

In contrast to the AB and CB, the integrationist stance was expressed more vocally by the members of the ABUG. The latter was a small organization numbering around one hundred members, located mostly in Jerusalem and Tel-Aviv. The organization was composed not only of university graduates, as the name indicated, but also of students and other people who aspired to find work as professionals, integrated into mainstream society. The ABUG activists maintained ties with members of the American National Federation of the Blind (NFB), that has an articulated disability rights platform. One of the ABUG leaders was himself an immigrant from the United States and a member of the NFB. The ABUG was also fueled from such indigenous sources as personal rivalries between individuals, who then became members of the rival association. Further, animosity between the associations was ramified by rivalries between individual sighted volunteers. Some of the latter, in their bickering, chose not to affiliate with the CB, as did most of the sighted volunteers, but to support the rival ABUG.

The ABUG activists criticized the CB harshly. In particular they felt that the CB ought to invest more effort in opening up new occupations for blind people and in developing vocational and professional training, leading to integration among the sighted. The ABUG activists were particularly sensitive to presentations of blind people that had degrading connotations. They were irate at the CB and the whole blindness system for expending what they considered, inordinate efforts in seeking philanthropic benefits, as against new work opportunities. To buttress its position with deeds, the ABUG made an effort to open the teaching profession to blind teachers. But nothing came of that. Thereupon the ABUG made a second attempt and launched an innovative project, an Everyman's High School in which students could study by correspondence toward a matriculation certificate. The salient point is the policy shift this entailed on the issue of integration: After the ABUG failed to integrate blind teachers into the general educational system, it strove to establish a niche that would be structured around the needs of its clients, unemployed blind teachers. But that position, contrary to ABUG's integrationist ideology, was a fusion of segregationist and integrationist positions.

The following is another instance of the potency of the segregationist stance within the integrationist ideology of ABUG. In a discussion about policy with regard to having Braille markings in public facilities, such as elevators, some ABUG people were in favor of demanding that elevator buttons be marked in Braille, but others objected. The latter felt that this would needlessly highlight blind people as being exceptional. In this case the integrationist stance, exemplified by a request that public facilities be structured with due consideration for the needs of the blind, was blunted by the age-old segregationist stance that ignored specific needs of the sightless.

Some of the ABUG activists objected particularly to having benefits extended into areas that are not inherently linked to sightlessness, for example taxation exemptions and minor financial privileges. They conceived the dispensation of these benefits to be based on a degrading and segregationist view of blind people. Such a view, the ABUG claimed, was held by the blindness workers who manage the CB (both blind activists and sighted philanthropists). The rationale for the CB's policy in the attainment of monetary benefits for its clients in fact was, that although in many Western countries blind people are indeed subject to regular taxation, they simultaneously enjoy generous material support from public sources. Therefore, the CB blindness workers claimed, those blind people had no need to lobby for privileges. But in Israel direct public support is much more limited and most blind people hovered on the fringes of poverty. Many ABUG activists, and others critical of the CB, were opposed in principle to tax exemption, but they never went out of their way so as not to benefit from it. These individuals evinced positions in which both integrationist and segregationist stances were inconsistently fused.

Inconsistency was common to both the ABUG and to its AB and CB opponents. The AB was, on several occasions, approached by groups and individuals who sought to prod it to greater activism for the attainment of benefits and tax exemptions. One such case was that of a man who had a rent income from a kiosk that he owned, and that someone else operated. The man requested that his tax exemption cover that income too. The existing regulations, however, permitted tax exemption only from salary gains, not from rent. The matter came to an AB board meeting and the discussants expressed objections to pursuing the matter. Some said that while the man might have a case, the matter was of concern to only a few individuals, and therefore not worthy of a sustained effort. Others said that the case lacked merit: Income from rent was different from income gained by one's own work, and should not be exempted. Altogether, the activists felt that there would be strong opposition to the motion on the part of the authorities, and that they did not stand a chance of succeeding. They decided to drop the case.

A similar decision was reached on a related issue. As a result of a national bank scandal in 1983, a certain type of savings that depositors had in the banks was frozen for three years. Senior citizens were partly exempted from this, on the assumption that the elderly were naturally likely to suffer from the freeze more than young people. Thereupon a group of blind people engaged in a press campaign, to be granted the same privilege as the elderly. There was no rationale specific to the condition of blindness to back this demand, beyond general neediness. The group appealed to the AB to adopt their cause, but again the AB declined to become involved. The AB activists were sensitive to what they felt were the limits of public acceptance to demands that they might raise. This sensitivity was a matter of both tactics of the AB activists, and of beliefs as to propriety and dignified self-presentation.

The diffusion of integrationist and segregationist stances was also evident in the area of recreation. In their drive to integrate into mainstream society and culture, many blind people participate occasionally in various outdoor activities. Some of these activities they genuinely enjoy, but some, I have come to conclude, they feign to enjoy. People may engage in these activities in order to present an integrationist stance, while they derive little intrinsic benefit from them. This emerges from the case of Menahem Bergman, the only son of middle-class parents. When he was a boy, Menahem's parents, who wanted to broaden their son's horizons, took him on a boat cruise.

However, Menahem did not recall the trip as memorable. Beyond experiencing the rolling motions of the vessel, he said, "It did not give me much".

Some years later Menahem married. Again, this time on his own initiative, he engaged in a standard activity of the sighted—he went with his blind bride, Shula, on a honeymoon trip to the distant resort town of Eilat. That trip, Menahem reported, he did enjoy. But when describing in detail what had made the experience enjoyable, he elaborated on points that were only tangentially relevant to the trip. He dwelt particularly on the warmth and friendliness the hotel staff extended to him and Shula, but not on any element intrinsic to the journey and stay in Eilat. The elements that made the trip a success Menahem could have been found closer to home, and at lower cost. Menahem's travels gave him relatively few returns. I suggest then, that such people engage in activities that, on the surface, appear as mainstream activities, leading to integration with the sighted, but in fact are experienced differently by the blind and the sighted. The accounts of Menahem indicate that the authenticity of an integrationist stance can be open to question.

Another example of a possibly inauthentic integrationist stance was that of a local American association of blind people that planned a group trip to Israel.[1] The association had delegated a regular travel agent with drawing up the details. The plan was routine, and focused on ordinary tourist sites. There was no evidence that consideration was given to the fact, that the group had specific needs in the selection of places to visit. The information leaflet describing the tour ignored the fact that the travellers were blind. It was illustrated with eighteen color pictures of tourist sites. Of these illustrations, seventeen featured tourists using cameras, giving vent to the snapshooting mania. The planners of the trip were oblivious of the fact that the group would not be attracted by the same visual stimuli as their other clients, and that they would not be carrying cameras.

The integrationist stance sometimes requires extraordinary strength of character, that only few can muster. One who did was Avraham San'ani who frequented a particular swimming pool. The approach to the pool was difficult because it necessitated crossing a wide plaza paved with small decorative tiles, and was occupied by patrons of open-air cafés that surrounded the plaza. The wide open space obviated convenient guide lines; the tiles were separated by narrow spaces in which the cane got stuck; and the randomly seated café patrons obstructed the route. All this constituted a complicated obstacle for a person navigating himself by cane. Nevertheless Avraham frequently negotiated this plaza. He would stumble onto people at their drinks, but that did not deter him; he would give some joking excuse and continue. But not everyone had Avraham's poise and strength.

Another example of this type of integration involved a group of young blind people, who spent a summer evening strolling along a street area where café patrons sat at sidewalk tables. The young people bumped onto café tables, but they joked about it, "We went on, stumbling and laughing, stumbling and laughing". These young people drew their resilience out of their communality, their not being isolated. Like the emotional resilience of Avraham San'ani, this also is a resource that is not available to everyone, nor at all times. The jolly behavior of the young people too, reflects an integrationist stance which is hyphenated, being dependent upon the presence of a group of supportive blind peers.

The predicament of accepting extraordinary material privileges is intertwined with the dilemma of emancipation of blind people. The burden of the age-old image of the blind beggar is prominent in the popular imagination as we saw in previous chapters.[2] Because of the grappling with this painful image, many blind people agonized over the issue of accepting any kind of support, not only from charitable, but even from impersonal public sources. Probably no other category of disabled people is as discomfitted by this as are the blind. I encountered the phenomenon of blind people indiscriminately grouping all types of private and public support into a single category that they sought to eschew. They developed a radical, but gratuitous and unrealistic integrationist stance.

To some extent, virtually all blind Israelis require public attention at some stage in life, in the form of assistance that is tailored to sightlessness. Only the most gifted, affluent and fortunate live a social and occupational life that is fully integrated among the able-bodied, and never require extraordinary consideration as disabled people. In fact, even most emancipatory stances, such as those of the disability rights movement, involve making certain demands of the public. However, many Israeli blind people were uneasy about this, as the following account exemplifies. Many of the demands of and on behalf of blind Israelis are made by the CB. One of the services, that cater to the condition of sightlessness, which the CB offers is the supply of basic equipment (i.e. canes, slates, tape-recorders), which is not manufactured locally and must be imported. Such goods are often priced beyond the means of the indigent clientelle, and in order to aid clients, the government subsidizes these goods, selling them through the CB.[3] Also, the CB lobbied for legislation to enable individuals to purchase new electrical appliances once every few years, with the government waiving the high import taxes. These appliances included both the aforementioned necessities for the sightless condition, as

well as general domestic amenities, such as electric cooking stoves.
The CB rationale for the latter was that sightlessness caused such
equipment to be safer and easier to use than gas stoves. The CB
policies thus wed both rehabilitative and traditional custodial-philan-
thropic elements. The latter, however, were objectionable to blind
individuals, of integrationist persuation. These people, many of them
members of the ABUG, claimed to be uncomfortable about using CB
services, but they did not refrain from doing so.

An arena in which the frustration of the integrationist stance
emerged was that of travel in public. Some blind people had reservations about not paying full fares on public transport, a privilege the
CB had achieved for its clients. The rationale for this was, that walking to one's destination was usually difficult for people using canes;
sometimes impossible. At best, cane-users are slow pedestrians. There
was therefore a constant need for travelling by bus, even for short
distances. However, some ABUG people were apprehensive about exercising their right to free travel. These people, upon boarding buses,
offered the driver payment. In doing so they created embarrassing
situations for themselves. Bus drivers sometimes reacted in confusion. One driver loudly retorted to Penina Danieli, "You people don't
pay on buses!" Penina had attempted to escape the category of blind
people who do not pay for public transport, but the driver's reaction
frustrated her effort.

The source of such people's frustration was not rooted only in the
doings of uncouth sighted people such as Penina's bus driver. It was
rooted also in the presentation practice of the CB as exemplified in
the following practice. In buses in Israel, the front seats which are
the most accessible as one boards, are marked "Reserved for the
Disabled". The rationale for this was formulated in a leaflet of the CB
published in 1980 (probably based on a publication of the American
Foundation for the Blind) for the information of the sighted. The
pertinent item runs as follows:

> How to offer a seat to a blind person: It is advisable to offer
> a seat to a blind passenger boarding a bus, particularly if
> he is elderly, because in case of unanticipated sudden brak-
> ing, his reaction might be slow. But it is sufficient if one
> passenger directs the blind man to a vacant seat, and places
> his hand there. Assistance offered by several people simul-
> taneously is apt to confuse the blind person.

Sudden braking is rarely anticipated and can jolt anyone, though
sighted passengers have some advantage, because they can sometimes more readily grasp a means of support. The rationale for extending seating privileges for blind people is therefore weak.

The practice is probably rooted in the propensity of the sighted to have the blind seated, as the former are commonly uncomfortable with blind people in their surroundings navigating themselves. The propensity to seat blind people is an aspect of the segregationist stance.[4] Several people of the ABUG circle objected to the extension of the seating privilege. Shlomo Deromi, who used a guide dog, found the front seat in buses inconvenient because the big animal lay in the way of boarding passengers; he preferred a rear seat. Yehezqel Mazuz impishly recounted how he enjoyed putting people in their places. When he boarded crowded buses together with Efrat, his sighted wife, people commonly rose to offer him their seat. Yehezqel usually accepted, but he never took the seat for himself; he gallantly used to offer it to Efrat, while he remained standing by her side.[5] From the point of view of integration among the sighted, the opposition to customary privilege is self-contradictory and problematic. While, for vigorous blind people and for guide dog users, the privilege may be inappropriate, it may be essential for frail people. The difference between the vigorous and frail is not always evident, and the integrationist stance places some blind people at a disadvantage. But the customary practice is indeed insulting to people such as Yehezqel going out with his wife, and inconvenient to Shlomo travelling with his dog.

Even such assertive people however, were usually inconsistent on the issue of accepting public support. Some who were vociferous when expressing views about the CB and its fundraising campaigns, would in the same breath talk of using CB services to obtain their necessary equipment. One man, Shime'on Serussi, in the context of a conversation on the CB and its public agitations, declared emphatically,

> "Never, never, would I participate in a demonstration of the blind! Only people who are unable to find work [in the open market] should receive state help!"

Yet this person used CB services to obtain equipment, oblivious to the fact that the tax rebate system was a direct outcome of a demonstration of blind Israelis, organized by the CB in 1980. This man also did not relate to the fact that, that demonstration had substantially improved the lot of people working in sheltered workshops, precisely those people who, he believed, were indeed entitled to public help. Many blind people sought to distance themselves from the annual Hannuka fundraising campaign, commenting as one activist did at a CB meeting: "The proceeds of the campaign are only for those who don't work. I don't need it! It is for others!" But a moment later he went on, "I just need the special equipment, nothing else." In fact, this man was also an avid client for another service funded by the annual campaign, the vacation program.

The CB annual fundraising campaign, which was anathema to many people, operated with the slogan "Light for the Blind" (*Or La'iver*), and was actually referred to as "the Light for the Blind campaign." The appeal avoided explicit stigmatizing expressions when referring to the beneficiaries of the campaign proceeds, but the name reflects powerful stigmatizing sentiments about blindness and blind people. In its timing the appeal is associated with traditional segregationist impulses. The 1983 CB appeal at Hannuka time featured the following publicity:

1. Eight thousand blind people live in Israel. Most of them, poor and needy, support themselves by relief or social security payments.

2. Many of them are out of work because of advanced age, disease and additional disabilities. These blind people require your help.

3. The income of the "Light for the Blind" campaign enables the CB and local voluntary associations to promote and develop services, aimed at improving the standard of living of thousands of blind people.

4. The following services are particularly important: opening places of employment, to provide additional income, in special workshops founded and managed by the local Association for the Blind. Importing and supplying special equipment to aid the studies, work and leisure of the blind. Establishing and maintaining endowments to extend loans and grants to the needy. Organizing vacation camps, and cultural and sports activities in social clubs. Extending legal assistance and advice to the blind and his dependents. Securing discounts and benefits, in taxation, public transport, communication services, housing, etc.

5. Contribute generously! Help the blind to help themselves!

While these terms of public presentation avoided explicit mystification of sightlessness, and touched on some of the particular positive needs of the condition, the ABUG is incensed anew each year by the appeal. The ABUG claims that besides being offensive, the campaign is superfluous. In 1983 the ABUG turned to the press at Hannuka time and smeared the campaign. Its spokesman was quoted in the mass circulation daily *Ma'ariv*, stating that the number of blind people in the country was lower than the figure of 8,000 cited by the CB, that the latter did not use its resources efficiently, and that it degraded blind people. The general slant of the interview was destructive. Some time thereafter the ABUG came out with threats that it would approach a foundation that was a major benefactor of the CB, with their grievances, and disrupt that source of support.[6]

To molify its opponents the CB introduced some changes in its publicity. In the 1984 version of the appeal, in item 1 the words, "most of them poor and needy" were deleted. Item 2 read briefly, "Many of them are out of work". Item 4 dealt with "special and expensive equipment to enable the blind to integrate into the community", and the final point about obtaining discounts and benefits was dropped altogether. The thread that runs through these changes is an avoidance of public statements that imply that blind people are pitiable. In 1985 the CB appeal was revised still further. Item 4 now detailed CB services as,

> treating about 500 blind and visually-impaired children . . . and providing equipment for assisting their successful integration into the population of school children.

The image of blind people that is projected is increasingly removed from that of the indigent and elderly. This shift is consistent with the preferences of a youth and child-oriented society, in which aged people and the attribution of old-age are discredited (see Hazan 1990).[7]

In the following final case, we observe a rare instance of cooperation on the part of CB and ABUG activists representing, respectively, relatively segregationist and integrationist stances. This highlights the thesis of this chapter: the small differences in practice—despite the ideological divergence and the verbose arguments. The issue was a problem that is specific to downtown Tel-Aviv. Traffic there had become extremely congested and motorists commonly parked on sidewalks. The chaotic conditions presented particular hazards to blind pedestrians. Encountering a vehicle unexpectedly parked on the sidewalk, or brushing along it, blind pedestrians often soiled their clothing. Sometimes blind pedestrians had to walk in the thoroughfare in the midst of traffic, thus endangering themselves.

Initially the CB has considered adopting the practice of some operators of parking lots who penalized illegal parkers by inconveniencing them by sticking warnings over the driver's windshield. This later requires drivers to busy themselves scraping off the paper and the glue. The proposition was rejected because of apprehension that angry drivers might develop an antipathy for blind people. The CB then formed a committee to formulate a recommendation. The committee session that I attended was composed of three activists: Avraham San'ani, who was a past employee of the CB, and Penina Danieli and Sion Yisraeli, both past ABUG activists, who were inclined to active positions over disability rights. The guideline of the discussion was that pedestrians who had been inconvenienced would leave a message under the vehicle windshield wiper. The discussion centered on the text of the message. Avraham suggested the following:

> I am a blind person. I stumbled on the vehicle that you parked on the sidewalk and endangered myself. I am sure that your intention was not malicious, and therefore I ask you to please refrain from parking in a way that endangers me and my blind friends.

The two ABUG discussants objected because they felt this text highlighted sidewalk parking as a problem peculiar to blind people. They argued that the problem affected other categories of pedestrians too, such as mothers pushing baby carriages. The appeal should therefore be formulated more broadly. Just as the segregationist CB, at an earlier stage of the deliberation, had ruled out using annoying stickers, Sion the integrationist now argued in a structurally similar way:

> The driver whom we appeal to, and ask to move his vehicle elsewhere may well be the person who one day will be requested to employ a blind person. Avraham's formulation is one that presents the blind person as pitiful; it damages the image of the blind person. It may cause that man not to give me employment, because he'll consider me pitiful (*miskein*).

It is questionable whether indeed all categories of pedestrians experience the inconvenience in the same way as implied by the ABUG argument. Blind pedestrians are clearly at a disadvantage. On the other hand, it is dubious whether blind pedestrians constitute a unique category as implied in Avraham's formulation. Rather, he and the ABUG activists were engaged in segregationist and in intregrationist image-building respectively. Avraham retorted to Sion:

> But all mobility is more dangerous for the blind![8] A blocked sidewalk forces us down into the thoroughfare! It is important to me that the vehicle-owner should know that a blind pedestrian left the note of complaint!

Thereupon Penina suggested a text that she had prepared, which ran as follows:

> I know you did not think of me as you searched for a parking spot. I am a pedestrian. Sometimes a blind person using a cane, sometimes a woman and child on a walk, sometimes a mother with a shopping bag and leading a carriage

with a baby, sometimes a blind person assisted by a dog. All
of us are disturbed by your vehicle parked on the sidewalk.
The blind person hurts himself, the women and children
must descend to the thoroughfare . . . Yet when pedestrians
walk in the middle of the road who but you is
inconvenienced? . . . Think about it, for only the sidewalk is
safe for us.

This was eventually the text that the committee recommended, to be
reproduced under the letterhead of the CB and signed by its direc-
tors.

Mobility on a crowded sidewalk and in the road is undoubtedly
more hazardous to blind pedestrians than to the other categories of
people mentioned. The latter at least are clearly visible to able-bodied
pedestrians and to drivers as traffic hazards, whereas the sightlessness of blind pedestrians is not as readily visible. The discussants
weakened their appeal by including in the text people who are not in
a position as hazardous as blind pedestrians. But for them the selection of texts was evidently a problem of public presentation, and that
governed their decision, no less than the specific traffic problem on
hand. Whichever particular public image was more effective in solv-
ing the problem was a question to which the discussants had no
answer; the public image they presented in the selection of texts was
not dictated by the parameters of the problem on hand. The protagonists of the differing positions, Avraham the segregationist and Sion
and Penina the integrationists, compromised. By agreeing to publish
the appeal under the CB letterhead, the committee made it clear that
the broadsheet was handed out by a blind person who had a particular interest in the matter; at the same time that blind person was, in
their view, not presented as unique, "pitiful".

In conclusion, the conflicting and sometimes convoluted attitudes
towards acceptance of aid should be viewed in their general context.
Namely, that of a society in transition between clearly defined segregation of disabled people and indeterminate vague integration. In
this social context blind people and blindness workers do not rely
exclusively on legislated public support to advance their interests,
but also on old-time philanthropy and charity. The conclusion is sobering: for all their squabbles the protagonists of opposing public
stances, the CB and the ABUG, do not differ much in practice. Those
who proffer a radical integrationist stance are not consistent, since
they are not able to effect such a policy in practice. In some spheres of
life the trend is towards segregation of the blind, in others the forces
for integration tend to act as a counter balance.

At present blind Israelis are not fully integrated into mainline
society. Blind people hold social positions in grooves that have been
opened by a society, that has come a long way from tradition and

from traditional roles for the blind. But Israeli society is still not a consistently plural society that affords equitable places to physically extraordinary people. Israeli society encourages blind people to leave the old segregated niches, but it does not particularly exert itself to that end. The emancipation of blind Israelis is indeterminate: elements of integration are evident, but the ultimate goal has not been clearly defined. Barring a clear definition, integration is, as we have seen, sometimes pictured by blind activists in unrealistic images. Segregation, now discredited, implied poverty, degradation, stigma. The price of integration, currently being moulded in Israel, can be stress and questionable authenticity.

Chapter Fourteen

Conclusion:
From Ethnography of Blindness to
Anthropology of Disability

We travelled along two main paths in these chapters. First, in terms of substance of the life experience of blind people, we started from the intimacy of the body, through private social domains and on to areas of public debate. Finally we focused on the major issue of the disability rights movement, integration among the able-bodied. The terrain that we covered contained issues that were salient in the lives of blind Israelis. They were important to blind people themselves, not just to the anthropologist who studied them. The salience of the issues of this study is demonstrated by the actions and the words of people reported in these chapters. The picture presented tends to be comprehensive and constitutes an ethnography of blind Israelis. The concluding paragraphs of this chapter indicate how such ethnographic work might contribute to the emergence of an anthropology of disability.

Along the second path, that of social theory, the study straddles the divide between the Goffman paradigm and post–Goffman work. In discussions such as on the use of the senses and on mobility-aids, the Goffman paradigm is implicitly accepted. But while Goffman's own substantive work on disability is focused primarily on general issues of social relationships and acceptance, we moved beyond it to explore other matters. Discussions such as in chapter 5 on raising children and chapter 10 on socializing among blind people, explored possibilities other than those of stigma and marginality. Presently, in concluding, I explicate the trajectory of the study beyond Goffman.

According to the Goffman paradigm, as also developed by others such as Davis (1961) and Levitin (1975), disabled people are commonly viewed as subordinate. Writing at a time when the Goffman paradigm was a fresh and powerful revelation, Robert Scott extrapolates it forcefully. Describing the operators of the blindness system, Scott sees them as

> ... active socializing agents that create and mould the fundamental attitudes and patterns of behavior that are at the core of the experience of being a blind man (1969: 121).

The main concern of this school of research is to uncover the strategies that disabled people employ to escape that situation. Hence the development of concepts such as "avowal" and "disavowal" of disability.

The present work did not focus on the blindness system and its workers. This led me to concerns other than the effect of the blindness system and issues of subordination. My location in the course of fieldwork was with the blind clients and only marginally with the sighted administrators of welfare services and workshops. My observations impressed me with the independent doings of the clients. But we also saw indications, similar to Scott, which underlined the dominant role of blindness workers, and sometimes also their prejudices. Thus, in chapter 9, we encountered a volunteer who insulted blind activists in an argument by saying they were "merely switchboard operators." Some volunteers attributed negative stereotypes to blind clients, such as their being suspicious, jealous and mean towards each other. On the other hand, the foregoing chapters are replete with indications of the independence and resourcefulness of clients of the blindness system. Those observations do not negate the perspective gained through the Goffman paradigm, but they do call for a more nuanced and balanced picture. The socialization of blind clients on the part of blindness workers, to which Scott drew attention, must be seen in the context indicated, which includes both subordination and assertion.

Blind Israelis are routinely categorized by public authorities, when they come to their attention, as welfare cases. This blanket categorization is one expression of the stigmatization which Goffman highlighted. Most of the public assistance available to blind Israelis necessitates that the applicant be certified as a blind person and that requires having a file with the welfare authorities. It is a matter of course for each and every blind Israeli to be registered as a client in some or all of the various agencies of the welfare bureaucracy (viz. local welfare offices, the national rehabilitation system, the payment office of the National Insurance Institute, the CB, not to mention the local volunteer association). During the course of fieldwork only one man, Yoram Peres, proudly claimed that he did not have a file at the local welfare office.

Numerous categories of able-bodied people in Israel draw public support for themselves, through an intricate network of grants, subsidies, and fringe benefits. Sometimes these benefits constitute barely disguised sinecures. These are people who obtain support under an imaginative variety of social labels. Thus, industrialists seeking support for a shaky plant, young couples requiring housing aid, unemployed workers, talmudical students engaged in putative indefinite study—all obtain public support through channels that are administratively labelled in a variety of ways, any but discredited "social welfare". Theoretically it is conceivable that blind, and disabled people generally, might obtain support in a similar way. But that is not the case. It is remarkable that blind people who approach the public authorities for non-blindness linked requests, such as employment, are unambiguously cast into the category of welfare cases, and are then processed through the welfare system. Even blind professionals, who are hardly indigent, have files in various offices of the blindness and welfare systems.

Another expression of the phenomenon of cultural conceptualization of blind people concerns the category of people who are visually-impaired, neither completely blind nor fully sighted. This category of disabled people has been driven to be identified either as blind or as sighted. The blindness system, being engaged with blindness, categorized the visually-impaired with blind people. Thus, in years past, one might encounter in the Jerusalem School for the Blind the phenomenon of visually-impaired youngsters who are taught to read Braille like blind pupils. But instead of doing so tactually, these students attempted to read the dots visually when their residual vision permitted. Optical equipment now available obviates such practice; it enables partially-sighted people effective usage of their residual vision, and to develop as such, not as blind people. However, like many institutions, the components of the blindness system have an inherent tendency to extend and ramify their activities, and hence to categorize as blind, people who in fact might be uncomfortable with the label. This practice of the blindness system is now changing, due to new optical aids designed for the needs of the visually-impaired. These function to obviate arbitrary categorization.

The context of the lives of the people that we have been considering is that of contemporary Israel. In terms of pertinent social policies, this context should be seen as lying at a point on a continuum between two poles. At one pole of the continuum lie systems of social policy where the lot of disabled people is structured in terms of charity, at the opposite pole are systems where the lot of the disabled tends, relatively, to be structured in terms of civil rights.

Under administrations of either of these systems, we encounter associations of disabled, specifically of blind people, that are unambiguous. In contemporary third world countries, we encounter groups of disabled people where disability is the base of association, unencumbered by special interests (such as those mentioned above in chapter ten). Blind people commonly band together in public, earning money by singing or begging, and also nurturing fellowship. This also was the type of association reported in early nineteenth century Cairo, where the blind people of the city coalesced en masse as a political force (Baer 1977: 233–234).[1] At the other end of the continuum, in contemporary disability rights movements, we again encounter the trait of fellowship of the disabled. Thus in the "Liberty Movement" in an American city, described by Goldin (1984), an advocacy group of blind people is conceived of in terms of "community". This is similar to developments in the contemporary feminist movement. The articulation of the lot of the disabled in unambiguous civil rights terms leads to internal association, the condition of disability being the essential base of fellowship.

How does the Israeli system fit into this scheme of a sociology of disability systems? The status and the other conditions of life of disabled people in Israel, as determined by the able-bodied, imply on the one hand, policies of a social welfare-type state, but on the other hand Israel lacks full-fledged movements for the emancipation and equal rights of disabled people. In addressing the question of mutual rejection as against association among the disabled in Israel, I suggest that the complex, ambiguous type of association uncovered, in chapter 10 is consistent with the attitude of the dominant able-bodied society toward the disabled, namely, a combination of social welfare ideology, with old-time charity, philanthropy and paternalism.

In the past decade, a number of developments in research have led disability studies to embrace such issues and to move beyond Goffman. Starting from the special *Journal of Social Issues* volume in 1948 through Edgerton's 1970 essay, cross cultural perspectives have been developed in the work of Groce (1985), Gwaltney (1980), Scheer and Groce (1988), and recently, the Groce and Scheer (1990) and the Bruun and Ingstad (1990) collections. These works have stimulated greater awareness of the range of variation in the situation of disabled people in various cultures and societies. The thrust of the cross-cultural studies is, that while symbolization to make disabled people distinctive is common, it is not universal. The new studies also highlight the notion that disabled people are not universally subordinate. That emphasis does not contradict Goffman's theory of stigma, but it corrects its imbalance. The Goffman paradigm lacks a cross-cultural perspective, since it is founded on empirical examples drawn from Western literature and from Goffman's own field observations in American settings. Another contribution of recent disability studies is that they focus more sharply on disabled people than on the able-bodied people in their environment (in their role as disability workers or as bystanders). More information is thus attained on the disabled people themselves, and not just on the environment and the reaction of disabled people to that environment. The new studies correct both the imbalance in the dominant theory in the field and also present a more realistic ethnographic perspective (see Raybeck 1988).

Moreover, in recent papers Bogdan and Taylor (1987, 1989) and Söder (1990) have exposed data from contemporary Western society that highlight, not the stigmatization of disabled people, but on the contrary, their acceptance. These studies argue that factors such as familism, religiosity, humanistic ideology and friendship can lead to acceptance of disabled people and integration among the able-bodied. Also, according to them, when disabled people fill a role in terms of exchange with the able-bodied they are likely to be viewed as individuals and not as undifferentiated disabled persons. Both this perspective, as well as the findings of the forementioned ethnographies, and that of the Goffman paradigm are valid. They all capture segments of social reality. But the studies do contradict each other, and for anthropologists they entail embarassment reminiscent of the classical controversy of Redfield and Lewis (Foster 1961; Lewis 1961), not to mention the Mead-Freeman storm.

The differences between the various studies are rooted in differences of detail between the various fields of the disparate researchers, but probably also in different theoretical and conceptual approaches and in individual idiosyncrasies. One of the aims of a mature anthropology of disability should be to harmonize varying sets of equally valid observations. Another aim should be to raise new questions, advancing knowledge beyond what it currently is. Some such questions I have formulated in the course of the preceding chapters.

New questions ought to be raised at disparate levels. At one level we want to approach highly delimited local issues. For instance in the area of mobility aids (see chapter 3), we saw that army veterans are disproportionately high users of guide dogs. Why is this so? Perhaps there are elements in the military sub-culture that predispose veterans to the kind of discipline and impersonality which is required for effective guide dog usage, in contrast to the effusive attitude of many owners toward their pet dogs. Another question within this specific field concerns the role of guide dogs in family relationships (in relationships between spouses and in relationships towards children). One might assume that the unique tie between user and animal will have an effect on other domestic relationships.

Within the field of blindness a major issue not approached in this monograph is that of intimate and marital relationships between couples in which one or both partners are blind. The nature of my involvement in the field was such that it did not afford me data in this sensitive area of adequate quality for a meaningful analysis. I eschewed the topic altogether, and it remains to be explored.

Another important issue to be explored is that of the nature of "the blindness system" and of the social welfare system generally among disabled people. Since the groundwork done by Scott over two decades ago not much has been achieved. Over the years there have appeared some provoking studies (Handelman and Leyton 1978, Flett 1979, Grillo 1980, Howe 1990), that have explored service providers in various areas of life and in various societies. The picture that emerges from these studies is that service-providers operate in a dynamic way and are not fully constrained or bound by the formal rules of their organizations. The conclusion is reasonable and should have been expected, because social workers are human no less than the people who are their clients. But it is of such major practical, social and moral import that it warrants reiteration. What we require at this point is more detailed insight as to the variety, the nature and the dynamics of the dominance of service-providers vis-à-vis clients, and particularly, the nature of the blindness system.

There is another level that also invites the formulation of new questions for research. Virtually all the topics that I approached in the foregoing chapters require to be studied cross-culturally, both in the conventional sense and in the particular one of disability studies. The conventional sense is virtually self-understood: We require studies of blindness in different cultural settings. In terms particular to disability studies, we need comparative examinations of particular topics in various disabilities. Thus, the issue of inverse inter-generational status that we discussed in the context of family life (chapter 5) ought to be explored comparatively in various disabilities, while keeping constant the factor of culture (in the conventional anthropological sense). Similarly, issues in the anthropology of work that were raised earlier (chapters 6 and 7) ought to be explored comparatively among people of various categories of disability. Questions of association among the disabled (chapter two), integration of the latter among the able-bodied, and so forth, all warrant study among people that have a hearing impairment, epilepsy, muscular and motor disability, dwarfism, speech impairment, obesity, etc.

Finally, the anthropological study of disability can lead to conclusions that have immediate practical import. Thus, to take a specific instance, the study of mobility aids (chapter 3) encourages a humanistically informed view of technological development in the service of disabled people. It demonstrates that people use material aids within given socio-cultural contexts which are inseparable from them. The material aids are prone to be culturally constructed, symbolized, by stigmatizing impulses, like the disabled individuals themselves (and their able-bodied companions). Hence the development and diffusion of these aids require as much sensitivity and imagination as do the personal aspects of the welfare of disabled people. Another example of practical import comes from the study of association among blind people (chapter 10). Those observations lead to the conclusion that grouping people together for remedial purposes requires consideration of the fact, that interactions among disabled people may be problem-ridden. One should not assume as a rule that interaction among disabled persons will be beneficial for rehabilitation.[2]

The doings of the people whom we studied were not random, inviting understanding only in terms of their idiosyncracies. Their doings were, moreover, not understandable merely in abstract terms of symbolic interactionism, "social construction of disability", and stigma. We learn from this study that by focusing sensitively upon the variety of activities related to disabled people, disability studies can be firmly anchored in general anthropology.

Notes

Chapter One

1. On epilepsy there is a fine, unfortunately unpublished ethnography, by Yael Fradkin-Mutzafi (1990).

Chapter Two

1. Studies of culture and immigrants in Israel are legion, but there is no complete overview. For one pertinent collection of studies see Deshen and Shokeid 1974.

2. Here is an illustration of the pertinent changes among Israelis of Middle-Eastern background: Traditionally in Morocco, ritual kissing of the head, cheeks and hands, in many contexts, was common among males. In the early years after immigration to Israel these practices continued, but over time they have become greatly constricted. Some forms of kissing have virtually disappeared.

3. Such assistance, besides being perceived as slighting, is inefficient because it stymies the sensitivity of the blind person to the guide's motions. The blind person is unable to anticipate the guide's steps, and may even have difficulty in just following the latter.

4. See chapter 6 for an account of stratification among blind Israelis.

5. The Akrams lived in Israel, a Westernized but relatively traditional society, and in a sleepy Tel-Aviv suburb. But a blind colleague, the late Hanan Selvin, who lived in a much more permissive New York City environment, expressed to me his experience with soliciting the assistance of strangers in a very different way. My colleague was jokingly expounding on "advantages" that the blind have. "You," he quipped, "can't just accost any woman on the subway and walk off with her arm-in-arm. But I can!" The comment entailed deliberate confusion of the request for guidance with a sexual advance, and it is evaluated differently in the New York and Tel-Aviv situations.

6. Accepted norms of behavior and values of blind Israeli people are described later in chapters 7 and 10.

7. Purim is a carnival-type holiday that commemorates an ancient deliverance of the Jewish people from destruction. Popularly, it is marked by masking and mild drinking and merry-making.

8. In the Israeli blindness system, described later in chapter 8, sighted benevolent volunteers are active side by side with blind activists.

9. I experienced this personally many times in the course of my work. Both academic colleagues and lay friends, who tried to be helpful by suggesting to me literary references to comparable fields, commonly cited to me works on the deaf. Hardly ever did people direct me to other physical disabilities.

10. See Sacks 1989, for graphic accounts of the social nature of deafness.

11. In actuality, the hearing of the blind in general is, if anything, inferior to that of the sighted, because certain eye conditions often also affect the sense of hearing. Also, age-linked sightlessness is often coupled with age-linked degeneration of other body functions, including hearing.

12. Similarly, blind people attempt to train their memory to its maximum since the ability of superior recall is admired and unhedged by cultural limitations. Switchboard-operators in particular occasionally develop high status at work among sighted colleagues, because of their astonishing command of memorized detail (see chapter 7).

13. The eight day long feast of Hannuka focuses on nightly ritual candle-lighting, in commemoration of a Jewish victory and miracle in antiquity. Similar to Purim it is currently marked by partying. In chapter 13 Hannuka figures prominently.

14. My information for the use of the olfactory sense is limited because of the invisibility of olfactory practice, and the reticence of people to volunteer information on practicing senses that are not considered genteel in their environment. Also on gustation I have no information. Audition on the other hand, is not overtly repressed, but the auditory sense of the blind is hampered by incidental practices of the sighted.

15. The implied dichotomy of the social roles of blind people being constructed not only by culture but also by nature, is founded on those physiological elements of the blind condition that cannot be reduced to societal imposition. Thus, the physiological state of sightlessness does not impose on a person roles such as seer, vender, or piano-tuner; those are socially imposed. But sightlessness does bar a person from becoming a surgeon.

Chapter Three

1. For a concise summary see Pfuhl 1980, particularly chapters 6 and 7, for later work see Jones et al. 1984, Ainlay et al. 1986.

2. These and other references in this chapter were suggested to me by my colleague Nurit Bird-David, who also offered useful comments.

3. The white cane, linking blind people with other categories of disabled people, had the effect of sustaining the erroneous popular notion that blindness implies diffuse invalidity.

4. The condition of rare individuals who move unaided where other blind people require mobility aids. Psychologists are of divided opinion about the phenomenon. Some explain it in terms of extraordinary sensitivity to changes in air pressure, that result from the position of obstacles. Others dismiss this and link the phenomenon to acute and disciplined audition (Supa et al. 1944, Kohler 1964).

5. Traffic crossings can be negotiated without having to wait for volunteered assistance and walking speed is increased. Mobility by guide dogs is also safer and more relaxed (Clark-Carter et al. 1986).

6. A striking illustration of this deep-rooted repugnance lies in one of the traditional Jewish explanations of the term 'mark of Cain' in the biblical story of the prototype fratricide (Genesis IV). Developing an idea that figures in much earlier sources, Nahmanides (Spain, thirteenth century) understands the mark of Cain to be a dog. Thus: God gives Cain a dog that would always precede him in his wanderings. Nahmanides writes:

> Wherever the dog would turn that would be the road that God had ordained for Cain to take...and the sages understood this despicable mark (*ot nivzeh*) to be appropriate to him (Nahmanides on Genesis IV:13).

Remarkably this image of the dog includes some elements of the modern guide dog, but it is wedded to a profoundly negative association and negatively evaluated. My then 15-year-old daughter Efrat brought this source to my attention. Eames and Eames 1989 have outlined cultural and other differences in the usage of guide dogs in the United States and Britain.

7. In a graduate paper devoted to guide dog usage in Israel Ronit Bar'am (manuscript) has outlined many pertinent situations, including similar ones to those which I have indicated. Bar'am (p. 57) demonstrates that owning a guide dog can be a burden to harmonious relations between spouses, because of both the intruding affective element and the daily domestic arrangements required for the maintenance of the animal.

8. Bar'am (p. 74) documents another symbolization of a guide dog: a woman talking about her dog repeatedly fell into a slip of the tongue, instead of saying *hakelev sheli* (my dog) she said *haben sheli* (my son).

9. People expressed the feeling of being superfluous not only in the context of actual viewing but also in the context of conversations that viewers held thereafter about the programs. Thus for one blind person, Fridays were annoying, because then sighted people talk about the weekly Thursday evening basketball game that is shown on TV.

10. There are very few detailed accounts of the integration of disabled people among the able-bodied in technologically undeveloped societies. But two extant ethnographies, one on blind and one on deaf people, provide dramatic views of the deeply-rooted integration of the disabled (Gwaltney 1970, 1980; Groce 1985).

Chapter Four

1. The factor of aristocratic lineage is important and pervades the traditional culture of Moroccan Jewry (see Deshen 1989).

2. It is plausible that the old social ties were pertinent and helpful to Re'uma's welfare, though I have no data to substantiate this.

3. Comparative research in the U.S. setting, despite the many socio-cultural differences from the Israeli setting, again indicates a similar situation. Gaudreau (1963, p. 61 seq.) reports that blind adolescents commonly complain that their kin lack understanding of their condition.

4. Stable cohabitation of unmarried couples involving either one or two blind partners, is uncommon. I encountered one such case where the blind partner was an impressive middle-aged widow and the sighted partner was a young man, inferior in terms of mental and physical health. The overall traditional family pattern of blind people is consistent with the generally conservative pattern they exhibit also in other activities, as seen below in chapters 11 and 12.

5. There are indications that the European situation is similar (Haugaan 1984); also the U.S. situation, at least as late as the 1960s. In observations of interpersonal relationships among young U.S. blind adults, there are accounts of young women who "feel they lack bargaining power" (Winton 1970: 77).

6. Safilios-Rothschild (1982) offers a comparative observation for the marriage pattern of the mentally retarded. She indicates a pattern which is obverse to the one I observed, namely that mentally retarded women, more than their male peers, tend to marry both normal and mentally retarded men. Safilios-Rothschild suggests the explanation that the disability of mental retardation interferes less grossly with the traditional female role than it does with the male role of breadwinner. Hence the acceptability of retarded women as spouses. The same variable thus explains the contrary realities of different disabilities.

7. I never heard that these marriages were anything other than stable.

Chapter Five

1. A recent survey of the social-psychological literature on blindness reflects this imbalance. The survey (Kemp 1981) lists about 150 items, of

which 43 focus on blind children. Not one is devoted to the sighted children of blind parents.

2. In Israel, as in much of the industrialized world, the usage of private cars is of great status significance. Also Edgerton (1967: 160–162) reports of the great importance of the lack of automobiles in the lives of the mentally retarded people whom he studied in 1960.

Chapter Six

1. Thus in Germany, national law obliges employers to hire a certain percentage of disabled workers among their employees. Failing that, the firm must pay an additional tax. In the USA, legislation is less sweeping and limited to federal government offices and suppliers of federal services; but it does require reserving certain positions for blind workers.

2. The estimate is based on the figure of about 8,000, as the total blind and visually-impaired population (State of Israel 1989:434). That figure includes many thousands of elderly people, of multiple disabled and of youngsters who do not pertain to an analysis of the working-age population of blind, but otherwise able-bodied people. The present study is based on fieldwork in 1983–84, and the data relate to that time.

3. Situations of married women who worked outside home while their husbands remained idle were rare: this clashed with traditional family norms. In one such case the woman resigned her position in favor of her husband, and thereafter satisfied herself with the position of a homemaker.

Chapter Seven

1. This sort of feeling of achievement at mastering complex equipment also lies behind Yoram Peres, whom we saw in the previous chapter, manipulating a job shift. Beyond the desire to avoid inconvenient travel, he was attracted to a position that because of its complexity afforded more self-respect.

2. The question whether in fact blind people constitute a community, and if so whether anyone represents it, is discussed in chapter 10, and need not concern us here. In the present discussion it is the fact of the belief that is salient.

3. The question whether in fact the thieves acted because of the blind man's condition, or whether it was not relevant in their choice of victim does not pertain to my analysis. The salient point is Yehezqel's view of the thefts, as inflicted upon him randomly, just as on other people in business. His further positive interpretation of this view is consistent with the superior self-image of this man.

Chapter Eight

1. The comparable figure that Scott (1969) gives for the U.S. is one for every thousand individuals (p. 61).

2. The major expenses for medication and schooling are usually provided for by the country's system of social welfare, so that remaining needs of this nature can be properly considered as incidental.

3. Scott (1969:60) summarizes the situation as follows:

... an aggregate of bureaucratic entities that share a common interest in the problems of blindness, but whose activities are not coordinated and integrated to any meaningful degree.

4. The project also provides for a sighted companion to accompany, at reduced price, a certain number of vacationers.

5. The sources give a stereotyped example of this: the wealthy person who was accustomed to luxurious food and clothing and then lost his wealth. Such a person should now be supported on a level approximate to his past situation, and not merely on a level that the philanthropist considers appropriate for the indigent. The subjective needs, as evaluated by the munificent, determine the extent of charitable assistance that tradition requires (Maimonides, *Mishne Torah, hilkhot matnot 'aniyim* VII, 3).

6. The *hevre*-type network is closely linked to *proteksia*-type nepotism as analyzed by Danet 1988. Both phenomena are part of a cluster of symbols, the details of which constitute core elements of Israeli popular culture. For an example of the operation of the hevre relationship in another context see Shokeid 1990.

Chapter Nine

1. The game is played in a closed space about thirty metres long and ten metres across. It consists of thrusting a large heavy ball along the floor, in vigorous motions, onto the wall behind the opposing team. The players seek to prevent the oncoming ball, which is audible in motion through bells placed inside, from hitting the wall behind them. The game requires good team coordination and a fine sense of hearing.

2. The workshop depended on suppliers for the provision of materials to assemble, and they were not very reliable. Supplies failing, the employees were left idle, but such was not the case on that particular day.

3. They seem to marry rather late by Israeli standards, so that their children are youngsters under ten-years old, whereas sighted men their age commonly have children in their teens or older.

4. The loudness of the knocking may well have been linked with a common assumption that blind people are poor of hearing and therefore must be addressed loudly.

5. Not surprisingly, the AB activists were not impressed by their visitors. In talking politics with people, I did not encounter a single blind person, among the AB activists or other blind people, who chose to support the Invalids' List. I return to the subject in chapter 12.

6. That is the vocational rehabilitation center near Haifa, about one hundred kms. from Tel-Aviv where the woman lived.

Chapter Ten

1. I realize that some of these statements, and the questions that follow below, may be objectionable from the perspective of the rights-for-disabled people movements. I refer back to my comments in the introduction.

2. A prominent ethnographer of deaf people summarizes:

Among the aged deaf I studied, being deaf is the single most important factor in their lives. One owes allegiance to deafness . . . One must further the good of the community, putting it before oneself . . . (Becker 1981: 23).

Only where the deaf are extraordinarily integrated among the able-bodied, as in the society depicted by Groce (1985), is evidence for such sociability minimal.

3. The basic datum that disabled people in general are often segregated into delimited social niches is well-documented (for the physically unusual in general see Goffman 1963 and for a recent revisionist view, Murphy et al. 1988).

4. The only positive stereotype I ever encountered among blind people about the blind, was the claim that blind workers are punctilious and devoted to their work. But I encountered little to substantiate neither that nor the negative images. (1) The behavior among people at work in the sheltered workshop was not particularly antagonistic. (2) The scope of interests of many of the blind people I came to know impressed me as broad, relative to that of sighted people of similar socioeconomic status. The reason for this may lie in the fact that Israeli blind people are avid radio fans, more so than sighted people (who view television). The local radio, in contrast to television, offers superior programs, including higher education courses, and there may be a link between the nature of the radio and the range of interests of local blind people. Previously (chapter 4), I noted the superior language usage of blind people.

5. Thus, a curse is often referred to as a blessing, a blind person as a *sagei nahor* ("much light"), and death as *bar-menan* ("away from us"). A recent extension of this is the practice of never using the word "cancer" for a malignant disease, but rather to use allusive euphemisms.

6. There is a parallel with the stereotype of dwarfs as being frequently engaged by circuses, exhibiting their condition. In reality, as Ablon (1984:71) shows, this is most unusual. Unfortunately Ablon does not offer comparable data pertinent to the question, whether the attitude of dwarfs to the circus occupation is in any way distinctive.

7. See note 3. We have seen stigmatization present even in the intimacy of family settings, in relationships between sighted parents and blind children (chapter 4). This is the background to the concern of the present chapter, relationships among blind people exclusively.

8. This group was referred to among the activists of the AB as "the Sifriya hamula". The term *hamula* technically applies to the traditional extended Arab family. In Israeli parlance it came to be loosely used at the time of mass immigration in the 1950s for any cohesive group of exotic immigrants. See Shokeid (in Shokeid and Deshen 1982, chapter 5) for an examination of the usage of the term. Since the Sifriya people are of an age group that experienced immigration as adults, cohere in an old-fashioned manner, and are now elderly, they are conceptualized condescendingly by other blind people who consider themselves superior to them.

9. In chapter 12, I describe one of the incidents that occurred in this group and which led people to drop out.

10. For two landmark discussions in the extensive literature on joking relationships see Radcliffe-Brown 1952 and Beidelman 1966.

11. For a recent account of these problems among deaf people, see Foster 1989.

12. The relatively weak tendencies for mutual association among blind people parallels those documented in studies of immigrants. In the United States, early in the century, mobile second-generation immigrants have been repeatedly described as succumbing to melting-pot type pressures, rejecting and transforming their ethnic allegiances.

Chapter Eleven

1. See also Herzog 1986 where this thesis is developed in a general way to interpret ethnic political phenonema in the pre-state period.

2. For a thoughtful and informative summary of the Israeli immigrant scene see Ayalon, Ben-Rafael and Sharot 1985.

3. I use the term "Middle-Eastern" in analytic contexts, but in quotations of informants other terms such as "Sephardic" and "Oriental" sometimes appear. Much ink has been spent in debates about the terminological usages. For purposes of the present discussion, however, this is immaterial and the terms are interchangeable.

4. One such person was Mazal Eini, under whom Nehama had done her switchboard operator apprenticeship, and whom she greatly admired, precisely because of her gregarious behavior.

Chapter Twelve

1. Upon reaching the age of eighteen, virtually the whole Jewish male population does three years of obligatory unpaid military service (girls serve two years and many are exempted). Thereafter, up to the age of fifty-five, men serve for yearly periods of thirty to sixty days.

2. The military authorities have sometimes been imaginative in availing themselves of the services of such volunteers. They have created adjunct positions in clerical work for young people, whose disability is not too serious and visible. Occasionally the press reports cases, such as that of a girl who suffered from a motor coordination condition and walked with difficulty, but whose determination drove the army authorities to find a role for her. Another celebrated case was that of an insistent, severely visually-impaired boy, for whom also a military niche was found.

3. This refers to protests by farmers against low market prices for their products, and the reluctance of government to subsidize agriculture.

4. The situation referred to is long past, and I could not reconstruct it reliably. But knowing Yael, I cannot conceive her actually "remaining silent". Had she done so, the local employees' association would probably have rallied to Yael's support in her disputes with her employers. It is reasonable to assume that factors additional to Yael's labor ethos led to her clashes at work, but it did contribute to them.

5. Migdalor is the name of a particular training center.

6. Job's three companions "sat down with him upon the ground seven days and seven nights, and none spoke a word to him; for they saw that his grief was very great." Job II:13.

7. If one considers that a list which garnered just 1% of the vote gained a Knesset seat, the Invalids did not, in terms of Israeli electioneering, fail to leave a mark on the voters.

Chapter Thirteen

1. This was pointed out to me by Professor Edwin Eames of California State University at Fresno.

2. There are indications that this situation is not unique to Israel. Thus Lukoff (1960), discussing blind people in the United States, emphasizes the problematic image of the blind beggar.

3. An example of this is a collapsible long cane, which in the United States was priced $20, was sold at the CB for $2.

4. To this is linked the tragi-comic practice of some public institutions to offer wheelchairs to blind people, and pressure them to use them. Such incidents figure in memoirs of the blind, and one of my informants told me that when he visited a Paris theater, although accompanied by a sighted girlfriend, he was, to his embarrassment, ordered to use a wheelchair. It is to the credit of Israeli institutions that my local material includes no such incidents.

5. For her part Efrat told me, that at such times passengers directed glowering stares at her. The question arises as to how such situations affect marital relations.

6. My informant in the CB told me that his organization planned to anticipate their opponents, and would inform the foundation of the ABUG's doings. I was not in a position to follow the matter further, and left it at that. The foundation has continued to support the CB.

7. Scott (1969) in his study of the American blindness system came to the same finding.

8. Avraham himself and other blind people of the study have suffered injuries as pedestrians in traffic accidents, some quite seriously.

Chapter Fourteen

1. This reference was brought to my attention by Professor Jacob Landau of the Hebrew University of Jerusalem.

2. But a major text on rehabilitation practice, dated but still cited, has the following dubious pronouncement:

Interaction with other disabled persons usually seems to present no problems to a disabled person but is, on the contrary, quite helpful in making it easier for him to accept his predicament. The "positive" influence of such interaction seems to occur either through identification with another disabled afflicted with the same type and degree of disability or through a comparison of his disability with that of a more seriously incapacitated disabled which produced a feeling of being "much better off" (Safilios-Rothschild 1970:121).

References

Ablon, J., 1984. Little People in America: The Social Dimensions of Dwarfism. Praeger, New York.

————, 1988. Living with Difference: Families with Dwarf Children. Praeger, New York.

Ainlay, S.C., 1981. "Intentionality, Identity and Aging: an Inquiry into Aging and Adventitious Vision-Loss." Unpublished Ph.D. dissertation, Rutgers University; also in, Day Brought Back My Night: Aging and New Vision Loss. Routledge, London, 1989.

————, Becker, G. and Coleman, L., eds., 1986. The Dilemma of Difference. Plenum, New York.

Appadurai, A., ed., 1986. The Social Life of Things: Commodities in Cultural Perspective. Cambridge University Press, Cambridge .

Ayalon, H., Ben-Rafael, E. and Sharot, S., 1985. "Variations in Ethnic Identification among Israeli Jews." Ethnic and Racial Studies 8:389–407.

Baer, G., 1977. "Popular Revolution in Ottoman Cairo." Der Islam 54:213–242.

Bar'am, R., 1988. "Guide-Dogs in the Lives of Blind People." Unpublished Tel-Aviv University term paper (Hebrew).

Becker, G., 1980. Growing Old in Silence: Deaf People in Old Age. University of California Press, Berkeley.

Beidelman, T., 1966. "Utani: Some Kaguru Notions of Death, Sexuality and Affinity." Southwestern Journal of Anthropology 22: 354–380.

Ben-Rafael, E., 1982. The Emergence of Ethnicity: Cultural Groups and Social Conflict in Israel. Greenwood, Westport, CT.

Berdichevsky, N., 1977. "The Persistence of the Yemenite Quarter in an Israeli Town." Ethnicity 4: 287–309 (also in Krausz, E., ed., Studies of Israeli Society: Migration, Ethnicity and Community. Transaction, New Brunswick, 1980, pp. 73–95).

185

Bogdan, R. and Taylor, S., 1987. "Toward a Sociology of Acceptance: The Other Side of the Study of Deviance." Social Policy, Fall, 34–39.

———, 1989. "Relationships with Severly Disabled People: The Social Construction of Humanness." *Social Problems* 36: 135–148.

Bruun, F.J. and Ingstad, B., eds., 1990. Disability in a Cross-Cultural Perspective. University of Oslo, Department of Social Anthropology, Oslo.

Bynder, H. and New, P.K., 1976. "Time for a Change: From Micro- to Macro-Sociological Concepts in Disability Research." *Journal of Health and Social Behavior* 17: 45–52.

Clark-Carter, D., Hayes, A.D. and Howarth, C.I., 1986. "The Stress Experienced by Independent Blind Travellers." *Ergonomics* 29:779–789.

Cohen, Yishaq Yoseif, 1982. "The Blind Person in Jewish Law." In *Sources and Events*. Re'uven Mass, Jerusalem, pp. 3–39 (Hebrew).

Csikszentmihalyi, M. and Rochberg-Halton, E., 1981. The Meaning of Things. Cambridge University Press, Cambridge.

Danet, B., 1988. Pulling Strings: Biculturalism in Israeli Bureaucracy. State University of New York Press, Albany.

Davis, F., 1981. "Deviance Disavowal: The Management of Strained Interaction by the Visibly Handicapped." *Social Problems* 9: 120–132.

———, 1963. Passage through Crisis: Polio Victims and their Families. Bobbs-Merrill, Indianapolis.

Deshen, S., 1970 . Immigrant Voters in Israel: Parties and Congregations in a Local Election Campaign. Manchester University Press, Manchester.

———, 1974. "Political Ethnicity and Cultural Ethnicity in Israel during the 1960's". In Cohen, Abner, ed., Urban Ethnicity, ASA Monograph 12. Tavistock, London, pp. 281–309 (also in Krausz, op. cit., pp. 117–145).

———, 1989. The Mellah Society: Jewish Community life in Sherifian Morocco. University of Chicago Press, Chicago.

———, and Shokeid, M., 1974. The Predicament of Homecoming: Cultural and Social Life of North-African Immigrants in Israel. Cornell University Press, Ithaca.

Douglas, M. and Isherwood, B., 1978. The World of Goods: Towards an Anthropology of Consumption. Penguin, Harmondsworth.

Eames, E. and Eames, T., 1989. "A Comparison of the Guide Dog Movements of England and the United States." *Journal of Visual Impairment and Blindness*, 83: 215–218.

Edgerton, R.B., 1967. The Cloak of Competence: Stigma in the Life of the Mentally Retarded. University of California Press, Berkeley.

————, 1970. "Mental Retardation in Non-Western Societies: Towards a Cross-Cultural Perspective on Incompetence." In Haywood, H. C., ed., Aspects of Mental Retardation. Appleton-Century-Crofts, New York, pp. 523–529.

Estroff, S., 1981. Making It Crazy: An Ethnography of Psychiatric Clients in an American Community. University of California Press, Berkeley.

Fischer, C., 1985. "Studying Technology and Social Life." In Castells, M., ed., High Technology, Space and Society. Sage, Beverly Hills, pp. 284–300.

————, and Glenn, C., 1988. "Telephone and Automobile Diffusion in the United States, 1902–1937." American Journal of Sociology 93:1153–1178.

Flett, H., 1979. "Bureaucracy and Ethnicity: Notions of Eligibility to Public Housing." In Wallman, S., ed., Ethnicity at Work. MacMillan, London, pp. 135–152.

Foster, G.M., 1961. "Interpersonal Relations in Peasant Society." Human Organization 19:174–178.

Foster, S., 1989. "Social Alienation and Peer Identification: A Study of the Social Construction of Deafness." Human Organization 48:226–235.

Fradkin-Mutzafi, Y., 1990. "Living in the Closet: How People with Epilepsy Cope with their Stigmatized Condition." Unpublished M.A. thesis, Tel-Aviv University (Hebrew).

Gaudreau, L., 1963. "Stereotypes of the Blind toward the Sighted in Contemporary American Society." Unpublished Ph. D. dissertation, Cornell University.

Goffman, E., 1963. Stigma: Notes on the Management of Spoiled Identity. Prentice-Hall, Englewood Cliffs, N.J.

Goldin, C., 1980. "Advocacy Organizing by the Blind: Responses to Stigmatization." Unpublished Ph.D. dissertation, University of Pennsylvania.

————, 1984. "The Community of the Blind: Social Organization, Advocacy and Cultural Redefinition." Human Organization 43: 121–131.

Greenberg, J., 1970. In This Sign. Avon, New York.

Grillo, R., 1980. "Social Workers and Immigrants in Lyon, France." In Grillo, R., ed., "Nation" and "State" in Europe: Anthropological Perspectives. Academic Press, London, pp. 73–87.

Groce, N., 1985. Everyone Here Spoke Sign Language. Harvard University Press, Cambridge.

―――― and Scheer, J., eds., 1990. "Cross-Cultural Perspectives in Disability." *Social Science and Medicine* 30:839–912.

Gussow, Z., 1989, Leprosy, Racism and Public Health. Westview Press, Boulder.

―――― and Tracy, G.S., 1968. "Status, Ideology, and Adaptation to Stigmatized Illness: a Study of Leprosy." *Human Organization* 17:316–325.

Gwaltney, J. L., 1970. The Thrice-Shy: Cultural Accommodation to Blindness and other Disasters in a Mexican Community. Columbia University Press, New York.

――――, 1980. "Darkly Through the Glass of Progress." Papers in Anthropology (Oklahoma) 21:91–100.

Hall, E.T., 1966. The Hidden Dimension. Doubleday, Garden City.

Handelman, D., 1975. "Expressive Interaction and Social Structure: Play and an Emergent Game Form in an Israeli Social Setting." In Kendon, A., Harris, R. and Ritchie Key, M. eds., The Organization of Behavior in Face-to-Face Interaction. Mouton, Hague, pp. 389–414.

―――― and Leyton, E., 1978. Bureaucracy and World-View. Memorial University of Newfoundland, St. John's.

Haugaan, E.M., 1984. "Mit einem blinden oder sehschwachen partner leben." Horus (Marburg) 46 (nr. 1): 1–6.

Hazan, H., 1990. "Victim into Sacrifice: The Construction of the Old as a Symbolic Type." *Journal of Cross-Cultural Gerontology* 5:77–84.

Herzog, H., 1986. "Political Factionalism: The Case of Ethnic Lists in Israel." *Western Political Quarterly* 38: 285–303.

――――, 1990. "Midway Between Political and Cultural Ethnicity: An Analysis of 'the Ethnic Lists' in the 1984 Elections." In Elazar, D., Penniman, H. and Sandler, S., eds., Israel's Odd Couple: The 1984 Elections and the National Unity Government. Wayne State University Press, Detroit, pp. 87–118.

Higgins, P., 1980. Outsiders in a Hearing World: A Sociology of Deafness. Sage, Beverly Hills.

Himelfarb, A. and Evans, J., 1974. "Deviance, Disavowal and Stigma Management." In Hass, J. and Shaffir, W. eds., Decency and Deviance: Studies in Deviant Behavior. McClelland and Steward, Toronto, pp. 221–232.

Hirbawy, S., 1987. Ha'sedeq ba'hasheikha. n. pub., Haifa (Hebrew).

Howe, L.E.A., 1990. Being Unemployed in Northern Ireland. Cambridge University Press, Cambridge.

Hyman, H., 1973. "Occupational Aspirations among the Totally Blind." *Social Forces* 51: 403–416.

Jones, E.J. et al., 1984. Social Stigma: the Psychology of Marked Relationships. Freeman, New York.

Kahanman, I., 1986. "The Cinema-Viewing Practices of Israelis." Research Report, May 1986, Israel Institute of Applied Social Research, Jerusalem (Hebrew).

Kemp, N.J., 1981. "Social Psychological Aspects of Blindness: A Review." *Current Psychological Reviews* 1: 69–89.

Klobas, L.E., 1988. Disability Drama in Television and Film. McFarland, Jefferson, N.C.

Kohler, I., 1964. "Orientation by Aural Clues." American Foundation for the Blind, Report 4:14–53.

Kutner, N.G., 1987. "Social Worlds and Identity in End-Stage Renal Disease." *Research in the Sociology of Health Care* 6:33–71.

Levitin, T., 1975. "Deviants as Active Participants in the Labelling Process: The Visibly Handicapped." *Social Problems* 22: 548–557.

Lewin, K., 1948. Resolving Social Conflict: Selected Papers on Group Dynamics. Harper, New York.

Lewis, O., 1961. "Some of My Best Friends are Peasants." *Human Organization* 19: 179–180.

Lewis, H., 1989. After the Eagles Landed: Yemenite Jews in Israel. Westview, Boulder Co.

Loeb, L., 1985. "Folk Models of Habbani Ethnicity." In Weingrod, A., ed., Studies in Israeli Ethnicity. Gordon and Breach, New York, pp. 201–215.

Lukoff, I., 1960. "A Sociological Appraisal of Blindness." In Finestone, S., ed., Social Casework and Blindness. American Foundation for the Blind, New York, pp. 19–44.

MacKenzie, D. and Wajcman, J., eds. 1985. The Social Shaping of Technology. Open University Press, Milton Keynes.

Michalko, R., 1982. "Accomplishing a Sighted World." *Reflections: Canadian Journal of Visual Impairment* 1: 9–30.

Mitteness, L.S., 1987. "So What Do You Expect When You're 85 Years Old?: Urinary Incontinence in Late Life." *Research in the Sociology of Health Care* 6: 177–219.

Montagu, A., 1971. Touching: The Human Significance of the Skin. Harper & Row, New York.

Murphy, C. and Cain, W.S., 1986. "Odor Identification: The Blind are Better." *Physiology and Behavior* 37: 177–180.

Murphy, R.F., 1987. The Body Silent. Holt, New York.

————, Scheer, J., Murphy, Y. and Mack, R., 1988. "Physical Disability and Social Liminality: A Study in the Rituals of Adversity." *Social Science and Medicine* 26: 235–242.

Musgrove, F., 1977. Margins of the Mind. Methuen, London.

Ogburn, W.F. and Gilfallin, S.C., 1933. "The Influence of Invention and Discovery." In President's Commission on Recent Social Trends. McGraw-Hill, New York, pp. 122–66.

Peres, Y. and Katz, R., 1981. "Stability and Centrality: The Nuclear Family in Modern Israel." *Social Forces* 51: 403–416.

Petrunik, M., 1974. "The Quest for Fluency." In Hass, J. and Shaffir, W. eds., Decency and Deviance: Studies in Deviant Behaviour. McClelland and Steward, Toronto, pp. 201–220.

Pfuhl, E.H., 1986. The Deviance Process. 2nd edition. Van Nostrand, New York.

Polhemus, T., ed., 1978. Social Aspects of the Human Body: A Reader of Key Texts. Penguin, Harmondsworth.

Radcliffe-Brown, A.R., 1952. Structure and Function in Primitive Society. Cohen & West, Glencoe, Ill.

Raybeck, D., 1988. "Anthropology and Labelling Theory: A Constructive Critique." *Ethos* 16: 371–397.

Roth, J.A. and Conrad, P., eds., 1987. The Experience and Management of Chronic Illness (*Research in the Sociology of Health Care,* vol. 6). JAI Press, Greenwich, Cn.

Roy, D., 1960. "Banana Time: Job Satisfaction and Informal Interaction." *Human Organization* 18: 158–168.

Sacks, O., 1989. Seeing Voices. University of California Press, Berkeley.

Safilios-Rothschild, C., 1970. The Sociology and Social Psychology of Disability and Rehabilitation. Random House, New York.

————, 1982. "Social and Psychological Parameters of Friendship and Intimacy for Disabled People." In Eisenberg, M.G., Greggins, C. and Duval, R.J., eds., Disabled People as Second-Class Citizens. Springer, New York, pp. 40–51.

Sagarin, E., 1969. Odd Man In: Societies of Deviants in America. Quadrangle, Chicago.

Scrambler, G. and Hopkins, A., 1986. "Being Epilectic." *Sociology of Health and Illness* 8: 26–43.

Scheer, J. and Groce, N., 1988. "Impairment as a Human Constant: Cross Cultural and Historical Perspectives on Variation." *Journal of Social Issues* 44: 23–37.

Schneider, J. and Conrad, P., 1983. Having Epilepsy: The Experience and Control of Illness. Temple University Press, Philadelphia.

Scott, R.A., 1969. The Making of Blind Men: A Study of Adult Socialization. Russell Sage Foundation, New York.

Sentumbwe, N., 1990. "Lovers, Mistresses and Wives: Marital Relationships for Visually Impaired Educated Women in Uganda." In Bruun, F.J. and Ingstad, B., op. cit., pp. 79–117.

Sharot, S., 1976. Judaism: A Sociology. David and Charles, London.

Shokeid, M., 1988. Children of Circumstances: Israeli Emigrants in New York. Cornell University Press, Ithaca, N.Y.

————,1990. "Generations Divorced: The Mutation of Familism among Atlas Mountains Immigrants in Israel." Anthropological Quarterly 63: 76–89.

———— and Deshen, S., 1982. Distant Relations: Ethnicity and Politics among Arabs and North-African Jews in Israel. Praeger, New York .

Shuval, J., 1966. "Self-Rejection among North-African Immigrants in Israel". Israel Annals of Psychiatry and Related Disciplines 4:101–111 .

Smooha, S., 1987. Social Research on Jewish Ethnicity in Israel, 1948–1986. Haifa University Press, Haifa.

Söder, M., 1990. "Prejudice or Ambivalence? Attitudes toward Persons with Disabilities." Disability Handicap and Society 5:227–241.

State of Israel, 1986. State Comptroller's Report. Government Printer, Jerusalem.

————, 1989. State Comptroller's Report. Government Printer, Jerusalem.

Steinberg, A., 1983. "The Blind Person in the Jewish Perspective." Tehumim (Jerusalem) 3: 186–227 (Hebrew).

Steiner, J. E., Ephrath, J. and Neustadt-Noy, N., 1988. "Olfactory Function in Blind and in Normal-Sighted Human Subjects." In Neustadt-Noy, N., Merin, S. and Schiff, Y. eds., Orientation and Mobility of the Visually Impaired. Heiliger, Jerusalem, pp. 35–39.

Stoller, P., 1989. The Taste of Ethnographic Things: The Senses in Anthropology. University of Pennsylvania Press, Philadelphia.

Supa, M., Cotzin, M. and Dallenbach, K.M., 1944. " 'Facial Vision': The Perception of Obstacles by the Blind." American Journal of Psychology 57: 133–183.

Walker, L.A., 1986. A Loss for Words: The Story of Deafness in a Family. Harper and Row, New York.

Watson, O.M., 1970. Proxemic Behavior: A Cross-Cultural Study. Mouton, Hague.

Weiss, M., 1985. "Infirmity and Identity: Handicapped Children as Perceived by their Parents." Unpublished Ph.D. dissertation, Tel-Aviv University; also in, Parents Coping with Deformed Children. Sifriat Ha'poalim, Tel-Aviv (Hebrew, in press).

Winton, A., 1970. "The Legally Blind Young Adult." Unpublished Ph.D. dissertation, University of California, Berkeley.

Index

Index